CHILDREN'S LITERATURE

The serious academic study of children's literature is an exciting, entertaining, and rapidly expanding field. This volume is a lucid statement of the 'purposes' of children's literature, and how it has developed, introducing the reader to the way in which the criticism of children's literature – and, indeed, the subject itself – has developed, particularly in the last forty years.

Out of the vast amount of critical material available, Dr Peter Hunt selects the most important landmarks – from key essays which synthesize and point forwards. There are extracts from Sarah Fielding, Ruskin, Chesterton, and Ransome, but most of the material is very recent. The pioneering work of Roger Lancelyn Green and John Rowe Townsend is included, as are major contributions to the theory of children's literature and directions for research by established authorities such as Aidan Chambers and Margaret Meek. New approaches to criticism are represented by important essays on psychology and response (Hugh Crago), feminism (Lissa Paul), and illustration (William Moebius). A discussion of the contemporary scene shows the many different ways in which the various problems in analysing children's literature are now being confronted.

This wide-ranging survey is a fascinating introduction to a new field of academic study.

Peter Hunt teaches English and Children's Literature at the University of Wales, Cardiff. He has lectured on the subject worldwide, and has published several novels and books for children and adolescents.

CHILDREN'S LITERATURE

The development of criticism

◆

edited by PETER HUNT

LONDON AND NEW YORK

First published 1990 by Routledge
11 New Fetter Lane, London EC4P 4EE
Simultaneously published
in the USA and Canada by
Routledge
29 West 35th Street, New York, NY 10001

Reprinted in 1993

© 1990 Peter Hunt

Printed in England by Clays Ltd, St Ives plc

British Library Cataloguing in Publication Data
1. Children's literature. Critical studies
I. Hunt, Peter
809'.89282

ISBN 0 415 02993 7 (hbk)
0 415 02994 5 (pbk)

Library of Congress Cataloging in Publication Data

also available

Contents

CONTENTS

Acknowledgements

We are grateful for permission given to reproduce extracts from the following:

Aidan Chambers, 'The Reader in the Book', *Booktalk; Occasional Writing on Literature and Children*, Bodley Head, 1985. First published in *Signal*, 23, Thimble Press, May, 1977.

Hugo Crago, 'The Roots of Response', *Children's Literature Association Quarterly*, vol. 10, no. 3, Fall, 1985.

Roger Lancelyn Green, 'The Golden Age of Children's Books', *Essays and Studies*, 1962. By permission of Richard Lancelyn Green (Literary Executor of Roger Lancelyn Green).

Felicity A. Hughes, 'Children's Literature: Theory and Practice', *ELH*, 45, Johns Hopkins University Press, 1978.

Margaret Meek, 'What Counts as Evidence in Theories of Children's Literature?' *Theory into Practice*, vol. 21, no. 4, 1982.

William Moebius, 'Introduction to Picturebook Codes', *Word & Image*, vol. 2, no. 2, April–June, 1986.

Lissa Paul, 'Enigma Variations: What Feminist Theory Knows About Children's Literature', *Signal*, 54, Thimble Press, September, 1987.

John Rowe Townsend, 'Standards of Criticism for Children's Literature', *The Signal Approach to Children's Books*, ed. Nancy Chambers, Kestrel Books, 1980. Text of the May Hill Arbuthnot Honour Lecture, delivered in Atlanta, Georgia, 1971. First published in *Top of the News*, American Library Association, June, 1971.

Introduction

1

This volume sets out to introduce the reader to the way in which the criticism of children's literature – and, indeed, the subject itself – has developed, particularly in the last forty years.

It is concerned with a complete species of writing, a species which parallels the rest of 'literature' from at least the mid-eighteenth century, and which encompasses virtually all genres and many thousands of authors. This is a species of literature whose boundaries are very hazy; it cannot be defined by textual characteristics either of style or content, and its primary audience, 'the child-reader', is equally elusive. As an outsider to the academic world, it does not fit neatly into any of the established 'subject' categories and has been positively snubbed by some of them.

'Children's literature', then, as a subject of study, has some awkward features. Much more than other literatures, there is a fracture between contemporary and historical works; some books seem to remain eternally in its living canon; other non-contemporary works in some senses cease to belong to the species. This is because the concepts of childhood which produces the conditions of production shift radically; similarly, the way texts are read, by both primary and secondary, and peer and non-peer audiences can be radically different.

All of this suggests a species of literature defined in terms of the reader rather than the authors' intentions or the texts themselves. It also demonstrates the closeness of the relationship between text and reader, and, consequently, the peculiar honesty and realism required of the children's book critic. It is obvious when an historical children's book ceases to be 'alive'; it is, perhaps, not so obvious when an adult one ceases to be so. How many of the works of the received canon are kept alive by artificial academic life-support systems?

But all this does not mean that we are dealing with a non-existent subject. It is clear that, at least since the mid-eighteenth century, there

1.

has been a huge output of text designed for the 'non-peer' audience. Much of it can, of course, be regarded in purist 'literary' terms as merely the matter of 'popular culture', but, of the current annual British output alone of somewhere around 2,500 volumes per year (and an in-print list of around 27,000), it is scarcely likely that all of the books can be dismissed in this way.

There can be no question that texts in this area are culturally formative, and of massive importance educationally, intellectually, and socially. Perhaps more than any other texts, they reflect society as it wishes to be, as it wishes to be seen, and as it unconsciously reveals itself to be. (Early nineteenth-century texts, for example, clearly saw themselves as firm and godly; they may now appear to be repressive and brutal.)

The criticism of children's literature has become a coherent discipline only as children's literature itself has emerged as a coherent field of study. There is a body of nineteenth-century criticism (anthologized definitively in Lance Salway's exemplary volume, *A Peculiar Gift*, Kestrel, 1976), some of which is represented here. As we shall see, it was clear to many writers even then that children's literature needed some special critical approach, and they rehearsed just the kinds of arguments that are heard today. As a phenomenon, both text and audience presented a new challenge. The perception that children's literature is not *lesser* but *different*, however, was rarely made. The problems were overcome by turning to didacticism, or to romantic concepts of the child, neither of which had much to do with the realities of reading.

Nevertheless, the criticism of children's literature involves a great deal of primary definition: what do we mean by 'literature'? What is the book *for*? Who and what is the audience, and how do they read? These questions have had to be asked, and answered, because the criticism has grown from writing designed almost exclusively for a pragmatic audience, 'practitioners' involved with children and books. As Stuart Hannabus observed of reviews:

> some criticism is very navel-contemplating, hieratic, self-consciously aware of other cognoscenti and all too little aware of the expectant and modest reader wanting help. Such modest readers are often practical people, with little time to spare, wanting the best advice quickly, eager to acquire the most effective books for the children in their care: people who can spend once and don't want to make too many mistakes. (Stuart Hannabus, 'Reviewing Reviews', *Signal*, 35, 1981, pp. 96–107: 97)

2

The result of this pragmatism has been, paradoxically, that children's literature critics have had to attend to philosophical and methodological questions which have been ignored for too long in the criticism of canonical literatures, and many of the essays represented here therefore begin with a certain amount of theorizing. This may seem at times, in academic terms, to be at a fairly fundamental level, but it would be interesting to see the result if critics of, say, Wordsworth or Dryden were called upon to justify their existence, without recourse to a canonical argument.

Only in the twentieth century, and, more specifically, post-1945, has criticism developed in a recognizably conventional direction, and it has developed in a way which parallels academic criticism. That is, there has been a divide between the scholarly–bibliographical–historical writers (who are dealing with a very different part of the forest), and the 'practitioners', who are concerned with 'living' texts. This second group has, in turn, over the last fifteen years, become increasingly sharply divided between those concerned with the books, and those concerned with the readers. Only very recently, as literary theory has approached what is, to most users of children's literature, the patently obvious position of necessary plurality of meaning and response, has children's literature criticism begun to find a unique voice, and these unfortunate divisions begun to disappear.

The landmark text in bibliographical terms was, and is, F. J. Harvey Darton's *Children's Books in England*, significantly subtitled *Five Centuries of Social Life* (CUP, 1932; 3rd edn, revised by Brian Alderson, 1982). This was the first example of extended first-class work in the field, and it has been followed by bibliographic, historic, and bibliophilic work which can stand beside any such work in any other area. Although there is a vast amount of unchronicled material to be explored, writers of the calibre of Darton and Alderson have laid an immaculate scholarly base for future work.

In Darton's original introduction, he wrote:

> Some provision is made for the book collector's point of view; not so much for the psychologist's, or the educational historian's. *Little is said about the aesthetic merits of children's books.* (p. vii, my italics)

This was not an evasion; it was not part of Darton's brief; the task, though, was and is still proving to be much more difficult than might have been supposed. Some measure of that difficulty will be found in this book.

3

Initially, those 'critics' who wrote about children's literature were regarded as eccentric, and, perhaps as a result, modelled their work on the most traditional of critical methods – a judicious mixture of biography and liberal–humanist literary evaluation – with the added (and often confusing) criterion of 'accessibility' and 'appropriateness'. Also, the lack of canonical status of the vast majority of children's books meant that there were few outlets for serious discussion of the texts. Even the pioneering *Junior Bookshelf* (1936 onward) was essentially a reviewing journal, and discussion of children's books, until fairly recently, was confined to corners of the review pages.

These are the reasons for the tone and stance of much of the criticism in this book. As we have seen, there has been a strong impulse to justify; the status of Milton, for example, is such that recent deconstructionist writers have felt it necessary to reread, or possibly to rewrite him, but rarely to question whether he has any particular right to be rescued from oblivion. Children's book authors have no such dubious privilege. Critical equality will only be reached when no one questions the right of, say, Farjeon to stand beside Wordsworth.

Similarly, the pragmatic audience can be positively anti-intellectual. I do not mean that the audience is in any way unintelligent; rather, it has been impatient with the pretentious and the theoretical (which too often go together in academic terms). It has also rejected the liberal–humanist value structure which has for so long underpinned the teaching of English. Once free of universities and examinations, which prescribe the 'correct' response, and what is canonical, teachers and librarians and parents not only have little use for predetermined 'right answers' about texts, but also can see that most of the well-worn judgement systems patently have little relationship to the responses of real readers.

This has had three very interesting effects, paralleled, perhaps, in what has happened to writing about popular culture. Two of them seem to me to be very positive. Writing about children's books (by writers whose primary interest *is* children's books) is notably readable, colloquial, and involved. There is little abstract pretension, and little use of impersonal constructions to confer a spurious universality of judgement. The audience continually challenges this, and, consequently, the style is commonly more robust, elegant, and clear. It may seem unacademic, but that seems to say more about the shortcomings of academia than about the validity of the criticism. Writers have no vested interest in obscurity or a distinctive dialect. Like children's literature itself, the critical discourse is different – perhaps more democratic, rather than less.

Similarly, the angle of approach to texts has been much wider than (until very recently) academic approaches. Because there has been a tendency to start with reader rather than text, and because there has been a practical end (acquisition of reading skills, or text skills, or social skills, or, merely and largely, entertainment), children's book critics have been forced to acknowledge and use a diversity of skills which elsewhere reside in discrete disciplines. Developmental psychology jostles politics and censorship; stylistics and readability go hand in hand with educational strategy; illustration and mixed-media studies have to sit with practical librarianship; reception theory faces the practicalities of response. The historical–bibliographic approach may seem to be the odd person out in this matrix, but writers in that area have been more aware of the social and cultural axes of their work than many another. Consequently, criticism of children's books has always been perhaps richer and more surprising than its mainstream counterpart.

We cannot, though, ignore the negative effects. There is a fine line between informality and casualness, and between enthusiasm and sloppiness. Anti-intellectualism has produced much so-called criticism which is simply impressionistic and popularist in the worst sense. Liberal–humanist judgements are reintroduced in the guise of forthright judgements; common-sense has replaced serious and empirical psychological insights. I would not care to argue that the proportion of trivial and pseudo-criticism is any higher or lower in children's literature studies than in any academic field; it is, however, a good deal more obvious, and, possibly, the more pernicious for being more easily accessible. I have some sympathy with the practitioners here; reception theory and writings on response in academic circles are comfortably divorced from real children. Pragmatic studies are dangerous, either because of the difficulties of empirical research (the answers are inherent in the questions), or because they are too parochial. They degenerate, as Brian Alderson put it, rather unkindly, 'into the customary waffle that is inseparable from most idea-swopping sessions on the subject of children's reactions to books' ('Literary Criticism and Children's Books; or, "Could Be Worse" ', in Geoff Fox *et al.* (eds), *Responses to Children's Literature*, Munich, K. G. Saur, 1983, p. 71).

Where there has been lax thinking, or 'soft' research, it has been particularly irritating to the historical and bibliographical scholars, who have seen their meticulous work downgraded by association. It remains to be seen whether the extension of reader-based criticism will validate itself, or whether criticisms which actually rest upon disguised ideological stances (which sometimes emanate from the scholars) will reveal themselves as such. It may also be dispiriting for the critic that, just as children's literature itself has always been a prime area for the amateur writer, so its criticism is the province of the amateur critic. Children's literature's major advantage as a subject area – that few people are afraid of it – has also worked to its disadvantage.

The problem of standards is one which crops up occasionally in the essays collected here. One which occurs far more often, and which lies behind some of the essays, is factionalism. Interestingly, it is not, as perhaps might be expected, academic respectability which has brought demarcation disputes. Children's literature studies have been seen academically as cross-disciplinary (which has brought practical problems of publishing and employment); rather, the basic function of children's literature and children's book studies has provoked intense argument. Who should be in control? Is the view of the psychologist more valid than that of the bibliographer? Does the lay parent 'know' more than the academic? There is, of course, a social axis here – which of the participants has the higher status, or publishes the books? In children's literature, which has, if anything, an even stronger impulse to award prizes to itself than the rest of the literary world, the annual arguments surrounding almost all the awards are not merely concerned with whether like is being compared to like, but about what criteria should be applied, and who should apply them. Several of the essays in this book try to resolve such problems. They cannot therefore be conventionally academic – nor, with few exceptions, do they wish to be.

Serious criticism of children's literature – perhaps because it sounds as if it is a contradiction in terms – has therefore had to be evangelical, and it is only very recently that the conditions of academic thought have changed sufficiently for this to be no longer a primary stance. Rather, the last ten years have seen a revolution in critical thinking in universities, which has, paradoxically, thrust children's books and their critics into the limelight.

Those aspects of literature and criticism which have been basic to all children's book practitioners – the meaning of 'value' (and, of course, the meaning of 'literature'); the part the reader plays; the problems of a multi-disciplinary approach – are now (at last) becoming fundamental to academic literary and cultural thinking.

The development of a coherent poetics for children's literature has had to wait, paradoxically, for the right academic conditions – for the academic world to catch up. However, because of the peculiar progress of the discipline, what we now see is a rich but unstructured area, and it is the object of many of the essays represented here to clear the ground, to define, and to seek an integrated and coherent development.

2

This book will present few surprises to experts in the field of children's books. Out of the vast amount of material available, I have attempted to select the most important landmarks (many of which have been frequently reprinted, although never together) and to select essays which seem to me to synthesize and to point forwards. I make no apology for this. I would like to think that the cause of children's literature is now won, and that its academic status is secure, but to very many readers it will be a new and questionable discipline, and its critical development needs to be laid out.

However, to talk of children's literature as a discipline is still to invite scorn from academics and non-academics alike. Jacqueline Rose, in her post-structuralist excursus into that unstable text, *Peter Pan*, wrote of:

> the ultimate fantasy, perhaps, of children's book criticism that it should come of age and do what the adults (that is adult critics) have been doing all along. (*The Case of Peter Pan, or, The Impossibility of Children's Fiction*, Macmillan, 1984, p. 154, n. 3)

At the other end of the scale is a writer like Robert Leeson, who is passionately involved in storytelling in schools; in making narrative accessible to the young; in preserving the book in the face of competing stimuli. In his polemical book, *Reading and Righting*, he asks:

> What future for the critic? Which critic, child- or book-centred? Eng-lit. critic or social critic? The critic who goes for rigour and respectability, or the one who goes for relevance and response? More importantly, the professional or the amateur?
>
> I see little future for the academic critic making an exhaustive study of *angst* in the writings of William Mayne, while I see an ever-expanding future for the librarian, the teacher, the parent,

above all, the child as critic. These I expect to become more active, informed, confident and demanding, as the former sort wilts on the vine. I hope DIY criticism will become the universal practice. Not before time, for I think a good deal of critical activity over the past 30 years has been misguided and has even done harm to the cause of the literature it champions. Criticism, taking its cue from the adult literary establishment, has failed to grapple with several basic contradictions in the historical development of fiction for the young. (*Reading and Righting*, Collins, 1985, p. 142)

Leeson undoubtedly underestimates the appetite of the academic world for small-scale territorial claims, but he states very trechantly the inbuilt prejudices which criticism has to overcome.

My argument that children's literature should have academic status does not, I hope, accord academia more importance than it should. I merely feel that with academic acceptance comes intellectual acceptance and, with that, a good deal of integrating power. The influence of literary theory over the last twenty years is a case in point; from being an eccentric minority sport, it has become a formative influence of contemporary thinking, at all stages of education. Until children's literature can cease to be on the defensive, and can cease to have to waste some of its time and space on self-justification, it will not have the influence which Leeson, for example, would like.

Consequently, this book sets out to present the background to the best of current thought in children's-literature criticism, and to review the arguments which have brought us this far. This is not mere historicism; without the landmark essays which spell out the difficulties encountered, there is an inevitable tendency for us to continue to reinvent the wheel, to have to reiterate the defences and arguments endlessly. Although some of the essays (notably 'The Reader in the Book', pp. 91–114) spend some time examining specific texts, I have not chosen essays which use textual analysis as their starting-points. Rather, it seems to me that most readers who are relatively new to the field will appreciate a clarification of theoretical positions, and that for them, applications will come second. Other readers may find the rehearsal of the key points useful.

There are five types of material included in this book:

1. The first section reprints illustrative extracts from early critical writing. The selection could be almost infinitely extended, but the point is soon made that, while there were obviously areas of text

thought appropriate for children, the way of talking about books was for the most part based solidly on the standard adult critical stances of the day, and with an arrogance which placed the child in a subordinate role. However, many writers were also aware that the material and audience implied differences in approach.

2. Apart from the work of Darton, which, as we have seen, was not concerned with literary standards and values, the first books to bring at least an attempt at literary criticism to children's literature were *Tellers of Tales* by Roger Lancelyn Green (Edmund Ward, 1946, 4th edn, 1965), and *Tales Out of School* by Geoffrey Trease (Heinemann Educational, 1949; 2nd edn, 1964). They are, in many ways, diametrically opposed texts. In its first three editions, *Tellers of Tales* was designed, rather avuncularly, for a child audience. Lancelyn Green was a bibliophile, whose own writing for children was largely based on traditional material, and who did not question any of the established values of literature. Trease, in contrast, took the position of a pragmatist and a politically motivated writer, and his large output of original writing (close on one hundred volumes to date), includes several books which challenge such conventional modes of thought. The contributions of these two writers to *Essays and Studies* are fair representations of the two divergent attitudes; both writers are responsible for much of the 'ordinary thinking' of children's literature. I have reprinted Green's essay, together with extracts from Trease, and from other cognate essays.

These essays were precursors of the current critical 'industry', as was Felicity Hughes' very intelligent approach from the academic side. Just as the fact that Trease and Lancelyn Green appeared in the pages of a distinguished literary annual is important in itself, so Felicity Hughes' contribution to the journal *English Literary History* broke down a major barrier. Similarly, John Rowe Townsend's Arbuthnot Lecture on standards of criticism moved the arguments on from Lancelyn Green's unacademic position and helped to define mainstream attitudes.

The writer and critic Aidan Chambers has a distinguished reputation for championing an eclectic and radical development of criticism. His article 'The Reader in the Book' demonstrates that he can work with equal skill from text and theory as well as from empirical data; but it is significant as one of the first, and probably the most important, articles to move literary theory into children's literature. As theory has moved on, Chambers' stance may seem, increasingly, to be simplistic, but it is not an historical piece; it is still influencing a new generation of children's-book practitioners.

3. Something of the range of preoccupations of children's book criticism will be indicated in the final section. Clearly, a case could be made for devoting space to a large number of genres and types – for example, fantasy, the fairy- or folk tale, the school story (for boys or girls), the 'adventure' story, the vast sub-species of the animal tale, or popular romance – and so on. However, I have selected two essays which treat in some depth broad topics particularly relevant to children's literature criticism; reception response, and illustration.

Aidan Chambers' article takes us some way towards the reader-oriented approach (of which Hughes, for example, despairs), and Hugh Crago's paper, which is indicative of the kind of research that is going on, takes the emphasis away from the book, more specifically to the reader.

William Moebius' important essay takes us towards a new and scarcely explored field, which is almost unique to children's literature, and which challenges our critical techniques and vocabularies – the picture-book (as opposed to the illustrated book).

4. The fourth type of material looks forward to the development of children's literature criticism. Again, I could have selected work on mixed-media texts, on psychological criticism, or on popular culture as particularly strong areas. Equally important, I think, is the use of other critical idioms for children's literature: hence the inclusion of Lissa Paul's feminist article.

Margaret Meek's essay is selected from a body of work which is based in empirical reading-education, but which draws eclectically upon the many disciplines involved. In 1980, at the first British Research Seminar on Children's Literature, Meek summed up the situation:

> Research into 'children's literature' is in its early stages. It is still most happily allied to historical studies of literature, from which one kind of security emerges, the natural-seeming alliance with developmental and cognitive psychology, as illustrated by Nicholas Tucker and Arthur Applebee. This uses a Piagetian model to account for 'staged' progression to adult literariness. Studies in 'response' generally imply a Freudian account of affective growth, influenced by writings of Singer, Winnicott and Bettelheim. In so far as literary criticism can be assumed to be a kind of research, the practitioners seem to want to divide themselves into those who argue a phenomenological stance, mostly prescriptive, towards the book as object, a kind of formalism . . . and those who feel that, if we are to distinguish

'children's literature' from literature in general, then the reader implied by the existence of such literature would *not* be an adult . . .

My general contention is that a model derived from historical studies, developmental psychology or literary criticism as such would be somehow inadequate to meet what is essentially *different* about children's literature. If we agree that it exists at all, then we need ways of looking at it which help us to understand its particularity, as well as its continuity with literature in general. (Margaret Meek, 'Prolegomena for a Study of Children's Literature', *Approaches to Research in Children's Literature*, Michael Benton (ed.), University of Southampton, 1980, pp. 29-30)

The article reprinted here demonstrates how far children's literature has progressed towards taking its place in the critical world, partly through a holistic approach.

5. The final section surveys briefly some of the other areas of criticism, and suggests the most useful introductory sources. Texts which have been mentioned in the body of the volume are not generally listed again.

3

The primary difficulty in assembling this volume has been to select essays which are sufficiently specific in their concern with criticism, and yet which make a general statement about what is clearly a very wide field. Previous collections have either attempted to include essays representative of many modes of criticism (*Signposts to Criticism of Children's Literature, Only Connect*), to argue a sustained thesis (*The Cool Web*), to collect opinions of authors (as might be expected, a popular form of book-making), or, most commonly, to represent the work from a particular journal (*The Signal Approach, Writers, Critics, and Children*, and *Good Writers for Young Readers*). (See Chapter 5 for full references.)

This last is symptomatic of the revolution in journal publishing, which has backed up the growth of educational and other activity in the field. In Britain, the major journal is *Signal, Approaches to Children's Books*, first published in 1970. This is emphatically NOT a reviewing journal (although The Thimble Press now publishes an annual review), and is a serious journal of the highest standard. *Children's Literature in Education* originated in the Exeter conferences on children's literature and, since 1970, has broadened its scope to take in all aspects of children's literature. Increasingly, reviewing journals, such as *Growing Point*, *Books for Your Children*, and *British Book News - Children's Books* (merged with *Books for Keeps* in 1988) have spent time on deeper examinations of books and issues, and the same can be said for general journals, such as *The Times Literary Supplement*. The changes in policy over the years with the *TLS*, which have variously accorded children's literature a separate sub-supplement (as befits its status), or which have refused to ghettoize it, incorporating reviews of children's books in the usual sections, are fairly indicative of the well-intentioned ambivalence accorded to the subject. (A very useful discussion of this ambivalence may be found in the editorial commentary of *Signposts to Criticism of Children's Literature*.) Children's books also feature in journals from not specifically literary disciplines, such as *Use of English*.

Elsewhere, there is a similar situation; a growing specialist interest, ranging from universities to local 'grass-roots' organizations, and peripheral contributions. In the USA, the oldest reviewing–critical journal is *The Horn Book*, but there are now many others, notably *The Lion and the Unicorn*. The Children's Literature Association produces a *Quarterly*, which is in the academic mainstream, and Yale University Press produces an annual journal, *Children's Literature*, in association with the Children's Literature Division of MLA. Material also appears in specialist journals of education, the International Reading Association, and so on. A similar picture could be drawn for Australia and New Zealand as well as for Europe, and the International Board for Books for the Young (IBBY) has national sections throughout the world.

This publishing activity supports, or results from, the span of interest which is perhaps broader than for any comparable subject. In Britain, the Confederation of Children's Book Groups consists of local organizations which raise money for books to be used in the community; there are groups representing children's rights; there are groups watching out for sexism and racism; the School Library Association, and many others. Across the world, there are major library and research collections and an International Research Society for Children's Literature. It is not surprising, then, to find that almost every conceivable subject and approach is to be found in the journals and specialist texts.

The articles and extracts presented here do not pretend to a complete examination of current publishing, but, rather, a broad map which may prove useful to those encountering the species for the first time, and a compendium which will be useful for children's book scholars.

Neil Philip wrote in a review of another collection of essays that, 'like all such culls from various sources and varied dates [the book] suffers from a lack of coherence which ultimately makes it seem less than the sum of the parts' ('This Way Confusion?', *Signal*, 43, 1984, p. 18). If this book suffers the same fate, it may be that the field of children's literature is now so wide and so well populated that no collection could adequately represent its diversity, and no anthologist could adequately comprehend the area well enough to adequately map it. If that is so, and I think that it now is, then the curious and anomolous thing that children's literature is – and which makes it a key study in the late twentieth century, in that it breaks down and crosses artificial demarcation lines between subjects – has in some sense reached maturity.

Finally, a few notes on what this book is not. It is not a history of criticism, or a history of children's literature. It is not intended to be comprehensive, or to suggest any particular partisan route to the understanding of the field of children's books. Rather, it attempts to give some characteristic points of view. The texts and extracts collected here either clear the ground or provide a foundation for future work.

Nor does this book, except by implication, explore the most advanced critical thinking. Children's literature should be the spearhead of criticism, and Chambers and Meek represent the springboards for work that is now in progress. This book shows how we have come this far, and gives a picture of the ways things have been and might be done.

1

Criticism before 1945

One of the principle demarcation disputes in establishing children's literature has been – where does it begin? This is, of course, a merely academic matter, because, with rare exceptions, pre-twentieth century texts are 'dead' to the contemporary primary audience. There have been revivals (for example, by Gollancz) of some texts for children, but most of the interest of early books is adult bibliographical and scholarly. The encounter with texts is inclined to be active rather than reflective.

This is a matter for brief discussion because, in looking for early examples of criticism, it is as well to decide which texts, and thus which commentaries on the texts, qualify. How far do we go back into history? Gillian Adams has suggested in her article 'The First Children's Literature? The Case for Sumer', *Children's Literature*, 14, 1986, p. 1, that we should consider texts as early as 2112 BC as part of the canon:

> Some scholars . . . believe that works from earlier periods routinely associated with children, even if their purpose is didactic or they were not written specifically for children, can also be classified as children's literature.

The early editions of the annual *Children's Literature* contain articles suggesting that Milton's *Comus*, for example, could be regarded as a children's book:

> The question is made credible first because the leading role and two important supporting roles were actually played by children and written as children's parts. Further, *Comus* has a very specific didactic quality emphasising problems of virtue and faith specifically pertinent to an adolescent girl. (Lee A. Jacobus, 'Milton's *Comus* as Children's Literature', *Children's Literature*, 2, 1973, p. 67)

Whatever the merits of such an argument, it seems to me that it casts the net of texts (and, consequently, criticism) far too wide to be conceptually manageable, or empirically useful. All literature - all texts - produced before the eighteenth century were, in the modern sense, not written for children; children, presumably, were a part of the audience in a primarily oral and aural society. We shall therefore confine our attention to the eighteenth and nineteenth centuries, beginning with, not a piece of criticism, but a prospectus or manifesto, which characterizes a whole century of writing for children.

Bettina Hurlimann begins her *Three Centuries of Children's Books in Europe* (trans. and ed. Brian Alderson, OUP, 1967), with reference to Comenius' *Orbis sensualium pictus* (1658). Comenius, she notes,

> was among the first to recognize the child as an individual . . .
> [T]he importance of the man lies in the effort which he made to introduce a new humanity into the idea of education at a time when Europe was still suffering from the effects of the Thirty Years War.
>
> The *Orbis pictus* long remained a unique achievement. The age once again forgot the child or saw him only as a damned soul who must be saved from perdition by a rigorous pietism. Children were not born to live happy but to die holy and true education lay in preparing the soul to meet its maker. The result of this was a crop of seventeenth-century books zealously depicting for children the holy lives and joyous deaths of their little contemporaries. Even the first half of the eighteenth century would have been a similar blank - or rather black - page in the history of children's books, had not Rousseau discovered *Robinson Crusoe* . . . and had not the fairy stories of Charles Perrault brought a little sweetness and light from 1700 onward.
> (p. xii)

Educational texts dominated writing 'for children'. The book commonly taken as a landmark in publishing for children, *A Little Pretty Pocket-Book* (1744), published by John Newbery, certainly pays lip-service to this. (For an account of publishing for children at this period, which places Newbery in his proper perspective, see Percy Muir, *English Children's Books 1600-1900*, Batsford, 1954, pp. 59-72.) Geoffrey Summerfield dismisses it trenchantly in his study, *Fantasy and Reason: Children's Literature in the Eighteenth Century* (Methuen, 1984):

> Whatever the archaeological interest of this and other Newbery volumes - and they are clearly considerable for some bibliographers - the philistinism of the *Pocket-Book*, the smell of the

shopkeeper that pervades the volume, has received remarkably little attention. Wittingly or unwittingly, it is a sneaky piece of work, and serves only to show how calamitous the didactic book for children could be, even when free of the gloomy puritanism of such as Watts. Whoever wrote the *Pocket-Book*, it is the work of a thoroughly trivial, commercial, and disinherited mind, and its continuing *succès d'estime* is something of a mystery. (p. 86)

To gain some idea of the best of thinking about children's books we can turn, in contrast, to 'one of the most popular and frequently imitated children's books [produced] at a time when the concept of "a literature for children" was only just beginning to emerge . . . [It is] the first novel in children's literature' (Jill E. Grey, 'Introduction' to Sarah Fielding, *The Governess or Little Female Academy*, OUP, 1968, vol. 1, p. 79. Another edition is in Pandora Books, RKP, 1987). Sarah Fielding's prefatory material characterizes the 'appropriate' attitudes which were regarded as requisite for the children's book, and which would have received approbation from critics – had there been any to give it. In the following extracts, I have omitted the illustrative fables.

Sarah Fielding
From the 'Preface' to *The Governess or Little Female Academy* (1749)

Before you begin the following Sheets, I beg you will stop a Moment at this Preface, to consider with me, what is the true Use of Reading; and if you can once fix this Truth in your Minds, namely, that the true Use of Books is to make you wiser and better, you will then have both Profit and Pleasure from what you read.

One Thing quite necessary to make any Instructions that come either from your Governors, or your Books, of any Use to you, is to attend with a Desire of Learning, and not to be apt to fansy yourselves too wise to be taught . . .

But take care, that instead of being really humble in your own Hearts, you do not, by a fansied Humility, run into an Error of the other Extreme, and say that you are incapable of understanding it at all; and therefore, from Laziness, and sooner than take any Pains, sit yourselves down contented to be ignorant, and think, by confessing your Ignorance, to make full Amends for your Folly. This is being as contemptible as the *Owl*, who hates the Light of the Sun; and therefore often makes Use of the Power he has, of drawing a Film over his Eyes, to keep himself in his beloved Darkness.

When you run through Numbers of Books, only for the sake of saying, you have read them, without making any Advantage of the Knowledge got thereby, remember this Saying, 'That a Head, like a House, when crammed too full, and no regular Order observed in the placing what is there, is only littered instead of being furnished.' . . .

The Design of the following Sheets is to prove to you, that Pride, Stubbornness, Malice, Envy, and, in short, all manner of Wickedness, is the greatest Folly we can be possessed of; and constantly turns on the Head of that foolish Person who does not conquer and get the better of all Inclinations to such Wickedness. Certainly, Love and Affection for each other makes the Happiness of all Societies; and therefore Love and Affection (if we would be happy) is what we should chiefly encourage and cherish in our Minds.

I depend on the Goodness of all my little Readers, to acknowledge this to be true. But there is one Caution to be used, namely, That you are not led into many Inconveniences, and even Faults, by this Love and Affection: For this Disposition will naturally lead you to delight in Friendship; and this Delight in Friendship may lead you into all manner of Errors, unless you take Care not to be partial to any of your Companions, only because they are agreeable, without first consider- ing whether they are good enough to deserve your Love: And there is one Mark in which you can never be deceived; namely, That whoever tempts you to fail in your Duty, or justifies you in so doing, is not your real Friend. And if you cannot have Resolution enough to break from such pretended Friends, you will nourish in your Bosoms Serpents, that in the End will fling you to Death.

The most expert commentary on nineteenth-century criticism is by Lance Salway, who opens his indispensible book, A Peculiar Gift *(Kestrel, 1976), thus:*

Children's books, it seems, are now being taken seriously and, although the level of criticism may not be as high as some commentators would wish, serious attention is, at least, being paid to the subject.

It is often assumed that all this commendable activity is a recent development, and that little notice was taken of chil- dren's books before the present deluge of publication and discussion. And yet, although specialist journals and societies did not exist, and few books were written on the subject, a great deal of critical attention was paid to children's literature during the nineteenth century. Reviews of recent books were published in the great literary journals of the day, and articles on children's books and their authors appeared in more popular periodicals. In many respects critical discussion of the subject was less restricted than it is now; books for the young were considered to be part of the general body of literature and writing about them was not confined to specialized journals and seasonal supplements. The works of Maria Edgeworth or Henty or Mrs Ewing were not considered to be less deserving of critical attention merely because they were directed principally at the young. (p. 11)

Perhaps characteristic of the early critics was Mrs Sarah Trimmer, whose importance, as Darton wryly observed, 'is that she was important'. She might be found, in 1803, reflecting on the rapid development of children's literature:

Formerly children's reading, whether for instruction or amuse-ment, was confined to a very small number of volumes; of late years they have multiplied to an astonishing and alarming degree, and much mischief lies hid in many of them. The utmost circumspection is therefore requisite in making a proper selec-tion; and children should not be permitted to make their own choice, or to read any books that may accidentally be thrown in their way, or offered for their perusal; but should be taught to consider it as a *duty*, to consult their parents in this momentous concern. (Sarah Trimmer, 'On the Care Which is Requisite in the Choice of Books for Children', *The Guardian Of Education*, 2, 1803, p. 407)

This is, of course, an attitude which is alive and well, and living not only in the USA.

In contrast, here are extracts from a remarkably modern piece which appeared in The Quarterly Review *in 1844, and which sets out most of the arguments for wide reading and free selection. The key statement that 'children are distinguished from ourselves less by an* inferiority, *than by a* difference *in capacity' is as apposite to current thinking as the wry note that this truth is 'seldom apprehended by juvenile book-writers'.*

Elizabeth Rigby
From 'Children's Books', *The Quarterly Review*,
74 (1844), pp. 1-3, 16-26

The attention of our readers has already been called to a subject, to which, the more it is considered the more importance must be attached – we mean that of children's books, which, no less in quality than in quantity, constitute one of the most peculiar literary features of the present day. The first obvious rule in writing for the amusement or instruction of childhood, is to bear in mind that it is not the extremes either of genius or dullness which we are to address – that it is of no use writing up to some minds or down to others – that we have only to do with that large class of average ability, to be found in children of healthy mental and physical formation, among whom in after life the distinction consists not so much in a difference of gifts as in the mode in which they have been led to use them.

Considering the sure sale which modern habits of universal education provide for children's books – the immense outfit required by schools and masters, and the incalculable number annually purchased as presents, it would be, upon the whole, matter of far more legitimate surprise if either the supplies were less abundant, or the suppliers, some of them, more conscientious. Ever since the days of Goldsmith the writing and editing of children's works has been a source of ready emolument – in no class of literature does the risk bear so small a proportion to the reward – and consequently in no class has the system of *mere manufacture* been carried to such an extent.

After the bewilderment of ideas has somewhat subsided which inevitably attends the first entrance into a department of reading so overstocked and where the minds of the writers are so differently actuated, and those of the readers so variously estimated, the one broad and general impression left with us is that of the excessive ardour for *teaching* which prevails throughout. No matter how these authors may differ as to the mode, they all agree as to the necessity of presenting knowledge to the mind under what they conceive to be the most intelligible form, and in getting down as much as can be swallowed. With due judgment and moderation, this, generally speaking, is the course which all instructors would pursue; nevertheless it is to the extreme to which it has been carried that parents and teachers have to attribute the stunted mental state of their little scholars, who either have been plied with a greater quantity of nourishment than the mind had strength or time to digest, or under the interdict laid on the imagination, in this mania for explanation,

19

have been compelled to drag up the hill of knowledge with a wrong set of muscles. Doubtless the storing up of knowledge at an age when the powers of acquisition are most ductile and most tenacious, is of the utmost moment; but a child's head is a measure, holding only a given quantity at a time, and, if overfilled, liable not to be carried steadily. Also, it is one thing to stock the mind like a dead thing, and another to make it forage for itself; and of incalculably more value is one voluntary act of acquirement, combination, or conclusion, than hundreds of passively accepted facts. Not that the faculties can be said to lie inactive beneath this system of teaching – on the contrary, the mere mental mechanism is frequently exerted to the utmost; but the case is much the same as in the present modern school of music, where, while the instrument itself is made to do wonders, the real sense of harmony is sacrificed . . .

As regards also the excessive clearness of explanation, insisted upon now-a-days as the only road to sureness of apprehension, it is unquestionably necessary that a child should, in common parlance, understand what it acquires. But this again must be taken with limitation; for Nature, not fond apparently of committing too much power into a teacher's hand, has decreed that unless a child be permitted to acquire beyond what it positively understands, its intellectual progress shall be slow, if any. As Sir Walter Scott says, in his beautiful preface to the Tales of a Grandfather, 'There is no harm, but, on the contrary, there is benefit in presenting a child with ideas beyond his easy and immediate comprehension. The difficulties thus offered, if not too great or too frequent, stimulate curiosity and encourage exertion.'

The truth is, though seldom apprehended by juvenile book-writers, that children are distinguished from ourselves less by an *inferiority* than by a *difference* in capacity – that the barriers between manhood and childhood are marked less by the progress of every power than by the exchange of many. A mere weaker decoction of the same ideas and subjects that suit us will be very unsuitable to them. A genuine child's book is as little like a book for grown people cut down, as the child himself is like a little old man. The beauty and popularity of Lamb's 'Shakespeare's Tales' are attributable to the joint excellences of both author and transposer, but this is a rare exception: – generally speaking, the way in which Froissart is cut into spoon-meat, and Josephus put into swaddling-clothes, has only degraded these authors from their old positions, without in any way benefiting the rising generation by their new. The real secret of a child's book consists not merely in its being less dry and less difficult, but more rich in interest

– more true to nature – more exquisite in art – more abundant in every quality that replies to childhood's keener and fresher perceptions. Such being the case, the best of juvenile reading will be found in libraries belonging to their elders, while the best of juvenile writing will not fail to delight those who are no longer children. 'Robinson Crusoe', the standing favourite of above a century, was not originally written for children; and Sir Walter Scott's 'Tales of a Grandfather', addressed solely to them, are the pleasure and profit of every age, from childhood upwards. Our little friends tear Pope's 'Odyssey' from mamma's hands, while she takes up their 'Agathos' with an admiration which no child's can exceed. Upon the whole the idea of a book being too *old* for a child is one which rests upon very false foundations . . .

We fear, in short, that parents are far more inclined to look on [the present liberty of indiscriminate reading] as a necessary evil than as an incidental good, and are by no means satisfied in their consciences as to the time spent in useless reading, or the risk incurred by pernicious. But may not these misgivings, like many another concerning the education of children, be traced to our giving ourselves too much credit for judgment, and them too little for discernment? As regards useless reading, so long as it does not interfere with habits of application, and powers of attention, we are but poor judges of its real amount. Children have an instinct of food which more cultivated palates lose; and many is the scrap they will pick from hedge and common which to us seem barren. Nor may the question of pernicious reading be left to its usual acceptation, more especially as what is so called deserves the epithet, not so much on account of any absolutely false principle as from a tendency to inflame the passions or shock the taste, and therefore falls innocuous on a mind where the passions are silent and the taste unformed. With the immense choice of irreprehensible works before us, no one would deliberately put those into a child's hands where much that is beautiful is mixed up with much that is offensive; but, should they fall in their way, we firmly believe no risk to exist – if they will read them at one time or another, the earlier perhaps the better. Such works are like the viper – they have a wholesome flesh as well as a poisonous sting; and children are perhaps the only class of readers which can partake of one without suffering from the other . . .

Upon the whole, we should be happy if, by calling attention to the real excellence and beauty of a genuine child's book, we could assist in raising the standard of the *art* itself – the only effectual way, it seems to us, of checking the torrent of dressed-up trumpery which is now poured upon the public. For on taking a retrospective view of the juvenile libraries of the day, it is very obvious that there are a set of individuals who have taken to writing children's books, solely because they found themselves incapable of any other, and who have had no scruple in coming forward in a line of literature which, to their view, presupposed the lowest estimate of their own abilities. Nor has the result undeceived them – on the contrary, they write simple little books which any little simpleton can understand, and in the facility of the task become more and more convinced of its utter insignificance. The whole mistake hinges upon the slight but important distinction between *childish* books and *children's* books. The first are very easy – the second as much the reverse – the first require no mind at all – the second mind of no common class. What indeed can be a closer test of natural ability and acquired skill than that species of composition which, above all others, demands clearness of head and soundness of heart, the closest study of nature, and the most complete command over your materials? A child's book especially requires that which every possessor of talent knows to be its most difficult and most necessary adjunct, viz. the judgment evinced in the selection of your ideas – the discretion exercised in the control of your powers. In short, the *beau-ideal* of this class of composition lies in the union of the highest art with the simplest form; and if it be absurd to expect the realisation of this more frequently in children's books than in any other, it is quite as absurd to attempt to write them without keeping it in any way in view.

Some of the most forthright and entertaining early pieces on children's literature concerned the fairy-tale. Of course, there has been much debate as to whether the fairy-tale can or should be regarded as part of the field of children's books at all. It is essentially of the oral tradition, collected by scholars or appropriated for courtly use. J. R. R. Tolkien made the fundamental points in his 1938 lecture 'On Fairy-Stories' (in Tree and Leaf, Allen and Unwin, 1964).

Is there any *essential* connexion between children and fairy-stories? Is there any call for comment, if an adult reads them for himself? *Reads* them as tales, that is, not *studies* them as curios. Adults are allowed to collect and study anything, even old theatre-programmes or paper bags.

Among those who still have enough wisdom not to think fairy-stories pernicious, the common opinion seems to be that there is a natural connexion between the minds of children and fairy-stories, of the same order as the connexion between children's bodies and milk. I think this is an error; at best an error of false sentiment, and one that is therefore most often made by those who, for whatever private reason (such as childlessness), tend to think of children as a special kind of creature, almost a different race, rather than as normal, if immature, members of a particular family, and of the human family at large.

Actually, the association of children and fairy-stories is an accident of our domestic history. Fairy-stories have in the modern lettered world been relegated to the 'nursery', as shabby or old-fashioned furniture is relegated to the play-room, primarily because the adults do not want it, and do not mind if it is misused.* It is not the choice of the children which decides this. Children as a class – except in a common lack of experience they are not one – neither like fairy-stories more, nor understand them better than adults do; and no more than they like many other things. They are young and growing, and normally have keen appetites, so the fairy-stories as a rule go down well enough. But in fact only some children, and some adults, have any special taste for them; and when they have it, it is not exclusive, nor even necessarily dominant. It is a taste, too, that would not appear, I think, very early in childhood without artificial stimulus; it is certainly one that does not decrease but increases with age, if it is innate.

It can be argued (although this is increasingly seen as simplistic) that fairy-tales have an appropriate structure, an emphasis on action and clear distinctions between good and evil, and clear allegorical or symbolic relevance to child development. The patterns which survive (perhaps vestigially) from the oral tale, make the books easy to comprehend and remember. A psychologist and children's literature specialist, Nicholas Tucker, considers the question of magic:

*In the case of stories and other nursery lore, there is also another factor. Wealthier families employed women to look after their children, and the stories were provided by these nurses, who were sometimes in touch with rustic and traditional lore forgotten by their 'betters'. It is long since this source dried up, at any rate in England; but it once had some importance. But again there is no proof of the special fitness of children as the recipients of this vanishing 'folk-lore'. The nurses might just as well (or better) have been left to choose the pictures and furniture.

The belief in magic in various forms that runs through so many fairy-tales may also be in accordance with how younger children themselves think about certain events in the outside world. Later on, children will start moving on to more logical thought, when they have attained a certain age and have more experience. Until then, fairy stories in particular may be essentially in tune with earlier modes of thought; far from confusing children, they may help to build the intellectual confidence that usually comes when young people are given material especially adapted to their current capabilities. An intellect encouraged in this sense, even though by a pre-scientific way of thought that will eventually be rejected, may do better than an intellect balked by forcible exposure to more complex ideas at too early an age. (*The Child and the Book*, CUP, 1981, p. 73)

Perhaps the most famous nineteenth-century contributions to the debate on children's books were from Dickens and Ruskin, who, like Coleridge and Lamb before them, were firmly on the side of freedom, and against the appropriation of the fairy-tale by moralists. Dickens' 'Frauds on the Fairies' was a criticism of George Cruikshank's Fairy Library, *which used some of the tales for moralistic purposes. Dickens' version of 'Cinderella', as told by one of 'the new and meritorious class of commercial travellers' is a neat lampoon (it is omitted here); for the purposes of criticism, Dicken's opening and closing remarks are of most interest.*

Charles Dickens
From 'Frauds on the Fairies', *Household Words*, vol. 8, no. 184 (October 1853), pp. 97–100

We may assume that we are not singular in entertaining a very great tenderness for the fairy literature of our childhood. What enchanted us then, and is captivating a million of young fancies now, has, at the same blessed time of life, enchanted vast hosts of men and women who have done their long day's work, and laid their grey heads down to rest. It would be hard to estimate the amount of gentleness and mercy that has made its way among us through these slight channels. Forbearance, courtesy, consideration for the poor and aged, kind treatment of animals, the love of nature, abhorrence of tyranny and brute force – many such good things have been first nourished in the child's heart by this powerful aid. It has greatly helped to keep us, in some sense, ever young, by preserving through our worldly ways one slender track not overgrown with weeds, where we may walk with children, sharing their delights.

In an utilitarian age, of all other times, it is a matter of grave importance that Fairy tales should be respected. Our English red tape is too magnificently red ever to be employed in the tying up of such trifles, but every one who has considered the subject knows full well that a nation without fancy, without some romance, never did, never can, never will, hold a great place under the sun. The theatre, having done its worst to destroy these admirable fictions – and having in a most exemplary manner destroyed itself, its artists, and its audiences, in that perversion of its duty – becomes doubly important that the little books themselves, nurseries of fancy as they are, should be preserved. To preserve them in their usefulness, they must be as much preserved in their simplicity, and purity, and innocent extravagance, as if they were actual fact. Whosoever alters them to suit his own opinions, whatever they are, is guilty, to our thinking, of an act of presumption, and appropriates to himself what does not belong to him.

We have lately observed, with pain, the intrusion of a Whole Hog of unwieldy dimensions into the fairy flower garden. The rooting of the animal among the roses would in itself have awakened in us nothing but indignation: our pain arises from his being violently driven in by a man of genius, our own beloved friend, MR. GEORGE CRUIKSHANK. That incomparable artist is, of all men, the last who should lay his exquisite hand on fairy text. In his own art he understands it so perfectly, and illustrates it so beautifully, so humorously, so wisely, that he should never lay down his etching needle to 'edit' the Ogre, to whom with that little instrument he can render such extraordinary justice. But, to 'editing' Ogres, and Hop-o'-my-thumbs, and their families, our dear moralist has in a rash moment taken, as a means of propagating the doctrines of Total Abstinence, Prohibition of the sale of spirituous liquors, Free Trade, and Popular Education. For the introduction of these topics, he has altered the text of a fairy story; and against his right to do any such thing we protest with all our might and main. Of his likewise altering it to advertise that excellent series of plates, 'The Bottle,' we say nothing more than that we forsee a new and improved edition of Goody Two Shoes, edited by E. Moses and Son; of the Dervish with the box of ointment, edited by Professor Holloway; and of Jack and the Beanstalk, edited by Mary Wedlake, the popular authoress of Do you bruise your oats yet.

Now, it makes not the least difference to our objection whether we agree or disagree with our worthy friend, Mr. Cruikshank, in the opinions he interpolates upon an old fairy story. Whether good or bad in themselves, they are, in that relation, like the famous definition of a weed; a thing growing up in a wrong place. He has no greater moral justification in altering the harmless little books than we should have in altering his best etchings. If such a precedent were followed we must soon become disgusted with the old stories into which modern personages so obtruded themselves, and the stories themselves must soon be lost. With seven Blue Beards in the field, each coming at a gallop from his own platform mounted on a foaming hobby, a generation or two hence would not know which was which, and the great original Blue Beard would be confounded with the counterfeits. Imagine a Total abstinence edition of Robinson Crusoe, with the rum left out. Imagine a Peace edition, with the gunpowder left out, and the rum left in. Imagine a Vegetarian edition, with the goat's flesh left out. Imagine a Kentucky edition, to introduce a flogging of that 'tarnal old nigger Friday, twice a week. Imagine an Aborigines Protection Society edition, to deny the cannibalism and make Robinson embrace the amiable savages whenever they landed. Robinson Crusoe would be 'edited' out of his island in a hundred years, and the island would be swallowed up in the editorial ocean . . .

Frauds on the Fairies once permitted, we see little reason why they may not come to this, and great reason why they may. The Vicar of Wakefield was wisest when he was tired of being always wise. The world is too much with us, early and late. Leave this previous old escape from it, alone.

Ruskin's somewhat portentous defence is valuable more for its views on the ideal childhood – a rather romantic view, but one whose exclusions as to subject-matter are very commonly held today.

John Ruskin
From 'Fairy Stories' (1868)

In the best stories recently written for the young, there is a taint which it is not easy to define, but which inevitably follows on the author's addressing himself to children bred in school-rooms and drawing-rooms, instead of fields and woods – children whose favourite amusements are premature imitations of the vanities of elder people, and whose conceptions of beauty are dependent partly on costliness of dress. The fairies who interfere in the fortunes of these little ones are apt to be resplendent chiefly in millinery and satin slippers, and appalling more by their airs than their enchantments.

The fine satire which, gleaming through every playful word, renders some of these recent stories as attractive to the old as to the young, seems to me no less to unfit them for their proper function. Children should laugh, but not mock; and when they laugh, it should not be at the weaknesses or faults of others. They should be taught, as far as they are permitted to concern themselves with the characters of those around them, to seek faithfully for good, not to lie in wait maliciously to make themselves merry with evil: they should be too painfully sensitive to wrong, to smile at it; and too modest to constitute themselves its judges.

With these minor errors a far graver one is involved. As the simplicity of the sense of beauty has been lost in recent tales for children, so also the simplicity of their conception of love. That word which, in the heart of a child, should represent the most constant and vital part of its being; which ought to be the sign of the most solemn thoughts that inform its awakening soul and, in one wide mystery of pure sunrise, should flood the zenith of its heaven, and gleam on the dew at its feet; this word, which should be consecrated on its lips, together with the Name which it may not take in vain, and whose meaning should soften and animate every emotion through which the inferior things and the feeble creatures, set beneath it in its narrow world, are revealed to its curiosity or companionship; – this word, in modern child-story, is too often restrained and darkened into the hieroglyph of an evil mystery, troubling the sweet peace of youth with premature gleams of uncomprehended passion, and flitting shadows of unrecognized sin . . .

And the effect of the endeavour to make stories moral upon the literary merit of the work itself, is as harmful as the motive of the effort is false. For every fairy tale worth recording at all is the remnant of a tradition possessing true historical value – historical, at least, in so far as it has naturally arisen out of the mind of a people under special circumstances, and risen not without meaning, nor removed altogether from their sphere of religious faith. It sustains afterwards natural changes from the sincere action of the fear or fancy of successive generations; it takes new colour from their manner of life, and new form from their changing moral tempers. As long as these changes are natural and effortless, accidental and inevitable, the story remains essentially true, altering its form, indeed, like a flying cloud, but remaining a sign of the sky; a shadowy image, as truly a part of the great firmament of the human mind as the light of reason which it seems to interrupt. But the fair deceit and innocent error of it cannot be interpreted nor restrained by a wilful purpose, and all addictions to it by art do but defile, as the shepherd disturbs the flakes of morning mist with smoke from his fire of dead leaves.

Beside Ruskin, Chesterton's prose shines as a model of life and ingenuity, but his discussion in the essay 'The Ethics of Elfland' extends the argument for the importance of the fairy-tale developmentally, socially, and politically. It is no accident, perhaps, that Todorov used the folk-tale as one of the basic exemplars of structuralism. Chesterton, by his usual device of multiple paradox, relates it to a political context. 'The Ethics of Elfland' is a discourse on Chesterton's own philosophy, and his remarks on fairy stories are only a part of this.

G. K. Chesterton
From 'The Ethics of Elfland', *Orthodoxy* (1908). Reprinted from *G. K. Chesterton, A Selection of his Non-Fictional Prose*, selected by W. H. Auden, Faber and Faber, 1970

My first and last philosophy, that which I believe in with unbroken certainty, I learnt in the nursery. I generally learnt it from a nurse; that is, from the solemn and star-appointed priestess at once of democracy and tradition. The things I believed most then, the things I believe most now, are the things called fairy tales. They seem to me to be the entirely reasonable things. They are not fantasies: compared with them other things are fantastic. Compared with them religion and rationalism are both abnormal, though religion is abnormally right and rationalism abnormally wrong. Fairyland is nothing but the sunny country of common sense. It is not earth that judges heaven, but heaven that judges earth; so for me at least it was not earth that criticized elfland, but elfland that criticized the earth. I knew the magic beanstalk before I had tasted beans; I was sure of the Man in the Moon before I was certain of the moon. This was at one with all popular tradition. Modern minor poets are naturalists, and talk about the bush or the brook; but the singers of the old epics and fables were supernaturalists, and talked about the gods of brook and bush. That is what the moderns mean when they say that the ancients did not 'appreciate Nature', because they said that Nature was divine. Old nurses do not tell children about the grass, but about the fairies that dance on the grass; and the old Greeks could not see the trees for the dryads.

But I deal here with what ethic and philosophy come from being fed on fairy tales. If I were describing them in detail I could note many noble and healthy principles that arise from them. There is the chivalrous lesson of *Jack the Giant Killer*; that giants should be killed because they are gigantic. It is a manly mutiny against pride as such. For the rebel is older than all the kingdoms, and the Jacobin has more tradition than the Jacobite. There is the lesson of *Cinderella*, which is same as that of the Magnificat - *exaltavit humiles*. There is the great lesson of *Beauty and the Beast*, that a thing must be loved before it is lovable. There is the terrible allegory of the *Sleeping Beauty*, which tells how the human creature was blessed with all birthday gifts, yet cursed with death; and how death also may perhaps be softened to a sleep. But I am not concerned with any of the separate statutes of elfland, but with the whole spirit of its law, which I learnt before I could speak, and shall retain when I cannot write. I am concerned with a certain way of looking at life, which was created in me by the fairy tales, but has since been meekly ratified by the mere facts.

It might be stated this way. There are certain sequences or developments (cases of one thing following another), which are, in the true sense of the word, necessary. Such are mathematical and merely logical sequences. We in fairyland (who are the most reasonable of all creatures) admit that reason and that necessity. For instance, if the Ugly Sisters are older than Cinderella, it is (in an iron and awful sense) necessary that Cinderella is younger than the Ugly Sisters. There is no getting out of it. Haeckel may talk as much fatalism about that fact as he pleases: it really must be. If Jack is the son of a miller, a miller is the father of Jack. Cold reason decrees it from her awful throne: and we in fairyland submit. If the three brothers all ride horses, there are six animals and eighteen legs involved: that is true rationalism, and fairyland is full of it. But as I put my head over the hedge of the elves and begin to take notice of the natural world, I observed an extraordinary thing. I observed that learned men in spectacles were talking of the actual things that happened - dawn and death and so on - as if *they* were rational and inevitable. They talked as if the fact that trees bear fruit were just as necessary as the fact that two and one trees make three. But it is not. There is an enormous difference by the test of fairyland; which is the test of the imagination. You cannot *imagine* two and one not making three. But you can easily imagine trees not growing fruit; you can imagine them growing golden candlesticks or tigers hanging on by the tail. These men in spectacles spoke much of a man named Newton, who was hit by an apple, and who discovered a law. But they could not be got to see the distinction between a true law, a law of reason, and the mere fact of apples falling. If the apple hit Newton's nose, Newton's nose hit the apple. That is a true necessity; because we cannot conceive the one occurring without the other. But we can quite well conceive the apple not falling on his nose; we can fancy it flying ardently through the air to hit some other nose, of which it had a more definite dislike. We have always in our fairy tales kept this sharp distinction between the science of mental relations, in which they really are laws, and the science of physical facts, in which there are no laws, but only weird repetitions. We believe in bodily miracles, but not in mental impossibilities. We believe that a Bean-stalk climbed up to Heaven; but that does not at all confuse our convictions on the philosophical question of how many beans make five.

Here is the peculiar perfection of tone and truth in the nursery tales. The man of science says, 'Cut the stalk, and the apple will fall'; but he says it calmly, as if the one idea really led up to the other. The witch in the fairy tale says, 'Blow the horn, and the ogre's castle will fall'; but she does not say it as if it were something in which the effect obviously arose out of the cause. Doubtless she has given the advice to many champions, and has seen many castles fall, but she does not lose either her wonder or her reason. She does not muddle her head until it imagines a necessary mental connection between a horn and a falling tower. But the scientific men do muddle their heads, until they imagine a necessary mental connection between an apple leaving the tree and an apple reaching the ground. They do really talk as if they had found not only a set of marvellous facts, but a truth connecting those facts. They do talk as if the connection of two strange things physically connected them philosophically. They feel that because one incomprehensible thing constantly follows another incomprehensible thing the two together somehow make up a comprehensible thing. Two black riddles make a white answer.

In fairyland we avoid the word 'law'; but in the land of science they are singularly fond of it. Thus they will call some interesting conjecture about how forgotten folks pronounced the alphabet,

Grimm's Law. But Grimm's Law is far less intellectual than Grimm's Fairy Tales. The tales are, at any rate, certainly tales; while the law is not a law. A law implies that we know the nature of the generalization and enactment; not merely that we have noticed some of the effects. If there is a law that pick-pockets shall go to prison, it implies that there is an imaginable mental connection between the idea of prison and the idea of picking pockets. And we know what the idea is. We can say why we take liberty from a man who takes liberties. But we cannot say why an egg can turn into a chicken any more than we can say why a bear could turn into a fairy prince. As ideas, the egg and the chicken are further off from each other than the bear and the prince; for no egg in itself suggests a chicken, whereas some princes do suggest bears. Granted, then, that certain transformations do happen, it is essential that we should regard them in the philosophic manner of fairy tales, not in the unphilosophic manner of science and the 'Laws of Nature'. When we are asked why eggs turn to birds or fruits fall in autumn, we must answer exactly as the fairy godmother would answer if Cinderella asked her why mice turned to horses or her clothes fell from her at twelve o'clock. We must answer that it is *magic*. Is is not a 'law', for we do not understand its general formula. It is not a necessity, for though we can count on it happening practically, we have no right to say that it must always happen. It is no argument for unalterable law (as Huxley fancied) that we count on the ordinary course of things. We do not count on it; we bet on it. We risk the remote possibility of a miracle as we do that of a poisoned pancake or a world-destroying comet. We leave it out of account, not because it is a miracle and therefore an exception. All the terms used in the science books, 'law', 'necessity', 'order', 'tendency', and so on, are really unintellectual, because they assume an inner synthesis, which we do not possess. The only words that ever satisfied me as describing Nature are the terms used in the fairy books, 'charm', 'spell', 'enchantment'. They express the arbitrariness of the fact and its mystery. A tree grows fruit because it is a *magic* tree. Water runs downhill because it is bewitched. The sun shines because it is bewitched . . .

This elementary wonder, however, is not a mere fancy derived from the fairy tales; on the contrary, all the fire of the fairy tales is derived from this. Just as we all like love tales because there is an instinct of sex, we all like astonishing tales because they touch the nerve of the ancient instinct of astonishment. This is proved by the fact that when we are very young children we do not need fairy tales: we only need tales. Mere life is interesting enough. A child of seven is excited by being told that Tommy opened a door and saw a dragon. But a child of three is excited by being told that Tommy opened a door. Boys like romantic tales; but babies like realistic tales – because they find them romantic. In fact, a baby is about the only person, I should think, to whom a modern realistic novel could be read without boring him. This proves that even nursery tales only echo an almost pre-natal leap of interest and amazement.

Anyone can see [the second great principle of the fairy philosophy] who will simply read *Grimm's Fairy Tales* or the fine collections of Mr. Andrew Lang. For the pleasure of pedantry I will call it the Doctrine of Conditional Joy. Touchstone talked of much virtue in an 'if'; according to elfin ethics, all virtue is in an 'if'. The note of the fairy utterance always is, 'You may live in a palace of gold and sapphire, *if* you do not say the word "cow" '; or 'You may live happily with the King's daughter, *if* you do not show her an onion.' The vision always hangs upon a veto. All the dizzy and colossal things conceded depend upon one small thing withheld. All the wild and whirling things that are let loose depend upon one thing that is forbidden. Mr. W. B. Yeats, in his exquisite and piercing elfin poetry, describes the elves as lawless; they plunge in innocent anarchy on the unbridled horses of the air –

> *Ride on the crest of the dishevelled tide,*
> *And dance upon the mountains like a flame.*

It is a dreadful thing to say that Mr. W. B. Yeats does not understand fairyland. But I do say it. He is an ironical Irishman, full of intellectual reactions. He is not stupid enough to understand fairyland. Fairies prefer people of the yokel type like myself; people who gape and grin and do as they are told. Mr. Yeats reads into elfland all the righteous insurrection of his own race. But the lawlessness of Ireland is a Christian lawlessness, founded on reason and justice. The Fenian is rebelling against something he understands only too well; but the true citizen of fairyland is obeying something that he does not understand at all. In the fairy tale an incomprehensible happiness rests upon an incomprehensible condition. A box is opened, and all evils fly out. A word is forgotten, and cities perish. A lamp is lit, and love flies away. A flower is plucked, and human lives are forfeited. An apple is eaten, and the hope of God is gone.

One of the major shifts in critical thinking over the last few years has been the rehabilitation of the author into the critical process. The

'New Criticism' of the 1930s outlawed any interest in intention, and thus in the author. Authorship itself, however, seems to have retained its fascination, and so biography and interview have led, as it were, a parallel existence of often dubious respectability beside criticism. However, modern criticism, including reader-response theory and deconstruction, have widened the scope of what is admissible as valid for the critical process.

Many books, of varying quality, have been assembled from the opinions, written or spoken, of writers for children, who have generally delighted in the opportunity to talk about themselves and their art. Perhaps the passage which sums up the most commonly expressed opinion (and one which has been challenged a good deal) was the letter written by Arthur Ransome to the editor of The Junior Bookshelf in 1937, the year in which Pigeon Post was awarded the first Carnegie Medal. This extract, together with the comments by Geoffrey Trease (pp. 48-9), may stand for all such declarations.

Arthur Ransome
From 'A Letter to the Editor', The Junior Bookshelf, 1 : 4 (1937)

First: on writing books for children. I do not know how to write books for children and have the gravest doubts as to whether anybody should try to do any such thing. To write a book *for* children seems to me a sure way of writing what is called a 'juvenile', a horrid, artificial thing, a patronizing thing, a thing that betrays in every line that author and intended victims are millions of miles apart, and that the author is enjoying not the stuff of his book but a looking-glass picture of himself or herself 'being so good with children' . . . a most unpleasant spectacle for anyone who happens to look over his shoulder. It is true that some of the best children's books were written with a particular audience in view - *Alice in Wonderland* and *The Wind in the Willows*, for example. Many others were not, and it is impossible to read even those that were without realizing that one member of that audience, and the one whose taste had dictatorial rights, was the author. Lewis Carroll was not 'writing down' further than to Lewis Carroll, and though Kenneth Grahame could count on a delighted listener in his small son, the first person to enjoy the exquisite fun of Mr Toad and his friends was Kenneth Grahame himself. Stevenson was stimulated to the writing of *Treasure Island* by the presence of a young stepson, greedy for the chapters as they came, but his first delighted public was Robert Louis Stevenson. 'If this don't fetch the kids,' he writes, 'why, they have gone rotten since my day.' And, 'It's awful fun, boys' stories; you just indulge the pleasure of your heart . . .' That, it seems to me, is the secret. You just indulge the pleasure of your heart. You write not *for* children but for yourself, and if, by good fortune, children enjoy what you enjoy, why then you are a writer of children's books . . . No special credit to you, but simply thumping good luck. Every writer wants to have readers, and than children there are no better readers in the world.

2

Key essays in children's literature criticism

The first essays in this section are landmarks in children's book criticism in the sense that they mark the graduation of the subject into the mainstream of academic writing.

Roger Lancelyn Green's work represents not only the earliest extensive 'criticism' of children's literature, but also a dominant mode, which has only been challenged very recently. His *Tellers of Tales* first appeared in 1946, as a book designed to be read by adolescents; it was revised and expanded as an adults' reference work, and had a wide influence on librarians and teachers throughout the 1950s and 1960s.

His position is broadly Leavisite, and he has little time for theory. Even the distinction between books for children and books for adults is unclear, and he operates with reference to his own extensive, and perhaps idiosyncratic reading. As a child in the 1920s, he was very familiar with the books he describes in this article. His critical approach, a judicious combination of biography and description, avoids any 'hard' judgements, and, particularly, blurs the distinction between books *for* children and books which *have been* for children. Although he is clearly a highly skilled and respected bibliographer, he may have left a slightly unfortunate legacy, in that children's books have continued to be described in vague and urbane terms, and social and political implications have been ignored.

Nevertheless, here we have the pattern for one side of children's literary 'criticism': highly conventional and respectable, but ultimately that of the talented amateur. If many of his followers were not so talented, we can still be grateful for Lancelyn Green's confident approach.

Roger Lancelyn Green
'The Golden Age of Children's Books'
in *Essays and Studies 1962*,
edited by Beatrice White, John Murray, pp. 59–73

Histories of Literature seldom mention books written primarily for children, except when in cases like *Tales from Shakespeare* and *The Rose and the Ring* they represent amiable eccentricities on the part of writers famous for other and adult works.

Of recent years one or two favoured volumes have been promoted: but even for such works as *Alice in Wonderland* and *The Wind in the Willows* it has seemed that an excuse must be found, and painstaking (and painful) efforts have been made to prove that they are really allegories, or deeply psychological parables, intended to convey disguised truths to initiated adults.

The consideration of children's literature as such found its most noteworthy exponent in F. J. Harvey Darton whose *Children's Books in England* was published in 1932. Even so, however, he felt constrained to add the sub-title 'Five Centuries of Social Life', and he does not in fact touch on anything which could be described as Literature until his last two chapters. Percy Muir's *English Children's Books 1600–1900* (1954) is written largely from the book-collector's point of view, and the delight in rare editions tends to divert both author and reader from consideration of content to that of format.

The most compendious and painstaking work on the subject was published in America in the previous year (1953), *A Critical History of Children's Literature*, a 'Survey' in four parts under the editorship of Cornelia Meigs.

Now while these excellent works describe the growth and development of writing for children over several centuries, they reveal curious differences in approach from any similar works on the whole or any section of adult literature. Not only are they apt to consider children's books as a separate species rather than a branch of literature, but they tend more and more to accumulate a vast sea of books in which the reader becomes lost as he struggles desperately between the few definite islands which are just allowed to emerge above the flood.

Under these circumstances there seems to be some point in attempting to write at least the first draft of what might be developed by some expert into a chapter in a future history of English Literature: an attempt to chart some of the more or less definite islands off a portion of the mainland of our more generally recognized literary heritage.

There were few books written before the middle of the nineteenth century which can be said to have more than an antiquarian interest today. Several adult books like *Robinson Crusoe, Gulliver's Travels* and *Baron Munchausen* which have become nursery property (usually now in abridged or simplified versions) are beside the point, as are ballads, popular rhymes and folk-tales. Beyond a few translations of foreign fairy tales (Perrault and Grimm) and of *The Arabian Nights*, Lamb's *Tales from Shakespeare* (1807) is the only book from before the middle of the century which is still read, or which deserves any place among children's classics. Apart from this, and from a few representative poems in anthologies, Marryat's *The Children of the New Forest* (1847) and Ruskin's *The King of the Golden River* (1851 – but written some years earlier) are the only islands still visible in those early waters.

The only book which hovers on the border between actual and academic interest is Catherine Sinclair's *Holiday House* (1839). From the historical point of view it is one of the most important books in the history of children's literature, for it was written with the intention of changing the quality and kind of reading supplied for young people, and it was so successful that not only did it achieve its purpose but it remained in print, and was read by children for precisely a hundred years.

At a time when 'informative' books (they are now called, significantly, 'non-fiction') are once again swamping the junior book-counters, it is worth looking at what Catherine Sinclair wrote (for parents) in her Preface: 'Books written for young persons are generally a mere dry record of facts, unenlivened by an appeal to the heart, or any excitement to the fancy . . . but nothing on the habits and ways of thinking natural and suitable to the taste of children. Therefore, while such works are delightful to the parents and teachers who select them, the younger community are fed with strong meat instead of milk, and the reading which might be a relaxation from study becomes a study in itself . . .'

'In these pages', she continues, 'the author has endeavoured to paint that species of noisy, frolicsome, mischievous children which is now almost extinct, wishing to preserve a sort of fabulous remembrance of days long past, when young people were like wild horses on the prairies, rather than like well-broken hacks on the road; and when, amid many faults and many eccentricities there was still some individuality of character and feeling allowed to remain.'

Her battle was not won without a long struggle, and her children seem fairly tame now in the light of subsequent developments. The only part of the book which stands out as a notable achievement that is still fresh and entertaining is the 'Wonderful Story' about Giant Snap-'em-up (who was so tall that he 'was obliged to climb up a ladder to comb his own hair') which is the earliest example of Nonsense literature, and a direct precursor of Lewis Carroll and E. Nesbit.

It was some time before either the nonsense fairy tale or the story of true-to-life childhood achieved any worthy representations; but meanwhile a new development was started by Marryat and developed by Charlotte Yonge – the simple historical romance, usually with a child hero. In any age when the Waverley Novels were read avidly even by young children (Mrs Molesworth, born 1839, was reading them at the age of six when *Peveril of the Peak* proved too difficult, though she had found *Ivanhoe* and *The Talisman* 'so much nicer and easier'), and when his followers such as Bulwer Lytton and Harrison Ainsworth were not forbidden like the majority of adult novels, it was natural that, sooner or later, such books would be written with the young reader specially in view. An obvious development came also by way of the 'desert island' story, since *Robinson Crusoe* and *The Swiss Family Robinson* had been followed by the intensely pious *Masterman Ready*: R. M. Ballantyne avoided the didactic brilliantly in *The Coral Island* (1858), and followed it with excellent adventure stories in other fields which, like the meticulously historical thrillers of G. A. Henty, grew together towards the close of the century into the semi-adult movement of the 'story-tellers' headed by Stevenson, Haggard and Conan Doyle.

The really distinctive children's book grew more slowly and in less expected forms. Traditional fairy tales and stories from myth and legend found a period of great popularity about the time of the first translation of Hans Andersen (1846) and of Kingsley's *The Heroes* (1856), the Kearys' *Heroes of Asgard* (1857), and Dasent's *Tales from the Norse* (1859). But the original tale of fantasy developed slowly. Probably the earliest of any was F. E. Paget's *The Hope of the Katzekopfs* (1844) which showed real imagination and invention, but gave way to an undue weight of direct moral teaching which cripples its last two chapters hopelessly. It has not been reprinted since a shortened version re-named *The Self-willed Prince* came out about 1908.

Ruskin's *The King of the Golden River* (1851), a brilliant imitation of Grimm, made the grade, though an interesting experiment in the Border Ballad tradition of Fairy tale, by Mrs Craik, *Alice Learmont* (1852), failed to hold its audience. But at Christmas 1854 (though dated 1855) Thackeray produced the first classic of fairy-tale nonsense, and set the stage for all future stories of the 'Fairy Court' with *The Rose and the Ring*.

Although there is a basic moral in Thackeray's fantasy, the story, the characters and the spirit of fun are all more important. With the paradox of all true originality, Thackeray owed several debts for the materials with which he built: the general fairy-tale background of writers like Madame d'Aulnoy and the pantomime tradition which was growing in the able works of Planché and H. J. Byron; perhaps *The Hope of the Katzekopfs*, certainly Fielding's heroic burlesque *Tom Thumb the Great* whose language is echoed in the royal blank verse and in the brilliant use of bathos ('He raised his hand to an anointed King, Hedzoff, and floored me with a warming pan!' 'Rebellion's dead – and now we'll go to breakfast').

The Rose and the Ring had very few direct followers, or few that survive. Tom Hood 'the Younger' wrote probably the best imitation, *Petsetilla's Posy* (1870), though it is too like its original to escape destructive criticism, and there were others of even less importance. It was not, in fact, until thirty-five years later that a major work in the same tradition appeared, Andrew Lang's *Prince Prigio* (1889) – which owes only the same kind of debt to *The Rose and the Ring* and the traditional fairy-tales as Thackeray owed to his sources. In each case a writer of real genius was using, as it were, the same company and setting to put on a play of his own devising, and such as only he could have written.

Thackeray's indirect influence may, however, be traced in another original if somewhat controversial genius, George MacDonald, whose first children's story *The Golden Key* (1861) was pure allegory in a setting only superficially that of any known fairyland, but who showed a strong dash of the comic Fairy Court tradition by the time he reached his third, *The Light Princess* in 1864 (written two years earlier). After this he attempted longer stories, beginning with the full-length *At the Back of the North Wind* (1870, dated 1871) which combines dream, allegory and fairy-tale in a not completely successful whole, but reached his real heights with the *The Princess and the Goblin* (1871) and its even better sequel *The Princess and Curdie* (1882, but serialized 1877).

Critical judgement of MacDonald's work is rendered difficult, as in the case of several writers with superlative powers of imagination which far out-run their skill as literary craftsmen. The classic example of this uncomfortable dualism is Rider Haggard whose amazing imagination and narrative powers would place him among the truly great did not his woefully inept use of language and creation of character press him back amongst the very minor novelists.

MacDonald's deficiencies are most notable in his adult novels and least apparent in his *Unspoken Sermons* and the best of his children's books and imaginative works.

The quality of the *Princess* books to a child is that of a haunted house – but a house haunted by entirely good and desirable ghosts. They leave behind a feeling of awe and wonder, the excitement of the invisible world (we may call it Fairyland at the time, but it is always something more) coming within touchable distance: the door into the fourth dimension is situated in the places that we know best – we may chance upon it at any moment, and with the thrill of delight and excitement quite divorced from any fear of the unfamiliar. Though the stories are not memorable, the experience and its enriching quality remain vivid, and MacDonald's greatness is shown by the fact that to re-read him in later life is equally rewarding and brings no sense of disppointment.

Two excursions into utterly different realms of the imagination which appeared at much the same time as MacDonald's finest children's books have also this quality of an appeal that continues through life: *Alice's Adventures in Wonderland* (1865) and *Through the Looking-Glass* (1871).

Coming when they did, these two books revolutionized writing for the young. They captured the irresponsible fantasy in the minds of most children, and with it the unrealized urge towards rebellion against the imposed order and decorum of the world of the Olympians: but the capture was made by a writer of exceptional powers, a scholar in love with the richness of language and the devastating precision of mathematics. This seemingly inharmonious concatenation of elements produced two masterpieces, of which the second, being a little farther away from the spontaneous inspiration of oral story-telling, is the more perfectly integrated whole.

It is unsafe to attempt to get nearer to Dodgson's sources of inspiration. There seems to be no doubt that he made up the stories on the spur of the moment, telling them to children who were supplying much of the inspiration while he told by the interruptions, suggestions and criticism which are inseparable from composition in this kind. It is also true that on account of his stammer, from which he was only free when talking to children, Dodgson was seeking an escape into childhood and thereby capturing or preserving his own to some extent past the normally allotted limits. The result is what matters, and in this case it was two of the best known, best loved and most often quoted books in the language.

Although 'Lewis Carroll' set free the imagination, he had no original followers, though his imitators were legion - 'People are always imitating *Alice*,' complained Lang in 1895. In fact the only writers to draw anywhere near him in his peculiar realm of fantasy, nonsense and felicitously haunting turns of phrase are Rudyard Kipling with the *Just So Stories* (1902) and A. A. Milne with his two *Pooh* books in 1926 and 1928. One has only to turn to Tom Hood again (*From Nowhere to the North Pole*, 1875) to see how completely impossible it is to write a memorable imitation of *Alice*.

Perhaps because of this impossibility, the last quarter of the nineteenth century tended to produce fewer and fewer examples of the child's quest for the 'perilous seas' of Fairyland and concentrate with more and more skill on the presentation of childhood in the world of every day.

This was the main theme of Catherine Sinclair's protest, but its application was slow and tortuous. Superficially it was not new, since Maria Edgeworth and Mrs Sherwood professed to be writing about real children in their daily lives. A distinct step forward was taken by Charlotte Yonge with her novels for teenage girls such as *The Daisy Chain* (1856) and in the following year by Thomas Hughes in his outstanding story of public school boys, *Tom Brown's Schooldays*.

Smaller children, however, were still being subjected to the lachrymose-pious as in *Jessica's First Prayer* (1867) and *Misunderstood* (1869), though a new writer first made her mark in the second of these years, Juliana Horatia Ewing (1841–85) with *Mrs. Overtheway's Remembrances*. She progressed to *A Flat Iron for a Farthing* in 1872, (which year also saw Elizabeth Anna Hart's one outstanding child-novel, *The Runaway*) and reached her greatest heights with *Six to Sixteen* (1875) and *Jan of the Windmill* (1876).

The impact of these first outstanding child-novels is shown by Kipling's reference to *Six to Sixteen* in his autobiography: 'I owe more in circuitous ways to that tale that I can tell. I knew it (in 1875) as I know it still, almost by heart. Here was a history of real people and real things.'

Although Mrs Ewing may have had a better style, and on a small scale could produce better work, she was far surpassed as a child-novelist by Mrs Molesworth (Mary Louisa, *née* Stewart, 1839–1921). Although several of her longer books remain popular and stand up to re-reading, Mrs Ewing is best remembered by her miniature novels, or long-short stories *Jackanapes* (1884) and *The Story of a Short Life* (1885); but their appeal is now more strong to the adult than the

41

child, since they both turn on child-deaths (*Jackanapes* in fact jumps into manhood before dying, but the effect is that of a child-death), which needs a conscious return to the days of high infant mortality on the part of the reader for any appreciation, and seem awkward and sentimental to a modern child. Though often derided, stories of this kind should not be condemned out of hand: Mrs Ewing's two remain classics, and they have close runners-up in Mrs Molesworth's *A Christmas Child* (1880) and Frances E. Crompton's *Friday's Child* (1889).

This was, however, almost the only death-bed in Mrs Molesworth's voluminous works for the young (two short stories and an opening chapter complete her list of early deaths, no parents meet their end during the course of any book, though a few endure dangerous illnesses, and only one child becomes a cripple): her greatness lies in the fact that she was at once the faithful mirror of her own age and yet wrote, at her best, about the universal aspects of childhood.

It is no exaggeration to describe Mrs Molesworth as the Jane Austen of the nursery. Although her works are to Jane's as the miniature is to the great painting, such books as *The Carved Lions* and *Two Little Waifs* and *Nurse Heatherdale's Story* are as nearly perfect in their small kind as the great novelist's are in hers. Like her novels they are 'period' without being dated; they appeal to the heart as well as to the intellect; they remain in the memory and enrich the experience; they not only played an important part in their own branch of our literature, but deserve an abiding place on our shelves to be read and re-read by young and old.

Not only is one told in Mrs Molesworth's stories what it was like to be a child seventy-five years ago; as one reads one can experience all the hopes and fears, all the miniature loves and hates, passions and despairs, plots and counterplots of that distinct, if rather restricted little world. She truly understood children and could see life again with their eyes, and give vividness and poignancy to their small troubles in such a way that even to the adult reader the suspense may be as strong and as compelling as if it were a matter of life and death among grown men and women. So many of the basic problems and conflicts of life make themselves felt at all ages that this novel view of them back through the telescope into the eye of childhood seems in her best work to clarify and accentuate their relevance.

Although after such early stories as *Carrots* (1876) and *Hoodie* (1881) Mrs Molesworth avoided any hint of direct preaching, there is always a certain underlying intention in her stories. Well though she and such writers as Mrs Ewing and Mrs Hodgson Burnett understood children, they had not quite escaped from the tradition of the child as a miniature adult, as always in training for grown-up life. This tends to make the children seem a little on their best behaviour, and it gives perhaps an undue emphasis to the continual moulding of character, occasionally an exaggerated importance to a small sin or back-sliding. The children are just a little better than ourselves: to some extent the same is still true in such recent masterpieces as Arthur Ransome's stories of holiday adventures, but most of the conscious recognition of and combat with temptation has now gone. Acute introspection plays a relatively small part, however, in Mrs Molesworth's stories, though one told in the first person like *The Carved Lions* (1895), which is probably her masterpiece, gains greatly by the insight into the heroine's mind which it allows.

For more pronounced introspection we must turn to Mrs Hodgson Burnett who wrote many minor works, but only three which are on the definitely higher level which still makes them vividly alive. The first, *Little Lord Fauntleroy* (1886), suffers both from its intractable material – the balance without sentiment or patronizing between the democratic child of America and the aristocratic child in England – and from its unenviable reputation derived mainly from its translation into a stage sweet-meat for sentimental adults. Given a sympathetic reader who is ready to accept the limitations imposed by its period, the book is still remarkably readable both by young and old. Less difficult, though less convincing to the adult, is her second major story, *A Little Princess* (1905 – but a revised version of an earlier book published in 1887), which exploits the theme of the lonely child fallen from high fortune to poverty and persecution and then rescued at the eleventh hour by means which seem supernatural until satisfactorily explained at the end. The book is brilliant fare for children, but not one which weathers the test of adult re-reading with complete success.

Her last book, *The Secret Garden* (1911), is one of great individuality and astonishing staying power. It is the study of the development of a selfish and solitary little girl later in contact with an hysterical and hypochondriac boy of ten: a brilliant piece of work, showing unusual understanding of introspective unlikeable children with a sincerity that captures many young readers and most older ones.

Children with a country upbringing have found a similarly satisfying quality in *The Carved Lions* with its less introspective and more sympathetic heroine, and Mrs Molesworth's less convincing *Sheila's Mystery* (also 1895) which deals not quite so happily with the salvation of one of her few unpleasant children. The significant difference is that while Sheila's solution is found for her by intelligent adults, Mary in *The Secret Garden* works out her salvation by herself – with the aid of an imposing array of coincidences. Between the writing of these two books another change had come over the child-novel and one of considerable importance: it seems to owe its main impetus to Kenneth Grahame's *The Golden Age*, also published in 1895.

Now *The Golden Age*, undoubtedly one of the most important landmarks in the history of children's literature, is not a children's book at all. Misguided parents have frequently thought that it was: so far as I can remember *The Golden Age* was the only book which, as a child, I really and violently hated. The reason, curiously enough, seems to be that Kenneth Grahame knew too much. Here was an adult writing in an adult style about things which touched the very heart of our mystery; he was profaning the holy places – perhaps (for his manner was elusive) he was laughing in his detestable Olympian fashion at the things which really mattered.

The Golden Age, said Oswald Bastable in *The Would-be-goods*, 'is A1, except where it gets mixed with grown-up nonsense.' Even E. Nesbit did not quite realize where the trouble lay, since she had never read it as a child. For to the older reader *The Golden Age* (with its sequel *Dream Days*, 1898) is, as Swinburne said of it, 'well-nigh too praiseworthy for praise': it is not merely one of the greatest books of its period, but a classic in its own right and an outstanding example of English prose.

Its importance in the present survey rests in its approach to childhood and its amazing understanding of the workings of the child's imagination and outlook. Hitherto the child had been pictured to a greater or less extent as an undeveloped adult, and all his books were intended in some degree to help force him into life's full flowering. Sheer instruction may have faded into the background, but an undercurrent of teaching in morality, in manners, in the sense of duty was always present. Even Mrs Molesworth never escaped from this background purpose, close though she came to the real thoughts and sensations of childhood – to the child looking forward to adulthood rather than the adult pushing the child into it. In the greater writers even the conscious push was not necessarily a blot: Mrs Ewing, Mrs Molesworth and Mrs Hodgson Burnett could make of it a triumph as, in a completely different way, could George MacDonald.

But *The Golden Age* suddenly presented childhood as a thing in itself: a good thing, a joyous thing – a new world to be explored, a new species to be observed and described. Suddenly children were not being written down to any more – they were being written up: you were enjoying the Spring for itself, not looking on it anxiously as a prelude to Summer.

The immediate result as a loosening of bonds similar to that wrought by the outbreak into mere amusement of *Alice* thirty years earlier. It had a marked effect even on writers already well in their stride; even Mrs Molesworth, nearing the end of her literary career, found it impossible to resist the new elixir altogether, and at least two of her later books, *The House that Grew* (1900) and *Peterkin* (1902) have a gaiety and a youthfulness that sets them among her half-dozen best child-novels. As for minor writers, one has only to compare the sickly sentimentality of S. R. Crockett's *Sweetheart Travellers* (1895) with the adventurous boyishness of *Sir Toady Lion* (1897) to see the difference at its most extreme.

The oddest omission from the majority of earlier child-novels which Kenneth Grahame brought into the front of the picture was the imaginative life of children, and its importance to the children themselves. It had cropped up in several books written with more than half an eye on the adult reader, notably in Dickens's *Holiday Romance* (1868), Jefferies' *Bevis* (published as a three-volume novel in 1882), and in Mark Twain's *Tom Sawyer* and *Huckleberry Finn* (1875, 1884). But when it appears in the child-novel proper, as in the first chapter of Mrs Molesworth's *Two Little Waifs* (1883), it is merely incidental, or a means (as in *Hermy*, 1881) of starting a train of incidents. Not until *The Three Witches* (1900) and *Peterkin* could she make it the centre of her story.

Grahame had many direct imitators, but only one broke away from imitation and produced great and original work, and that was Edith Nesbit. She had been a hack journalist, whose ambition was to be a poet, for nearly twenty years when, in July 1897, a series of reminiscences of her schooldays in *The Girl's Own* ran away with her when she came to write of her childhood games of 'Pirates and Explorers'. From this grew the idea of producing sketches or short stories of the Golden Age variety, but purporting to be written by one of the children concerned. Most of Oswald Bastable's earlier adventures were contributed to the *Windsor* and *Pall Mall* magazines, both intended purely for adults, and only in the autumn of 1899 did she revise and link them, with a little re-written, earlier material from *The Illustrated London News* and several of *Nister's Holiday Annuals*, as *The Story of the Treasure-Seekers*.

A few reviewers took it as an adult book: 'Don't be content to read

The Treasure Seekers, but give it also to children. They will all bless the name of Mrs Nesbit,' wrote Andrew Lang, who described the Bastables as 'perfect little trumps' and preferred them to the heroes of *Stalky & Co.* which appeared at the same time. He went on to describe it as 'a truly novel and original set of adventures, and of the finest tone in the world'.

Lang himself was of an older generation and could still not quite reconcile the apparent lack of a moral with a children's book about contemporary children. Albeit with a twinkle in his eye, he had looked for and found a moral in his own original fairy stories (just as Dodgson had done with *Alice*, many years after its publication) and could at least make excuses for the moral short-comings of such traditional tales as *Puss in Boots*.

E. Nesbit, though she could lapse into sentimentality with the best, made the shift from conscious 'elevation' to unconcious improvement, substituting tone for teaching with the untidy impetuosity which characterizes even her best work. In the second Bastable compilation, *The Would-be-Goods* (1901) she even rounded on the moral tale, made a face at *The Daisy Chain* and (apart from the one monumental lapse over the supposed, dead Boer War hero) wrote her best non-magical children's book. Most of the Bastable stories were based on incidents or inspirations from her own childhood, and the thorough assumption of the child's outlook in the person of the narrator, Oswald, allowed her to use the joyous freedom and colloquial verve which carried the child-novel right out into the Spring sunshine once and for all.

In the 'real-life' line she could not follow up her initial success: *The New Treasure Seekers* (1905) already shows strain and self-imitation, and *The Railway Children* (1906) tends to lapse back into the sentimentality from which she was usually able to escape. Moreover surprisingly few child-novels followed hers that win anywhere near the status of classics (apart from *The Secret Garden*, 1911) until Arthur Ransome produced *Swallows and Amazons* in 1930.

Apart from achieving complete freedom, E. Nesbit's real claim to greatness lies, however, in her series of Wonder Tales. Short stories in the Fairy Court tradition accompanied the earlier Bastable tales into the world (they were collected as *The Book of Dragons*, 1900, and *Nine Unlikely Tales*, 1901) and she continued writing them, producing as many again over the next dozen years. The best of these would have assured her of a place not so very much lower than Thackeray and Lang; but by combining her styles and expanding her scope she produced eight full-length stories in which magic is introduced into family circles and surroundings as convincingly and prosaically real as those of the Bastables.

Magic to most children is only just out of reach: it fills their imaginings and informs their games. With the sure, deft touch and the rather pedestrian matter-of-factness which she knew so well how to use to advantage, E. Nesbit turned the games and the imaginings into actual events. 'Actual' is the key word; here she has never been equalled. She may have learnt how convincing magic can be, if strictly rationed and set in the most ordinary surroundings possible, from 'F Anstey' (Thomas Anstey Guthrie 1856-1934) of *Vice Versa* and *The Brass Bottle* fame; she certainly knew and admired Mrs Molesworth's blendings of fact and fantasy such as *The Cuckoo Clock* and *The Tapestry Room* – the Cuckoo and Dudu the Raven are close relations of the Psammead, the Phoenix and the Mouldiwarp: but the total effect is, at its best, original with the originality of sheer genius.

Her mounting skill is shown in her first series of three, *Five Children and It* (1902), *The Phoenix and the Carpet* (1904), and [*The Story of*] *The Amulet* (1906), each better than the last. Then came perhaps her supreme achievement, *The Enchanted Castle* (1907), with a delightful new family, unexpected and most credible magic, and a really cohesive plot instead of the string of adventures in her other books. *The House of Arden* (1908) and its overlapping sequel *Harding's Luck* (1909) keep to the same high level, though the construction begins to falter; and then the decline continues through *The Magic City* (1910) to *Wet Magic* (1913), after which she had written herself out.

The period ends sharply with E. Nesbit. But to follow out her career three notable writers have been shouldered aside, each authors of individual works of such recognized importance and popularity as to need no comment: Kipling with *The Jungle Books* (1894-5), *Stalky & Co.* (1899), *Just So Stories* (1902) and *Puck of Pook's Hill* (1906); Kenneth Grahame for that ambivalent masterpiece *The Wind in the Willows* (1908), an adult's book for children written by one of the few adults who could re-enter childhood at will; and Beatrix Potter, the only writer for very small children to produce works of real literature which adults can still enjoy – helped perhaps by her inseparable and equally outstanding illustrations.

Finally, spilt over from another medium, comes *Peter Pan*, the essence and epitome of all that the writers of the Golden Age were striving to capture. 'It has influenced the spirit of children's books,' wrote Harvey Darton, 'more powerfully than any other work except

the *Alices* and Andersen's *Fairy Tales.*' From its shores (the play has
been revived every year but one since it began in 1904, and the book,
Peter Pan and Wendy, 1911, is only a little less immortal) we may sail
adventuring in I know not how many directions, but to the Never,
Never Land we shall always return – led away for magic moments by
the Boy who wouldn't grow up, before turning refreshed and re-
invigorated to seek those joys in the world of real men and women
from which he was for ever shut out. For such, to all of us, of whatever
age, is the true message of the great children's books.

---

*It is interesting to contrast Lancelyn Green's attitudes with the overtly
political approach of Geoffrey Trease in the other article on children's
literature to appear in* Essays and Studies, *in 1973.*

*In it, he recollected the state of children's books in 'the depressed
nineteen-thirties':*

> If there was no fame, there was not much fortune. Children's
> books were commonly published under the old system long
> abandoned for other types of book. The author sold his
> copyright for a single payment of perhaps fifty pounds . . . It
> was small wonder that so much of children's literature was
> hackwork. (pp. 99–100)

His own introduction to radical readings of history is instructive:

> How did one write for children? To entertain them was
> essential. At that date I knew there was a prejudice against
> historical fiction, which was associated with compulsory holiday
> reading, long-winded descriptive passages, and archaic diction,
> especially in the dialogue. There were too many varlets crying
> 'quotha!' Too many writers slipped into a stilted, didactic style
> which set up an unnecessary barrier between them and their
> readers. A conscientious author of those days, Gertrude Hollis,
> in *Spurs and Bridle*, would produce a sentence like this:

>> 'Yonder sight is enough to make a man eschew lance and
>> sword for ever, and take to hot-cockles and cherry pit,'
>> exclaimed the Earl of Pembroke, adding an oath which the
>> sacred character of the building did not in the least
>> restrain.

> An obliging footnote informed the young reader that, 'hot-
> cockles and cherry pit' were 'popular games'. (p. 101)

He also has some practical answers to the question of how to write for children:

Granted, it is fatal to write down. 'When you write for children,' said Anatole France, 'do not adopt a style for the occasion. Think your best and write your best.' That is a splendid thought, something to cling to in hesitant moments, but for the practising craftsman it is not a sufficient guide.

Granted, too, that the 1973 ten-year-old is more sophisticated than his counterpart forty years ago, and in some respects genuinely more mature, which is by no means the same thing. Childhood, to many people's regret, has been telescoped into a much shorter period by varied factors ranging from earlier puberty to the pressures of television and advertising.

Grant that in any generation children may be more intelligent than their parents, more literate, better informed (especially about new scientific and technical developments) and more fully endowed with that quality of 'apprehension' which Walter de la Mare distinguished from 'comprehension'.

Grant all this, yet the writer is left with one obvious and inescapable difference between child and adult readers: the former have not lived so long, and in the nature of things they cannot have built up the same mental and emotional capital of background knowledge and first-hand experience. They were not alive fifteen years ago. To them, 'all our yesterdays' are already history that has to be learnt.

This is not to say that every 'i' must be dotted. A book, Alan Garner has said, 'must be written for all levels of experience'. There must be, as he rightly insists, a text that works 'at simple plot level', to make the reader turn the page. 'Anything else that comes through in the book is pure bonus. An onion can be peeled down through its layers, but it is always, at every layer, an onion, whole in itself. I try to write onions.' (pp. 102–3)

One of the most basic elements of children's literature criticism has been the problem of defining the field – or at least, marking out the administrative divisions. Unfortunately, there has been a tendency to try to define the books in terms of characteristics, sometimes in apposition to 'adult' literature, as though it were possible to define the characteristics of that. Two of the most famous and succinct statements are by Dennis Butts and Myles McDowell.

Reflecting on the post-Second World War 'second golden age' of children's literature, Butts noted (in 1977) 'a good deal of uncertainty

about the methodology and criteria for talking about children's books'.
He explored the possibilities of dealing with the subject by using the
same criteria and methods as for adult fiction, and by using child-
response to assess texts. The first method 'ignores the many necessary
differences in literary form' between the two types of text; the second
ignores the problem of articulation and experience in the readers
(pp. 9–10). (See Alderson, pp. 53–5.) Butts continues:

Because of the limitations of these approaches towards the
discussion of children's books, a third approach, although not
yet clearly articulated, is gradually appearing, based upon the
recognition of children's books as a literary *genre*. This
approach regards children's books as a sub-division of literature
proper, like, for example, the pastoral elegy, with its own
conventions and characteristics, which are neither good nor bad
in themselves, but exist only as the framework by which the
author expresses his view of life. Value judgements derive,
therefore, from trying to assess the writer's point of view and
how successfully he used the conventions to express it, as with
other forms of literature, and without criticising a work for
following the conventions of its *genre*.

Among the characteristics of the *genre* of children's fiction,
for example, are such obvious factors as the presence of child-
protagonists, greater flexibility about the probability of
narrative events, and recurring plot-elements such as the quest,
the journey through time, falls and rises of fortune, and various
kinds of initiation into adult life. Because of children's immatur-
ity, some linguistic, emotional, and intellectual limitations are
inherent in the *genre*, though this is by no means certain. Few
people, for example, would once have expected sexual relationships to have been dealt with so sensitively in a children's book
as they are in Paul Zindel's *I Never Loved Your Mind*. And
indeed Myles McDowell has argued in a recent essay that while
an adult novelist might draw attention to the complexity of
experience in a fairly raw way, and leave the reader to draw his
own conclusions and comfort, a good children's writer will also
make that complex experience available but perhaps in a
slightly different, more guarded way. This is clearly an aspect of
genre-theory which needs further clarification, but its defenders
would argue that all *genres* have some limitations, such as the
realistic novel's inability to deal with fantasy or farce's rejection
of grief.

(Introduction to *Good Writers for Young Readers*, Hart-Davis Educational, 1977)

This pragmatic approach was also used by Myles McDowell in his article 'Fiction for Children and Adults: Some Essential Differences' (Children's Literature in Education, *10, March, 1973, and reprinted in Geoff Fox* et al. (eds) Writers, Critics and Children, *New York, Agathon; London, Heinemann Educational, pp. 140–56*).

The only definition of a children's book, John Rowe Townsend avers, in *A Sense of Story*, Longman, 1971, p. 10, is that its name appears on a publisher's list of children's books. The distinction between adult and children's fiction is an artificial one maintained for administrative convenience. Now there is enough of truth in this to make us stop and ask, is there really no difference at all? But it seems to me to be the sort of special pleading to expect from one who is known as a writer for children, and is hardly the assertion one would expect from a purely 'adult' novelist. Townsend's statement is more important for the questions it raises than for the truth it contains, for while clearly the line between children's and adult fiction is blurred and broad, equally clearly there are vast numbers of books that fall very definitely on one side or the other. For the sake of examples one might pick, almost at random, Joyce's *Ulysses* and Clive King's *Stig of the Dump*. Now this is not to say that there is nothing in *Stig* that an adult might read with pleasure and profit, nor indeed that there are not bits of *Ulysses* that a child might confidently approach. C. S. Lewis was undoubtedly right to claim that a book that could only be read by a child was a poor children's book, but he might have added that an exclusive diet of children's fiction can hardly be satisfying to an adult, any more than an exclusive diet of the 'available bits' from adult books is a satisfactory diet for a child. An adult reading *Stig* does not read it as a child, full of wonder and delight and discovery, but as one perhaps blandly aware (because it is a rather 'thin' book), of an evocation of childhood, and aware too of some rather naively oblique comments on the Consumer Society. Neither does the adult read *Stig* as he reads and adult book. His mental approach and his expectations would be markedly different.

Nevertheless, there are *differences, however blurred, between the two broad categories:*

> children's books are generally shorter; they tend to favour an active rather than a passive treatment, with dialogue and incident rather than description and introspection; child protagonists are the rule; conventions are much used; the story

develops within a clear-cut moral schematism which much adult fictions ignores; children's books tend to be optimistic rather than depressive; language is child-oriented; plots are of a distinctive order, probability is often disregarded; and one could go on endlessly talking of magic, and fantasy, and simplicity, and adventure. The point here is not to legislate for essential differences but simply to note observable general orders of differences between the large body of children's fiction and that of adult fiction. The question immediately to be raised is how far these observable differences are inherent rather than accidental or conventional. Must a child's book necessarily be different from an adult book, or are the reasons for the differences merely conventions introduced by publishers, or by teachers, librarians, parents or others who direct choice and influence the supply?

Of the several critical directions that might be taken from this starting-point, two might be noted here. One is to dismiss the question of classification as totally invidious, as does Isabel Jan in On Children's Literature *(Allen Lane, 1969, pp. 142–3):*

It should by now be clear that since what is known as 'literature' does not and never did, in fact, exist, it is absurd to imagine that any sort of initiation can be required; that the emotions we experience through reading develop by stages, each stage represented by the various examinations leading from primary school to university entrance, and that an understanding of what we read can only be acquired the hard way through a succession of school essays and literary comprehensions. Children's literature is not a temporary substitute for something which the novice in a great, mystical scheme for the gradual achievement of transcendental knowledge is not yet ready to tackle. Critics – always ready to distribute either good or bad marks – are prepared to judge this 'by-product' by academic standards and to declare that one of its productions is or is not 'literature', is or is not 'well-written', and that it stands or does not stand a chance of becoming a 'classic'.

Scholastic disputes of this order only disguise the truth, which is that such works exist in their own right and not as rungs on the ladder to adult reading or that of middle-class citizens reared on the humanities. To say that a book is a 'first step' or that an author is an 'initiator' is to subscribe to a preposterous belief in a formidable staircase negotiated easily by some – who take it merrily two steps at a time – while others puff and plod or simply settle down contentedly on the first flight. Such assertions imply a difference in the quality of emotions experienced by children and adults, and indicate an attempt to put a value even on sensibility.

*Another is to face the question of how far children can be usefully incorporated into the critical process. Possibly the most influential short article on this subject is by Brian Alderson, who, in 'The Irrelevance of Children to the Children's Book Reviewer', (*Children's Book News, *January/February, 1969, pp. 10–11) attacked what he saw as the soft-centred approach of children's-book critics. This is a theme to which he has returned (see, for example, 'Opinions Are Free: Facts Are Expensive' in Peter Hunt (ed.)* Further Approaches to Research in Children's Literature, *UWIST, 1982, pp. 77–82), but the frequency with which Alderson's first article is mentioned suggests an impact out of proportion to its length. Brian Alderson is one of the great bibliographical critics, and he has been a trenchant upholder of the verities of text-based criticism in its various forms. In view of the work of Michael Benton, Chambers, and others in refining our analyses of children's responses, and in view of the general acceptance of a democratization of criticism Alderson's remarks may seem to be extreme. Nonetheless, what he has to say needs to be restated, because the malaise which he attacks so scathingly is still widespread in the less thoughtful areas of criticism, and the whole subject is denegrated by association.*

The question of how individual responses (which are not generalizable) can be weighed against abstract judgements (which may not apply to the individual) is one which 'conventional' criticism has been allowed to ignore, and one with which children's literature criticism is forced to grapple.

There has always been a tendency among the critics of children's books to invoke the response of particular children to support their assessment of works under review. Superficially, this may seem a perfectly acceptable practice since the books, after all, are intended for children, so why not canvass the customers in the approved psephological manner? Furthermore, it has often been observed that the children's book reviewer (like everyone else in the children's book business) subsists in a slightly unreal world, where time, brains and energy are expended on behalf of a vast and largely non-participating audience. The more valuable therefore, runs the argument, that the voice of this submerged public should be allowed to express some opinions for itself.

Confined to remarks like 'My Euphemia loved the tasteful blues and yellows' this procedure is innocuous if pointless: but when the critic seeks to use child-response to establish or refute a critical position, it can be much more dangerous. At best it forms a type of special pleading foreign to the art of criticism (how many reviewers of adult books cite their grandmothers' opinions as a serious yardstick for assessing books for old ladies?) and at worst it supplies a neat opportunity for the critic to welsh from his duties.

There is no doubt that the situation of reviewing has improved since Alderson made these comments, but it is equally clear that the reviewing of adult texts draws upon a far more 'agreed' set of critical tenets. Any distinction between 'reviewers' and 'critics' is ignored here:

Critics who abdicate their responsibilities like this probably forget a number of things that are of considerable importance if the adult is to be of any help in creating intelligently literate young people. In calling upon the views of children he may forget that he is almost bound to receive opinions that are immature and often inarticulate. They may be true for the people expressing them, but they will hardly serve as the basis for a sound critical assertion. More important, he may forget how easy it is for the inquiring adults to influence the views of the specimen children. I am inclined to think that, within reason, you can sell most young people anything, provided you are sold on it yourself – or conversely you can put most children off anything provided that you find it off-putting yourself.

Ultimately, of course, the referral of critical issues to young readers themselves raises the question of the validity in critical terms of majority opinions. If it is deemed acceptable to condemn to perdition, say, the choir school stories of William Mayne because a class of school children cannot understand them, it will presumably be acceptable to canonize Anthony Buckeridge because the same class reads him to pieces. The adage that 'we needs must love the highest when we see it' has always seemed to me of doubtful application and it is at its most doubtful applied to children when they are left to themselves among books. But for the critic to collapse under popular clamour for the lowest is not only undignified, it is also evidence of his failure to analyse where his position lies in the no-man's-land between young readers and literacy.

At this point, Alderson is confronting the central question in children's book criticism, the question of use. *Alderson (although he may appear to be) is not attacking those who use children's books as a vehicle for education; he is attacking 'the present bane of adult ignorance'. Alderson's 'purist' approach is one which is difficult to sustain, but one which is a necessary corrective. He goes on:*

It may be objected that to assess children's books without reference to children is to direct some absolute critical standard relating neither to the author's purpose nor the reader's enjoyment. To do much less, however, is to follow a road that leads to a morass of contradictions and subjective responses, the most serious result of which will be the confusion of what we are trying to do in encouraging children to read. From the tone of reviews in the popular press our aim would appear to be not much more than that of keeping the children quiet for half an hour or fitting them out to be competent participants in a bureaucratic society. But once one assigns to reading the vital role, which I believe that it has, of making children more perceptive and more aware of the possibilities of language, then it becomes necessary to hold fast to qualitative judgements formed upon the basis of adult experience. Naturally a knowledge of and sympathy with children (beyond mere remembrance of things past) must play a vital part in this judgement, but just as vital is a personal response based upon knowledge of the resources of contemporary children's literature.

This theme is echoed, perhaps a little less aggressively, by Wallace Hildick (Children and Fiction, *Evans Brothers, 1970, pp. 140–2):*

At one end of the scale, for instance, books might be given to children to review, and especially to the children of celebrities – a procedure that has the added advantage of seeming to be completely logical. So it is of course, up to a point – that point being where a skilled adult reviewer finishes canvassing his own children's or his friend's children's opinions and begins to take them into account when making his *own* assessment, which will naturally envisage other children, with other tastes or reading abilities. As they stand, however, the fifty or so solemn words by Adrian (aged 11) or Sara (who is 8¼) are about as likely to be useful as a review of *Lord Jim* by a deck hand, or *Lady Chatterley's Lover* by a gamekeeper. Then at the other end of the scale we have the well-known critic of adult books charged with the task of being mistily reminiscent or waspishly sociological or brilliantly facetious according to his usual persona.

Where more sympathetic and knowledgeable skilled critics are used, they are still rarely given the space for lengthy quotation and analysis – and it should be especially noted here that the duality of concern in children's fiction, the intertwined questions of social and artistic responsibility, often require the lengthy disentangling of the various threads, through extensive quotation, in order that a work be properly appraised. Granted, even adult-fiction reviewers are seldom given the space in which to delve deeply, through analysis, but there is a whole field of criticism in volume form in which they may extend themselves and their inquiries, to say nothing of the literary quarterlies and similar journals. By comparison, the books on children's fiction and the journals willing to find room for the subject form a tiny, almost negligible patch. And even here, the habits formed in the workhouse of the more popular sections of the press seem to cling, so that comparatively little advantage is taken of their opportunities by critics who are given their head. Broad surveys are undertaken rather than studies in depth, with the result that each book discussed is so often given little more space than it would have had in a friendly newspaper or weekly review. The squaring of children's preferences and needs with artistic accomplishment in relation to single books or authors – a subject requiring whole chapters or volumes – tends to be ignored or skated over. And where lengthy quotations are given they are too often presented only in the course of paraphrasing a plot or as the subjects of eulogy. Again and again one comes across quotations heralded or followed by such thin unsubstantiated comments as: 'What child could resist the following pen-picture?' or 'This is a masterly piece of writing' or 'Here is a characteristic example' or 'The social milieu is indicated in the second paragraph' or 'Just how far from real children they were will be seen from the following extract' or 'Here is how the author describes the scene' or 'A fine piece of realistic observation'. What we wish to know is *why* the critic thinks a piece of writing is 'masterly' or 'fine' or 'characteristic' or 'irresistible to a child'. We need closely pursued investigations and closely argued conclusions.

The major points made in this area of discussion were brought together in John Rowe Townsend's 'Standards of Criticism for Children's Literature' in 1971.

John Rowe Townsend is a distinguished novelist for children, his best work, perhaps, being The Intruder *and* Goodnight, Prof. Love. *He has risked the ephemerality of writing books dealing with fashionable topics, the best of which is probably* Hell's Edge. *But his reputation may well stand on what is still the definitive writing of children's book history,* Written for Children, *now in its third edition.*

Townsend is in the line of Lancelyn Green, but with much sharper concentration on the text. His definition of children's books, in his collection of essays, A Sense of Story *(Longman Young Books, 1971) (cited by McDowell, p. 51), has justifiably become a standard dictum:*

> Although the distinction is administrative rather than literary, it must have some effect on the way books are written. Yet authors are individualists, and still tend to write the book they want to rather than one that will fit into a category. Arguments whether such-and-such a book is 'really for children' are always cropping up, and are usually pointless in any but organizational terms. The only practical definition of a children's book today – absurd at it sounds – is 'a book which appears on the children's list of a publisher'. (p. 10)

However, in delivering the 1971 May Hill Arbuthnot lecture (Arbuthnot being one of the pioneering American librarians who set the standard for children's book criticism in the USA), Townsend made a definitive statement on the position of both writer and critic. Only recently, with radical shifts in critical thinking, has this article been surpassed, and then probably not in any single text. This version is reprinted (slightly edited) from Nancy Chambers (ed.), The Signal Approach to Children's Books, *1980. It has been reprinted several times, but I make no apology for reproducing it here; it remains a centrally important statement.*

John Rowe Townsend
'Standards of Criticism for Children's Literature', from ALA Children's Services Division, *Top of the News*, June 1971

To give the May Hill Arbuthnot Honour Lecture is the greatest privilege that can fall to a commentator on books for children. It is with some idea of matching my response to the size of the honour that I have decided at last to attempt the largest and most difficult subject I know in this field: namely, the question of standards by which children's literature is to be judged. This is not only the most difficult, it is the most important question; indeed, it is so basic that none of us who are professionally concerned with children and books ought really to be functioning at all unless we have thought it out to our own satisfaction and are prepared to rethink it from time to time. But, as in many other areas of life, we tend to be so busy doing what we have to do that we never have time to stop and consider why and how we do it. True, Mrs Arbuthnot herself had a good deal to say on the subject of critical standards, but she would not have claimed to say the last word.

It seems to me that the assessment of children's books takes place in an atmosphere of unparalleled intellectual confusion. There are two reasons for this. One is a very familiar one which I need not elaborate on. It was neatly expressed by Brian Alderson in an article in *Children's Book News* when he said that 'everyone in the children's book business subsists in a slightly unreal world, where time, brains and energy are expended on behalf of a vast and largely non-participating audience'. It has been pointed out time and time again that children's books are written by adults, published by adults, reviewed by adults, and, in the main, bought by adults. The whole process is carried out at one, two, three, or more removes from the ultimate consumer.

This situation is inescapable, but it is an uneasy one. Most of us think we know what is good for ourselves, but the more sensitive we are, the more seriously we take our obligations, the less we feel sure we know what is good for others.

The second cause of confusion is that children's literature is a part of the field, or adjoins the field, of many different specialists; yet it is the *major* concern of relatively few, and those not the most highly placed in the professional or academic pecking-order. Furthermore, the few to whom children's literature is central cannot expect, within one working lifetime, to master sufficient knowledge of the related fields to meet the experts on their own ground and at their own level. And yet, while the children's literature person obviously cannot operate at a professional level in all these various fields, the people operating in the various fields can and quite properly do take an interest in children's reading as it affects their own specialities, and quite frequently pronounce upon it. But, understandably, such people are often unaware of or have not thought deeply about the aspects of children's literature that do *not* impinge upon their own field. The subject is one on which people are notoriously willing to pronounce with great confidence but rather little knowledge. Consequently, we have a flow of apparently authoritative comment by people who are undoubtedly experts but who are not actually experts on *this*.

I am not here to quarrel with those who see children's literature in terms of social or psychological adjustment, advancement of deprived or minority groups, development of reading skills, or anything else. I have said in the foreword to my book, *A Sense of Story*, that 'most disputes over standards are fruitless because the antagonists suppose their criteria to be mutually exclusive; if one is right the other must be wrong. This is not necessarily so. Different kinds of assessment are valid for different purposes.' I would only remark that the viewpoints of psychologists, sociologists, and educationalists of various descriptions have rather little in common with each other or with those whose approach is mainly literary.

We face, in fact, a jungle of preoccupations, ideas, and attitudes. I should like to begin my discussion by clearing, if I can, some small piece of common ground which will accommodate most of us who care about children and books.

Let me borrow a phrase used by Edgar Z. Friedenberg, in a book entitled *Coming of Age in America*, published in 1965. I do not agree with all that is said in the book, but I think the phrase I have my eye on is admirable. Friedenberg used it to describe the true function of the schools; I would use it to describe the duty of all of us, either as parents, or, in a broad sense, as guardians. This aim, he said, was 'the respectful and affectionate nurture of the young, and the cultivation in them of a disciplined and informed mind and heart'.

Extending this formulation to cover the special interest which has brought us here today, I should like to add that in furtherance of these ends we would wish every child to experience to his or her full capacity the enjoyment, and the broadening of horizons, which can be derived from literature. Diffidently I invite my hearers, and my readers, if any, to subscribe to this modest and unprovocative creed. What it asks is the acceptance of literary experience as having value in itself for the general enrichment of life, over and above any virtue that may be claimed for it as a means to a non-literary end. Anyone who cannot accept the proposition is of course fully entitled to stand aloof: but I cannot think of anything to say to such a person, because if literature is *solely* a means to an end, then the best literature is the literature which best serves that end, and the only matters worth arguing about are whether the end is a good one and how effectively it is served. Furthermore, those points cannot be argued in general terms, but only in relation to a particular cause and a particular book.

I wonder if from the tiny clearing we have made we can begin to find a way through the tangle that surrounds us. Let us try to consider what literature is, what it offers and what is children's literature. I do not want to spend a lot of time on questions which, although they may present theoretical difficulties, are not really perplexing in practice. I am going to define literature, without appeal to authority, as consisting of all works of imagination which are transmitted primarily by means of the written word or spoken narrative — that is, in the main, novels, stories and poetry — with the addition of those works of non-fiction which by their qualities of style or insight may be said to offer experience of a literary nature. This is a rather loose definition, but in practical terms I think it will do.

What does literature offer? Summarizing ruthlessly, I will say that it is, above all, enjoyment: enjoyment not only in the shallow sense of easy pleasure, but enjoyment of a profounder kind; enjoyment of the shaping by art of the raw material of life, and enjoyment, too, of the skill with which that shaping is performed; enjoyment in the stretching of one's imagination, the deepening of one's experience, and the heightening of one's awareness; an enjoyment which may be intense even if the material of the literary work is sad or painful. I should add that obviously not all literature can offer such a range of enjoyment; that no work of literature outside such short forms as the lyric poem can offer these enjoyments throughout; and that the deliberate restriction of aim is often necessary in children's literature as in much else.

What in particular is children's literature? That is quite a hard question. There is a sense in which we don't need to define it because we know what it is. Children's literature is *Robinson Crusoe* and *Alice* and *Little Women* and *Tom Sawyer* and *Treasure Island* and *The Wind in the Willows* and *Winnie-the-Pooh* and *The Hobbit* and *Charlotte's Web*. That's simple: but it won't quite do. Surely *Robinson Crusoe* was not written for children, and do not the *Alice* books appeal at least as much to grownups?; if *Tom Sawyer* is children's literature, what about *Huckleberry Finn*?; if the *Jungle Books* are children's literature, what about *Kim* or *Stalky*?; and if *The Wind in the Willows* is children's literature, what about *The Golden Age*?; and so on.

Since any line-drawing must be arbitrary, one is tempted to abandon the attempt and say that there is no such thing as children's literature, there is just literature. And in an important sense, that is true. Children are not a separate form of life from people; no more than children's books are a separate form of literature from just books. Children are part of mankind; children's literature is part of literature. Yet the fact that children are part of mankind doesn't save you from having to separate them from adults for certain essential purposes: nor does the fact that children's literature is part of literature save you from having to separate it for practical purposes (in the libraries and bookshops, for instance). I pondered this question for some time while working on *A Sense of Story*, and came to the conclusion that in the long run children's literature could only be regarded as consisting of those books which by a consensus of adults and children were assigned to the children's shelves – a wholly pragmatic definition. In the short run it appears that, for better or worse, the publisher decides. If he puts a book on the children's list, it will be reviewed as a children's book and will be read by children (or young people), if it is read at all. If he puts it on the adult list, it will not – or at least not immediately.

Let us assume that we have found, in broad terms, a common aim; that we know roughly what literature is and the nature of the experience it offers: that we have a working definition of children's literature, even if it is more pragmatic than we would wish. Can we now make some sense out of the question of differing standards? So far I have tried to examine what exists rather than to project a theoretical system out of my own head. We all know how often the application of a new mind to an old problem will fail because the new thinking is insufficiently grounded in what has been thought and done before; indeed, it often overestimates its own originality.

When we look for individual assessments of actual books (as distinct from general articles on children's literature and reading) we find that most of what is written comes under the headings of (a) over-whelmingly, reviews, (b) aids to book selection, and (c) general surveys. There is little writing that I think could be dignified with the name of criticism, a point to which I will return later. While examining reviews, selection aids, and surveys, in both the United States and Britain and in relation to imaginative literature, I asked myself not whether they were sound and perceptive or whether I agreed with them, but what they were actually doing and what their standards appeared to be. I was aware that similar enquiries had been carried out by others, and more thoroughly; but I was aware, too, that my findings would be matters of judgement which were not of simple fact, and the scheme of my over-all study required that the judgements should be my own. I will spare you the raw material of my investigation and will keep my conclusions brief. I found, naturally, some differences between reviews in general and specialist publications, but from my point of view they were not crucial.

What the reviewers and selectors were largely concerned with, more often than not, it seemed to me, was telling you what the story was about: a necessary activity, but an evaluative one. I came to the conclusion that where they offered judgements the writers always concerned themselves with one or more of four attributes, which I do not place in order of importance of frequency. These were (1) suitability, (2) popularity, or potential popularity, (3), relevance, and (4) merit. 'Suitability' is rather a blanket term, under which I include appropriateness to the supposed readership or reading age or purpose, and also attempts by the reviewer or selector to assign books to particular age groups or types of child. 'Popularity' needs no explanation. By 'relevance' I mean the power, or possible power, of theme or subject-matter to make the child more aware of current social or personal problems, or to suggest solutions to him; where a story appears to convey a message I include under 'relevance' the assessment of the message. Finally, by 'merit' I mean, on the whole, literary merit, although often one finds that what might be called undifferentiated merit is discerned in a book.

Of the four attributes I have mentioned (please remember that my classifications are arbitrary and that there is some overlap) it may well have occurred to you that the first three are child-centred: suitability to the child, popularity with the child, relevance to the child. The fourth is book-centred: merit of the book. This is an important distinction: failure to perceive it has given us a great deal of trouble in the past, preventing us from understanding each other and understanding what we are about. In an article in *Wilson Library Bulletin* for December 1968 I rashly coined a phrase about 'book people' and 'child people'. 'Book people', I said, were those primarily concerned with books: authors, publishers, a great many reviewers, and public librarians. 'Child people', I said, were those primarily concerned with children: parents, teachers, and (in England at any rate) most school librarians. This division was useful in a way, because it helped to account for two diametrically opposed views of the state of English children's literature: that it was in a very healthy state, with so many good books being published; and that it was in a very unhealthy state, because so many children didn't find pleasure in reading. 'Book people', I thought, tended to take the former view; 'child people' to take the latter. Incidentally, it was reflection on the fact that such totally opposite views could be held that led me to feel we needed an examination of standards and, in part, led me to offer my present hesitant contribution to that formidable task.

However, I did not and do not intend to set any group against any other group, and I must say at once that all children's 'book people' I know are also 'child people' in that they care about children; and all the 'child people' I know who are interested in books are on that account 'book people'. And I will repeat here what I said earlier in another context: that different kinds of assessment are valid for different purposes. Not only that, but different standards can co-exist within the mind of the same person at the same time. This is why we get mixed up. Our judgements are rarely made with a single, simple purpose in mind, and we do not stop to separate our purposes any more than we normally stop to analyse our own processes of thought. Because we are both 'book people' and 'child people' and because we care about both books and children, book-centred and child-centred views are all jumbled together in our heads. Is it a good book, will children like it, will it have a beneficial effect on them? We ask ourselves all these questions at once, and expect to come up with a single answer.

It is easy for mental sideslips to occur, even when we are writing for publication. A simple instance (one of many that could be cited) is in the London *Times Literary Supplement* of 16 April 1970, where the anonymous reviewer of a book of verse by Alan Brownjohn discusses the book with much intelligence in the language of literary criticism, and finishes by saying that 'this is a book all children will most definitely enjoy'. The statement is unrelated to the rest of what is said and, unfortunately, cannot be true. Nobody has yet found a book that 'all' children enjoy, and if there were such a book I do not think it would be a book of poems. The reviewer cannot have *thought* before writing that: he or she has made the remark either as a general expression of approval or as an unrealistic inference: 'It is good, so they will all enjoy it.'

There are people – Brian Alderson in an article provocatively entitled 'The Irrelevance of Children to the Children's Book Reviewer'; Paul Heins, if I understand him correctly, in two articles in the *Horn Book* called 'Out on a Limb with the Critics' and 'Coming to Terms with Criticism', in June and August 1970, respectively – who maintain that reviewing should be strictly critical. Alderson says: 'It may be objected that to assess children's books without reference to children is to erect some absolute critical standard relating neither to the author's purpose nor to the reader's enjoyment. To do much less, however, is to follow a road that leads to a morass of contradictions and subjective responses.'

I do not wish to prolong my discussion of a subject already so much discussed as reviewing. On the whole I agree with Heins and Alderson, whose positions, I think, can fairly be described as purist. I would prefer the reviewer to address himself sensitively to the book which is there in front of him, rather than to use his space for inevitably crude assessments of suitability for some broad notional category of child or speculations that the book will or will not sit long on the shelf, or that it will or will not help its readers to adjust to reality or understand how the other half of the world lives. Readers can use their intelligence and make these assessments or pursue these speculations for themselves. I suspect that library systems can manage the practical task of book selection without undue dependence on the individual reviewer. What they need to know from him, if they need to know anything from him (and if it isn't too late anyway by the time the review appears), is: does the book have literary merit?

Suitability, popularity, relevance – are these not questions for the buyer, and perhaps above all for those who are closest to the ultimate consumer? 'Will this be suitable for *my* child, will this be popular with *my* class, will this be relevant to the children in the area served by *my* library?' Surely only the parent, teacher or librarian there on the spot can find the answer. He will find it in his own judgement and experience. And he will soon learn whether he was right.

I hope I have cleared the ground sufficiently to allow myself to move on to a discussion of critical principles in relation to children's literature. I am not sure whether I have sufficiently indicated the *usefulness* of the critical approach. If I have not, then I ought to do so: for although some of us would no doubt practise it quite happily for its own sake, if it is not useful we cannot reasonably expect others to give their time and attention, their paper and print, to the result of our endeavours. So I will suggest first that a standard of literary merit is required, and indeed in practice is accepted, as the *leading edge*, so to speak, of book assessment, since non-literary standards relate so largely to specific aims and situations, times, places and audiences. Literary standards are not fixed forever, but they are comparatively stable; that is part of their essence. Without this leading edge, this backbone if you prefer it, there can only be a jumble of criteria, a haphazard mixture of personal responses. And I have found in my own numerous discussions with people concerned with various aspects of books for children, that even those who most strongly condemn what they consider to be an excessively literary approach do in fact take it for granted that there is some independent standard of quality other than what children like or what is good for them or what brings them face to face with contemporary issues. 'Wonderful stuff, but not for *my* kids' is a frequent comment.

I would suggest, too, and have suggested in the introduction to *A Sense of Story*, that a critical approach is desirable not only for its own sake but also as a stimulus and discipline for author and publisher, and, in the long run, for the improvement of the breed. Donnarae MacCann, introducing a series of articles in the *Wilson Library Bulletin* for December 1969, made this point and quoted from Henry S. Canby's *Definitions* (second series, 1967):

> Unless there is somewhere an intelligent critical attitude against which the writer can measure himself . . . one of the chief requirements for good literature is wanting . . . The author degenerates.

Donnarae MacCann goes on to say that 'there is no body of critical writing to turn to, even for those books which have been awarded the highest literary prizes in children's literature in Britain and America'. That seems to me to indicate a serious lack, and to suggest a further use for the literary criticism of children's books: to help them to achieve their proper status. There is a parallel between the standing of children's literature now and that of the novel a hundred years or so ago. Listen to Henry James in *The Art of Fiction* (1884):

> Only a short time ago it might have been supposed that the English novel was not what the French call 'discutable' . . . there was a comfortable, good-humoured feeling abroad that a novel is a novel as a pudding is a pudding, and that our only business with it could be to swallow it . . . Art lives upon discussion, upon experiment, upon curiosity, upon variety of attempt, upon the exchange of views and the comparison of standpoints . . . [The novel] must take itself seriously for the public to take it so.

We can apply Henry James' statements to children's literature today. As yet, it is barely discussible at a respectable intellectual level. But if we are to move onward from kiddy lit and all that the use of that squirmy term implies, then children's books must be taken seriously *as literature*, and this means they must be considered with critical strictness. Vague approval, praise for the work of established writers because they are established and, above all, sentimental gush will get us nowhere.

I have suggested, diffidently, what I consider to be literature and what I believe in broad terms to be the nature of literary experience. From the latter it would be possible to derive, in equally broad terms, an elementary criterion for the assessment of literary merit. But we need something more detailed and sophisticated, which could hardly be drawn by legitimate processes of deduction from my simple premises; and I feel even more diffident when I think of the amount of distinguished American and British literary criticism in print. Is this even a case where the construction and application of abstract rules are proper? Perhaps we ought to see what some of the critics say.

We find in fact that the literary critics, both modern and not-so-modern, are rather reluctant to pin themselves down to theoretical statements. In the introduction to *Determinations* (1934), F. R. Leavis expresses the belief that 'the way to forward true appreciation of literature and art is to examine and discuss it'; and again, 'out of agreement or disagreement with particular judgements of value a sense of relative value in the concrete will define itself, and, without this, no amount of talk about values in the abstract is worth anything'. The late T. S. Eliot was elusive above critical standards, but when he did make a firm statement it could be startlingly down-to-earth. He said, in *The Use of Poetry and the Use of Criticism* (1933):

> The rudiment of criticism is the ability to select a good poem and reject a bad poem: and its most severe test is of its ability to select a good *new* poem, to respond properly to a new situation.

I should mention that Eliot, like many other critics, sometimes used the word, 'poem' as shorthand for any work of imaginative literature. Whether he was doing so here I am not sure, but his statement is a statement about criticism, not about poetry, and if for 'poem' you substituted 'novel', 'painting', or 'piece of music' it would be equally true.

In the same book, Eliot remarked that 'if you had no faith in the critic's ability to tell a good poem from a bad one, you would put little reliance on the value of his theories'. I do not recall that Eliot ever explained by what standard you were to judge whether the critic could tell a good poem, but obviously it was some standard other than the person's own theory and, in fact, I am fairly sure that it was the consensus of informed opinion over a period of time. And that comes originally from Dr Johnson, who said in the *Preface to Shakespeare* that the only test that could be applied to works of literature was 'length of duration and continuance of esteem'; and also, in the *Life of*

Gray, that 'it is by the common sense of readers uncorrupted by literary prejudice that all claim to literary honours is finally decided'.

Matthew Arnold in *The Study of Poetry* (1880) proposed, as aids to distinguishing work of the highest class, not rules but touchstones, examples from the great masters. Arnold says:

> Critics give themselves great labour to draw out what in the abstract constitutes the character of a high quality of poetry. It is much better simply to have recourse to concrete examples; – to take specimens of poetry of high, the very highest quality, and to say: The characters of a high quality of poetry are what is expressed *there*. They are far better recognised by being felt in the verse of the master than by being perused in the prose of the critic . . . If we are asked to define this mark and accent (of 'high beauty, worth and power') in the abstract, our answer must be: No, for we should thereby be darkening the question, not clearing it.

Here Arnold was undoubtedly talking about poetry and not using the word as shorthand. His touchstone principle could be extended to prose, although it strikes me as not entirely satisfactory anyway since it would not help you to judge really original work. The main point is, however, that Johnson, Arnold, Eliot, Leavis – and Henry James, too, if I correctly interpret his critical writings – are reluctant to prescribe an abstract framework against which a work of literature can be measured. They see the danger. 'People are always ready,' T. S. Eliot said, 'to grasp at any guide which will help them to recognize the best poetry without having to depend upon their own sensibility and taste'. Once establish a formula (this is myself speaking, not Eliot) and you open the door to bad and pedantic criticism by people who rely on rules instead of perceptions. Not only that but you risk creating a structure within which writers can be imprisoned. Writers should never be given the idea that there is one approved way of doing things. Far better to keep an open critical mind and encourage them with the words of Kipling:

> There are nine and sixty ways of constructing tribal lays,
> And – every – single – one – of – them – is – right!

Am I, you may ask, suggesting that there should be no formal standards at all? Well, not quite that. It depends on the critic. Some find formal principles helpful in organizing their thought. Mrs Arbuthnot did; and I am sure the 'criteria for stories' which she sets out on pages 17–19 of *Children and Books* have been valuable to a great many people, especially those who are feeling their way into the subject. Mrs Arbuthnot suggests looking at stories with an eye to theme, plot, characters, and style, and that is excellent; it gives you somewhere to start; it gets you moving. The guidelines for the award in England of the Carnegie Medal are almost identical and are laid down with staccato brevity; they are not expanded and explained, as Mrs Arbuthnot expanded and explained hers. But I believe that Mrs Arbuthnot's standards are less valuable than her example, as seen in the perceptive, practical literary criticism and, I might add, art criticism all through her book. It may well be that the British Library Association realized that what mattered for the Carnegie were not a few bald words about plot, style, and characterization, but the knowledge and judgement of the people who were appointed to apply them. The terms of the *Guardian* award for children's fiction, with which I am associated, say only that it is to go to an outstanding work; everything else is left to the judges, and I see nothing wrong with that. A good critic will indeed be aware of theme, plot, style, characterization, and many other considerations, some of them not previously spelled out but arising directly from the work; he will be sensitive; he will have a sense of balance and rightness; he will respond. Being only human he cannot possibly know all that it would be desirable for him to know; but he will have a wide knowledge of literature in general as well as of children and their literature, and probably a respectable acquaintance with cinema, theatre, television, and current affairs. That is asking a lot of him, but not too much. The critic (this is the heart of the matter) counts more than the criteria.

He will have his standards, but they will have become part of himself; he will hardly be conscious of them. Certainly he will not cart them around with him like a set of tools ready for any job. He will, I think, if I may now quote myself again from *A Sense of Story*, approach a book with an open mind and respond to it as freshly and honestly as he is able; then he will go away, let his thoughts and feelings about it mature, turn them over from time to time, consider the book in relation to others by the same author and by the author's predecessors and contemporaries. If the book is for children, he should not let his mind be dominated by the fact, but neither, I believe, should he attempt to ignore it. Just as I feel the author must write for himself yet with awareness of an audience of children, so I feel the critic must write for himself with an awareness that the books he discusses are children's books.

This last point gives me my cue to return very briefly to an issue which I touched upon but put aside at its logical place in my discussion, because I wanted to keep some edges clear and I feared it might blur them. I think I can now safely go back to it. When I indicated that a critical approach was book-centred rather than child-centred, when I said I agreed on the whole with the purists, I did not, emphatically not, mean to imply that the book exists in some kind of splendid isolation, and that whether it actually speaks to the child does not matter. Rather, I think that purists can go too far in their apparent disregard for popularity. There is a sense in which the importance, the value even, of a work, is linked with its capacity to appeal to the multitude. To take some exalted examples: does not common sense tell us that part of the greatness of a Beethoven, a Shakespeare, a Michelangelo lies in the breadth of their appeal, the fact that their works are rewarding not only to a few *cognoscenti* but to *anyone* in possession of the appropriate faculties? A book is a communication; if its doesn't communicate, does it not fail? True, it may speak to posterity, if it gets the chance; it may be ahead of its time. But if a children's book is not popular with children here and now, its lack of appeal may tell us something. It is at least a limitation, and it *may* be a sign of some vital deficiency which is very much the critic's concern.

Those of us with purist tendencies are also perhaps too much inclined to turn up our noses at the 'book with a message'. For the message may be of the essence of the work, as in the novels of D. H. Lawrence or George Orwell. The revelation of the possibilities of human nature for good or ill is a major concern of literary art, probably *the* major concern of literary art. If the writer engages himself with a contemporary problem, he may be engaging himself most valuably with the mind and feelings of the reader; and to demand that he be neutral on the issues raised is to demand his emasculation. Nevertheless, it needs to be said from time to time that a book can be good without being immensely popular and without solving anybody's problems.

You will have noticed that in this talk, now drawing to a close, I have refrained from discussing specific contemporary books for children. This has been a self-denying ordinance. We would all rather talk about books than principles. But to illustrate adequately – not just casually – the various general points I have made would require reference to many books and to many pieces of writing about them; it would be the task of a course of lectures, not a single one. And so, having reluctantly maintained a somewhat abstract level throughout, I want to finish, as it were, on the theoretical summit of children's literature. T. S. Eliot, in the book already cited, remarks that:

69

In a play of Shakespeare you get several levels of significance. For the simplest auditors there is the plot, for the more thoughtful the character and conflict of character, for the more musically sensitive the rhythm, and for the auditors of greater sensitiveness and understanding a meaning which reveals itself gradually.

Now authors cannot all be Shakespeares, nor for that matter can critics all be Eliots. And even within our own limitations we cannot aim at the peaks of achievement all the time. But no one compels us to be modest in our ambitions; no one has compelled me to be modest in making claims on behalf of children's literature, nor have I any intention of being so. Let's all remember with pride and pleasure that children's books of the highest merit will work on several levels; they will work indeed on the same person at successive stages of development. The best children's books are infinitely rereadable; the child can come back to them at increasing ages and, even as a grownup, still find new sources of enjoyment. Some books, a few books, need never be grown away from; they can always be shared with children and with the child within. The writer for children need feel no lack of scope for high endeavour, for attempting the almost but not quite impossible. For of books that succeed in this comprehensive way, that bind the generations together, parents with children, past with present with future, we are never likely to have too many.

A more academic and theoretic approach is Felicity Hughes' highly intelligent and justly celebrated 'Children's Literature, Theory and Practice', which first appeared in ELH. *It differs from all the other essays in this book by being clearly written from an academic, rather than 'children's literature' stance, and, as a sub-text, we can see the need for intellectual and academic justification. It is a microcosm of a struggle that is still going on.*

The essay draws from the conventional criticism of its day, and thus lacks the confidence of contemporary writers, who would read her quotation from Henry James quite differently:

> The sort of taste that used to be called 'good' has nothing to do with the matter: we are so demonstrably in the presence of millions for whom taste is but an obscure, confused, immediate instinct.

Similarly, Hughes' reading of history might appear rather simplistic to the reader in the 1990s; nevertheless, she sets the development of

the children's book as a distinctive entity in a valid context. The essay,
incidentally, demonstrates the strength and importance of Australian
criticism of children's literature.

Felicity A. Hughes
'Children's Literature: Theory and Practice', *ELH,* 45,
Baltimore, MD, Johns Hopkins University Press
(1978), pp. 542–61

The theory of Children's Literature has been for some time in a state
of confusion. That so many good and important works of literature
have been produced in that time is a cheering reminder that art can
survive even the worst efforts of critical theorists. There are no
grounds for complacency in this state of affairs, however, because
although theoretical confusion may not stifle good art, it can impose
significant constraints and directions upon it.

I suggest that the origin of some confused beliefs, including the
belief that there is, in some significant literary sense, such a thing as
children's literature at all, is to be found in the theory of the novel.
The history of children's literature coincides, more or less, with that
of the novel. What historians of children's literature often call the
first real children's book, Newbery's *A Little Pretty Pocket-Book* was
published within a decade of Richardson's *Pamela*. It is probable that
more than mere coincidence is involved since similar social conditions
are conducive to both. In fact, the development of a separate body of
literature addressed to children has been crucially associated with that
of the novel, and the critical fortunes of the one have been strongly
affected by those of the other. In this paper I shall discuss that
dependence with respect to twentieth-century novels for children, and
argue that it accounts for some of the many confusions which hamper
attempts to construct theories of children's literature.

The crisis in the novel which occurred in the eighteen eighties is
generally agreed to have determined the development of the
twentieth-century novel. In that decade a new view of the novel is
held to have triumphed over an older one. David Stone writes of the
eighties, 'with the deaths of the established Victorian novelists, not
only a younger group of novelists, but an entirely new set of attitudes
towards fiction appeared'.[1] John Goode suggests that the change
involved 'a reappraisal of the possibilities and responsibilities of the

novel which is important because it represents the beginning of the dividing line between the Victorian novel and the twentieth century novel'.[2] The emergent view is characterised by Walter Allen as 'a heightened, more serious conception of the novel as art'.[3] Further, it is agreed by these and other writers that this change came about at least partly in response to changing social conditions and in particular what were seen as profound changes in the readership of the novel. I propose to consider the implications of this crisis for the development of a separate literature for children.

From its inception in the eighteenth century the novel had been seen in England as at least potentially *family* reading. A glance through the material collected in Ioan Williams' *Novel and Romance 1700–1800* will amply bear this out.[4] The words 'young people' or 'our youth' appear in virtually every review or essay. The debate on the relative merits of Richardson and Fielding seems to have revolved around the question of which novel was more appropriate for the moral, social and literary education of British youth. In spite of occasional deprecatory murmurs, Victorian novelists also accepted the constraints that a family readership was held to impose on them. In light of this it is clear that Moore, when he protested in 1885 that 'never in any age or country have writers been asked to write under such restricted conditions' was either taking a very large view of his 'age' or wrong.[5] Judgement of novels had always involved a hypothetical young reader.

Moreover, throughout the same history, the status of the novel as a genre was comparable to that of the bourgeoisie it largely predicted. In spite of its rapid rise to dominance as preferred reading, it failed to gain the accolade of critical and learned opinion. Lacking the long and distinguished classical ancestry of poetry and drama, the novel was engaged in a struggle to live down the stigma of being a 'low' form, not art but entertainment. Critics turned their attention to novels cursorily and with distaste, real or feigned, recommending the best novels only in the context of a general caveat against the genre.

The crisis of the eighties effected changes in both these circumstances. By the turn of the century it was clear that at least some English novelists would no longer allow themselves to be held responsible for the moral welfare of the nation's youth. By about 1910, moreover, the novel seemed to have risen above its old inferior status. It received more critical recognition; it was old enough to have something of a history; it had, as Allen Tate later put it, 'caught up with poetry'.[6] There was acknowledged to be an 'art of fiction' and there were some novels that could be referred to as 'art novels' or 'serious novels'.

It was also true that by the turn of the century something was emerging that might be called 'children's literature'. Just as D. H. Lawrence's titles seem to proclaim themselves as 'M', for mature readers only, so Edith Nesbit's books equally clearly announce themselves as 'C', for child readers only. Stevenson's *Treasure Island*, which had been read with pleasure by Henry James, was reclassified as a 'children's classic' and the days when novels could confidently be dedicated to 'boys of all ages' were over.

I doubt whether this particular development, initiating as it did a trend in fiction writing which has continued to the present, was a mere accident of literary history. I suggest that a plausible explanation of it can be found in the acceptance by writers and critics of a theory about fiction which directly attributed the low status of the novel *to* its family readership. The theory in question is that developed by Henry James in his essays. Setting aside, for the moment, the question of whether the theory is true or false, I shall argue that one major consequence of its acceptance was that novelists, in a bid for critical respectability, tried to dissociate the novel from its family readership and redirect it towards what was seen as art's traditional elite audience of educated adult males outside the home, at court, the coffee house, or the club. The 'serious novel' would have to earn its laurels, or win its spurs, at the cost of being unsuitable for women and children – beyond their reach not only because it dealt with facts of life from which such people had to be 'protected', but because it was too difficult, requiring not only maturity but discrimination beyond the reach of all but the highly educated. Since no-one can start off life highly educated, children are *ipso facto* disqualified.

The implications of this particular aspect of the crisis in the novel can best be studied by a consideration of the controversy between James and R. L. Stevenson. It is generally agreed that James was making a bid to establish the novel as serious art in his manifesto, 'The Art of Fiction'.[7] In that essay, it will be remembered, he claimed that the novelist's function was 'to attempt to represent life' and that the novel should not be presented by its author as 'just a story' or as 'make believe', but as something akin to history. Novel-writing being an art which 'undertakes immediately to reproduce life', it must take itself seriously if it wishes to be taken seriously and, in particular, 'it must demand that it be perfectly free'. 'It goes without saying', he says, 'that you will not write a good novel unless you possess the sense of reality.' He gave *Treasure Island* only qualified praise, saying that it is delightful 'because it appears to me to have succeeded wonderfully in what it attempts', and compared it to its disadvantage with a story by a French writer which attempted to 'trace the moral consciousness of a child'. Although he acknowledged that the French story failed in what it attempts', he nevertheless preferred it to *Treasure Island* because he could measure it against his own sense of reality; 'I can at successive steps . . . say Yes or No, as it may be, to what the artist puts before me.' In *Treasure Island* he could not make that decision, because 'I have been a child in fact, but I have been on a quest for buried treasure only in supposition'. James here suggests a criterion for critical approval which would exclude all stories except those the reader can measure against his own sense of reality. It may be inferred from this that a 'sense of reality' is required of the reader as well as of the writer, so that he is actually as well as theoretically able to say 'Yes or No' to what the writer offers. Writer and reader, then, are to enter into a sophisticated contract by which, although illusion is held to be the object of the exercise, no one is actually taken in, the reading having constantly to judge the merit of the novel *as illusion* by measuring it against something else.

Since James' principal criterion for the seriousness of a novel was the degree to which it gave the illusion of portraying real life, when Stevenson came to answer the essay he found himself in the position of defending the notion of the novel as 'make believe'. He called it 'a peculiarity of our attitude to any art' that 'No art produces illusion'.[8] Yet his requirement of the reader seems to require the involuntary assent appropriate to illusion. In '*A Gossip on Romance*', he wrote,

> In anything fit to be called by the name of reading, the process itself should be absorbing and voluptuous; we should gloat over a book, be rapt clean out of ourselves, and rise from the perusal, our mind filled with the busiest kaleidascopic dance of images, incapable of sleep or of continuous thought . . . It was for this pleasure that we read so closely and loved our books so dearly, in the bright, troubled period of boyhood.[9]

Stevenson admired novels which made intense demands of sympathy and identification, whereas James required that characters in novels be presented 'objectively' in a way that prevents the reader from entering into any extraordinary sympathy with them. Their disagreement over *Crime and Punishment* was reported by Stevenson in a letter thus:

> it was easily the greatest book I have read in ten years. Many find it dull. Henry James could not finish it: all I can say is that it

nearly finished me. It was like having an illness. James did not care for it because the character of Raskolnikov was not objective: and at that I divined a great gulf between us and . . . a certain impotence in many minds of today which prevents them from living *in* a book or character, and keeps them standing afar off, spectators of a puppet show.[10]

While it is difficult to see the consistency of either writer's position, it is clear enough that they were opposed on the two points under discussion. James claimed that novels are serious in so far as they attempt to provide 'the intense illusion of real life'. Stevenson denied this claim. Secondly, James required characters to be 'objective' and the reader to be detached, impartial and sceptical, whereas Stevenson saw reader involvement and the submersion of self to be the triumph of art.

In reviewing this controversy we should also bear in mind that other great item of discussion in the eighties and nineties – the early years of State Education in England – the spread of literacy, which was assumed to be proceeding rapidly through the agency of universal compulsory education. By the turn of the century these two issues had come together in James' thinking in a way that was to be widespread not long after his death. The attitude I wish to discuss is that expressed in an essay called 'The Future of the Novel' which he published in 1899.[11] What that essay expresses is an undisguised dismay at the galloping popularity of the novel, the great increase in novel readers, which he attributed to the fact that

The diffusion of the rudiments, the multiplication of the common schools, has more and more had the effect of making readers of women and of the very young. Nothing is so striking in a survey of this field . . .

and he observes the growth of writing for children in these terms:

The literature, as it may be called for convenience, of children is an industry that occupies by itself a very considerable quarter of the scene. Great fortunes, if not great reputations, are made we learn, by writing for schoolboys . . . The published statistics are extraordinary and of a sort to engender many kinds of uneasiness. The sort of taste that used to be called 'good' has nothing to do with the matter: we are so demonstrably in the presence of millions for whom taste is but an obscure, confused, immediate instinct.

The distaste and even fear of the mass of women and children readers which James manifests here springs, I suggest, from his suspicion that the popularity of the novel will diminish its chances of finding the elite audience the existence of which will justify its status as art. He thinks that being exclusive is a necessary condition for novels being serious. Popular novels cannot be good, they must be vulgar. Commercial success therefore is a sign of declining standards:

> The high prosperity of our fiction has marched very directly, with another 'sign of the times', the demoralisation, the vulgarisation of literature in general, the increasing familiarity of all such methods of communication, the making itself supremely felt, as it were, of the presence of the ladies and children - by whom I mean, in other words, the reader irreflective and uncritical.

So serious a menace did James take this to be that he prophesied on the brink of this century:

> By what it decides to do in respect to 'the young', the great prose fable will, from any serious point of view, practically see itself stand or fall.

He refrains from making any specific suggestions as to what should be done with respect to the young but his general drift is clear when he goes on to demand again 'freedom' for the serious novelist. If the novelist's business is to present 'life' he must be able to select his material from the whole of life: nothing must be prohibited. And he refers to the 'immense omission in our fiction'. It was, he claimed, 'because of the presence of ladies and children' that in novels 'there came into being a mistrust of all but the most guarded treatment of the great relation between men and women, the constant world-renewal'. In fact James' solution seems to be the same as that suggested by Moore in 1885:

> We must write as our poems, our histories, our biographies are written, and give up at once and forever asking that most silly of all silly questions 'Can my daughter of eighteen read this book?' Let us renounce the effort to reconcile these two irreconcilable things - art and young girls. That these young people should be provided with a literature suited to their age and taste, no artist will deny; all I ask is that some means may be devised by which the novelist will be allowed to describe the moral and religious feeling of his day as he perceives it to exist, and to be forced no

longer to write with a view of helping parents and guardians to bring up their charges in all the traditional beliefs.[12]

In the course of their respective essays, Moore and James both imply that keeping children in heavily guarded ignorance is not only bad for the novel but bad for the children. Neither chooses to pursue that point, however, since, unlike their eighteenth-century predecessors, they are exclusively concerned about the rights of novelists. Hence the proposed solution is not that adults should allow formerly prohibited topics to be discussed in front of the children, but that [the] child should be excluded so that adults can discuss such matters among themselves. The children are to be sent away to play, with their mothers presumably, so that the serious novelist can be free to pursue his art and write about sex.

Within twenty years of the publication of 'The Future of the Novel', the views expressed in it were widespread; in particular the view that the serious novel is one that children cannot read was generally accepted among writers and critics. The impact that this exclusion has had not only on the development of children's literature, but on attitudes towards it is still overwhelming. The segregation of adult's and children's literature is rationalised, even celebrated on all sides. It has assumed the status of a fact, a piece of knowledge about the world, that children read books in a different way and have to have special books written for them.

The consequence of this *de facto* segregation of children's literature from the rest can be seen in general aesthetic theory, in literary theory, in the theory and criticism of children's literature and in the literature itself. I shall deal briefly with the first two and more fully with the last two.

In aesthetic theory it is a not uncommon assumption that children cannot have aesthetic satisfactions. Professor F. J. Coleman, for instance, introduces aesthetics in *Contemporary Essays in Aesthetics* (1968) by suggesting that we can rank pleasures in a sequence which 'depends on the degree of intelligence and discrimination needed to experience the feelings those terms designate':

> The lowest pleasures would be those that any sentient human being can feel – children, idiots, the senile; they are such pleasures that do not require any power of discrimination. To call a pleasure an 'aesthetic' pleasure is to imply that it would fall on the highest end of the continuum; therefore aesthetic pleasures are those that require discrimination, intelligence and imagination to be experienced. For surely we do not speak of

children or the mentally deficient as *experiencing* art, though of course they may *hear* a symphony or see a painting . . .[13]

Professor Coleman's argument is circular and proves nothing, but it at least affords a clear view of the prejudice under discussion.

Children have also continued to figure as scapegoats in the controversy over 'aesthetic distance' raised in the debate between James and Stevenson. In literary theory, the question is 'what constitutes a proper attitude on the part of the reader: detachment (which James felt to be characteristic of the good reader) or involvement (which Stevenson preferred and was universally believed to characterise the child reader)?' Over the last few decades the requirement that the mature reader, qualified to be discriminating, keep his proper distance has been increasingly questioned. It is acknowledged that even the most judicious readers do become involved in the books they read. But, even so, the children have not been rescued from the scapegoat role in this debate. It seems that the prejudice against child readers is so strong that it will be the last element in the theory to be relinquished. For instance, the celebrated attack on the theory in Wayne Booth's *The Rhetoric of Fiction* turned on an analysis of Jane Austen's *Emma* in which he showed that during the course of the novel 'our emotional reaction to every event concerning Emma tends to become like her own'.[14] It seems then that Booth is acknowledging that even critics do identify with characters in books – that it doesn't make one an inferior reader to do so. *But*, that is only the last half of the sentence, the first half of which goes, 'While only immature readers ever really identify with any character, losing all sense of distance and hence all chance of an artistic experience . . .' Even Booth feels he has to make a concession to the prejudice he is trying to overcome, and the concession he chooses to make is once again to deny 'immature readers' any chance of 'an artistic experience'.

If the assumptions outlined here were held universally, then we would not be able to talk of children's literature but only, as James would have it, of the children's book industry. Critics and theorists who want to talk about 'children's literature' have had to find a way round this pervasive prejudice. Few have been bold enough to take issue with authorities such as Professor Coleman. Many have taken a way out by arguing that children *do* have aesthetic satisfactions but that these are different in kind from those of adults. Cornelia Meigs, for example, introducing a critical history of children's literature, says:

> Just as children, in spite of having long been treated as no more
> than smaller and more helpless editions of their elders, have

always been *something apart* in vigour of personality, of vision,
and enterprise of mind, so has the reading of their choice, even
though unrecognised as something separate, had its own characteristics, its own individuality, and its own greatness.[15]

This is to make the best of a bad thing and it leads to a great deal of
effort on the part of such writers to give an account of the
mysteriously different way of experiencing books that children are
supposed to have. Criticism, it may be noted, becomes virtually
impossible in the face of this supposed fundamental difference
between adults' and children's responses to the same book. Some,
despairing of bridging the gap, have suggested that only children
should review children's books. Such reviews are invariably disappointing to their advocates because they give no evidence
whatsoever of a fundamentally different way of responding to books.
Rather than explain this away on the grounds of teacher interference,
we should regard the original hypothesis that children's responses are
different in kind from those of adults as not proven.

The exclusion of children's literature from the class of serious
literature has of course resulted in its being classed as a branch of
popular literature. Just as the unsubstantiated claim that the aesthetic
experiences of adults are not available to children created a need for
theories of what children do experience, so the equally arbitrary
categorisation of children's literature as 'popular' has fostered the
belief that the popularity of a children's book is a proper index of its
worth which has in turn attracted the curious explanation that
children, unlike adults, are possessed of natural good taste in reading,
hence if they generally approve of a book it must be good. Further
confusions arise from the fact that at times 'popularity' is understood
as a set of critical criteria rather than a function of sales and readers.
Kipling, for instance, had considerable respect for Rider Haggard and
tried to base a theory on Haggard's writing. In a letter, Kipling
exclaimed:

How the dickens do you do it? How do you keep and outpour
the vitality and the conviction and *how* do you contrive to nail
down and clinch the *interest* that keeps a man lying along one
elbow till the whole arm is tone-cramped? I don't pretend to
judge the book in the least. I only know in my own person, that
it held me as a drug might – but it was a good drug – . . . You
have the incommunicable gift of catching and holding . . . [16]

Although at the time of writing Kipling was himself a top best-seller whilst Haggard's popularity was declining, Kipling still regarded Haggard as the master popular writer, indicating that for him the popularity of a novel could be determined by criteria other than its sales. What these were may be deduced from Haggard's *Autobiography* in which he tries to communicate the incommunicable gift:

> the story is the thing and every word in the book should be a brick to build its edifice . . . Let the character be definite, even at the cost of a little crudeness. Tricks of style and dark allusions may please the superior critic; they do not please the average reader, and . . . a book is written to be read. The first duty of a story is to keep him who peruses it awake . . . 'grip' is about everything.[17]

This passage is interesting in that, if you replace 'the superior critic' by 'the adult reader' and 'the average reader' by 'the child reader' it could be interpolated without being noticed into any textbook on children's literature. Nor is that because the audience for such textbooks are assumed to be interested in writing for children as a commercial venture. A recent critical book dealing with a handful of the best authors of books for children was called *A Sense of Story*.[18] It is thought to be the prerequisite for the good children's writer in the way that James required the 'sense of reality' in the serious novelist. The source of the requirement lies in the perception of children's literature as a branch of popular literature.

This perception originated, I suggest, in the vagueness with which the group of unwelcome new readers was perceived in the eighties by those who felt threatened by them. Class, sex, and age were conflated as causes of a supposed inability to appreciate the best in art and literature, those 'millions to whom taste is but an obscure, confused, immediate instinct', Walter Allen, writing in 1954 saw the class division as most important:

> It was probably not accidental that this heightened, more serious conception of the novel as art should have triumphed in the eighties, for the split between the old novel and the new coincided with a cultural revolution. Forster's education Acts of 1870 provided compulsory primary education for all, and the result, over the years, was an enormous increase in the reading public. But the gap between the best education and the worst was so great that the highbrow-lowbrow dichotomy with which we are now wearisomely familiar was inevitable. Before 1870, the poor man who strove to learn to read and, having done so, went on to read beyond the newspapers, did so because he was

to some degree a superior man. To be able to read was a key to enfranchisement; it opened the door to a better position as a tradesman or to succeed in business; it was essential to the politically minded working man who dreamed of power for his class; and for a few more disinterested spirits it offered the freedom of a culture traditionally an upper-class preserve. But whatever the motive for learning to read, the Victorian working man, by and large, accepted the cultural standards of classes higher in the social scale. After 1870 this was no longer necessarily so. The provision of reading matter for a semi-literate public became the concern of a vast industry which set its own standards, standards which had nothing to do with the literary and artistic standards as normally understood. Indeed the notion of a single standard ceased practically to exist, and perhaps this was inevitable, for when you give a semi-literate person the vote and persuade him that thereby he is an arbiter of his countries [*sic*] destiny, it is not easy at the same time to convince him that he is not also the arbiter of what is excellent in art: there is a natural tendency for every man to believe that what he prefers must be the best.[19]

In the closing sentences of this passage, Allen echoes James, who wrote of 'an industry that occupies a very considerable quarter of the scene' with which 'the sort of taste that used to be called "good" has nothing to do'. Allen similarly writes of 'a vast industry' setting 'standards which had nothing to do with literary and artistic standards as normally understood'. James had in mind the child reader, Allen the enfranchised adult male working-class reader, but from the point of view of literary theory they are treated as interchangeable.

It was claimed at the beginning of this paper that theoretical confusion can impose significant constraints on art. One of the most striking features of English children's literature is the amount and quality of fantasy offered to children especially in the last quarter century. The prominence and excellence of fantasy in children's literature has often been remarked on, yet the criticism of those works has been confused and superficial. I believe that both of these phenomena can be explained in terms of the theory I have offered in this paper.

I have shown that the exclusion of children from the readership of the serious novel was associated with the acceptance of a version of realism. One consequence of the acceptance of realism was that fantasy was immediately déclassé. Since fantasy can be seen as the antithesis of realism, it seemed to follow, to those who espoused the realist cause, that fantasy was also the opposite of serious, i.e., trivial or frivolous. That is precisely how Forster used the term in *Aspects of the Novel*.[20] In that book, he devoted two chapters to non-realistic aspects of the novel, one called 'Fantasy' and one called 'Prophecy', characterising both by what they require of the reader. Fantasy, he says, 'asks us to pay something extra'. It is, he suggests, 'like a side-show in an exhibition where you pay sixpence as well as the original entrance fee'. The analogy is damaging, raising the question as to whether the show is worth even sixpence. He divides the potential audience into two groups. Of the first group, those who 'pay with delight' (i.e. enjoy fantasy), Forster claims, 'it is only for the side shows that they entered the exhibition', i.e., a taste for fantasy precludes a taste for other literature; to the second group who 'refuse with indignation' (i.e., detest fantasy), he offers 'our sincere regards, for to dislike the fantastic in literature as not to dislike literature. It does not even imply poverty of imagination, only a disinclination to meet certain demands that are made on it.' So, while a taste for fantasy is said to be incompatible with a taste for any other literature, a distaste for fantasy is said to be quite compatible and, not surprisingly, wins Forster's regard. Although he finds the demands made by fantasy unfulfillable, he admits that he cannot show that they are unreasonable:

> No doubt this approach is not critically sound. We all know that a work of art is an entity, etc. etc.; it has its own laws which are not those of daily life, anything that suits it is true, so why should any question arise about the angel etc., except whether it is suitable to its book? Why place an angel on a different basis from a stockbroker – once in the realm of the fictitious what difference is there between an apparition and a mortgage? I see the soundness of this argument, but my heart refuses to assent. The general tone of novels is so literal that when the fantastic is introduced it produces a special effect.

In comparison with fantasy, Prophecy is, according to Forster, a much more serious affair and demands to be taken seriously. Fantasy and prophecy are said to be 'alike in having gods, and unlike in the gods they have'. In comparison with the gods of prophecy, those of fantasy are 'small'. 'I would call them fairies if the word were not consecrated to imbecility.' He suggests that fantasies should be saved from 'the claws of critical apparatus', that 'their appeal is specially personal – they are side-shows inside the main show'. The implication here is that the appeal of fantasy is so ephemeral that critical inspection would destroy it - show it to be a trick, an illusion, a device. In fact, he suggests that fantasy can be identified by its 'devices' and 'the fact that their number is strictly limited is of interest'. Prophecy, on the other hand, demands of the reader, 'humility and a suspension of the sense of humour'. It is interesting to note that in this case Forster feels that *refusal* to submit is childish:

> Humility is a quality for which I have only a limited admiration. In many phases of life it is a great mistake and degenerates into defensiveness and hypocrisy. But humility is in place just now. Without its help we shall not hear the voice of the prophet, and our eyes will behold a figure of fun instead of his glory. And the sense of humour - that is out of place: that estimable adjunct of the educated man must be laid aside. Like the school-children in the Bible, one cannot help laughing at the prophet - his bald head is so absurd - but one can discount the laughter and realise that it has no critical value and is merely food for bears.

In *Aspects of the Novel*, 'Fantasy' and 'Prophecy' together represent a by-way in Forster's train of thought on the novel - he calls them interludes 'gay and grave'. Neither can be dealt with properly by his critical equipment, which was designed for novels that are 'literal in tone', though prophetic novels induce him to consider the possibility that this critical equipment is not the best, or that there may be no such thing as critical equipment at all. Such doubts are momentary, however, and characteristically, brushed off with a sigh. 'It is a pity that Man cannot be at the same time impressive and truthful.'

In those 1927 lectures Forster reflected and helped disseminate a widespread prejudice against fantasy. A consequence of the prejudice that fantasy is childish has been that the writer of fantasy has been directed into writing for children no matter how good he or she might be. The realistic writer has had a choice and indeed been encouraged to regard writing for adults as more satisfying. In writing for children the realistic writer has been conscious of taking second best since realism was defined in terms which excluded children as readers hence 'real' realism was impossible in a children's book. The fantasist has written under no such shadow - has had no such option - all fantasy goes on the children's list. Some excellent writers have found themselves writing for children for this reason, which partially explains the high amount and quality of fantasy in children's literature this century.

Moreover, writers of children's literature have been able to turn to advantage the fact that a work which announces itself as fantasy is deemed frivolous, childish and not worth critical attention. Edith Nesbit referred to this situation at the beginning of *Five Children and It*:

> I could go on and make this into a most interesting story about all the ordinary things that the children did – just the kind of things you do yourself you know – and you would believe every word of it, and when I told you about the children being tiresome, as you are sometimes, your aunts would perhaps write in the margin of the story with a pencil 'How true!' or 'how like life!' And you would see it and very likely be annoyed. So I will only tell you about the really astonishing things that happened, and you may leave the book about quite safely, for no aunts and uncles either are likely to write 'How true!' on the edge of the story.[21]

Using fantasy thus as a protective cover to save the work from prying adult eyes, writers have managed to extend considerably the range of subjects dealt with in children's literature.

An inevitable consequence of the way that children's literature came into being was that a certain restraint has been imposed on children's writers in the realist tradition when it comes to topics such as terror, politics and sex. That such censorship has been found too restrictive by some writers is clear from books like William Mayne's *A Game of Dark* (1971) and Philippa Pearce's *A Dog so Small* (1962). The protagonist of the former is schizoid, of the latter, obsessive, which enables the writers to present intense fears and resentments. But such shifts are of limited use: one can't write about deranged people all the time, nor is it true that only the mad get frightened. What is clear is that these devices will never accommodate what are, after all, incompatible demands made on the writer in this tradition, that he be true to life and also that he avoid certain topics. Moore's solution was to exclude the children: the children's writer's solution is to turn to fantasy. Even Mayne, who is inventive enough to write a highly schematic book like *Sand* (1970) or a mythopoeic book like *The Jersey Shore* (1973) and remain, technically, within the conventions of realism-for- children, found it necessary, in order to deal with the more terrifying aspects of his earlier preoccupation, the alien time-scheme of the earth, to resort to fantasy, in *Earthfasts* (1966).

The so-called 'new realism' in children's books proves on inspection, to be an attempt to introduce adolescent sex into children's books. In fact the acclaimed writers of the 'new realism' have a long way to go before they can deal with the range of sexual feelings including jealousy, possessiveness, despair and the desire for liberation that Alan Garner dealt with in *The Owl Service* (1967) by using fantasy.

Political topics such as class and race have recently been self-consciously injected into children's realistic fiction, but again the fantasists have set the standard to be met. Those writers who are attempting accurate description of working class life in realistic terms are only attempting what Mary Norton did so brilliantly in the Borrowers series (1953 *et seq.*) in which, by one fantastic stroke, she invented a way of presenting the experience of being small and propertyless in a society in which that entails constant vulnerability. Accounts of dispossession and exploitation given in fantasy by Mary Norton and by Russell Hoban in *The Mouse and His Child* (1969) are much more penetrating that those given in books like Serrailler's *Silver Sword* (1956) and Rugters Van der Loeff's *Children On the Oregon Trail*, (*Oregon at Last*) (New York, 1961) though the latter make the strongest claim to verisimilitude – that of being based on the real experiences of real children. Similarly, in *A Stranger at Green Knowe* (1961) Lucy Boston depicts the relationship between a Chinese boy and an escaped gorilla in a way that makes the self-consciously anti-racist realistic literature look crass.

A preoccupation with the role of the imagination in relation to time would appear unduly sophisticated in a realistic children's book as is suggested by the reaction of reviewers to Mayne's *The Jersey Shore*. So Philippa Pearce was able to contribute to that immemorial topic only by writing fantasy in *Tom's Midnight Garden* (1958). Finally and by a just revenge, fantasy gives cover to parody, the children's own traditional weapon, to mount attacks on the pretensions of adult art and artists in Randolph Stow's *Midnite* (Melbourne, 1967) and Hoban's *The Mouse and His Child*.[22]

These admirable novels have not received the critical appreciation they deserve. I suggest this also stems from the fact that the rejection of the child reader by influential critics and writers was accompanied by the rejection of fantasy and the associated claim that fantasy does not appeal to the mature mind. Scholes and Kellogg's *The Nature of Narrative* is often cited as a work which challenges the domination of realism in the novel. In so far as they champion Romance, however, it is with a reservation similar to that made by Booth concerning reader-involvement and identification:

Romance, the only narrative form which is ineluctably artistic since it is the product of the story telling impulse at its purest, diminishes in interest as its perfection carries it too far from the world of ideas or from the actual world. A pure story, without ideas or imitation of actuality to tie it to human concerns and experiences would be, if such a possibility were realized, totally uninteresting to adult readers. In some children's stories this infinitude of inanity is approached. But in general, narrative artists have sensed the dangers of purity in their art and shied away from it consciously or not.[23]

The use of the term 'inanity' here is reminiscent of Forster's identification of fairies with 'imbecility' and Coleman's association of 'children, idiots, the senile'. A tendency to class children with the mentally defective seems to have supplanted the older prejudices which classed children with women or with working class men. From the point of view of thinking clearly about children as readers this can hardly be counted progress.

The first and major impediment to useful criticism, then, lies in the acceptance by critics of the idea that fantasy is peculiarly suitable for children, not for adults. In order to interpret this supposed fact in a way that attributes no inferiority to children (a considerable feat) many critics rely on some version of the 'culture epoch' theory which states that individual human development recapitulates the development of the race. According to this view children are primitives and are most appropriately served by primitive literature – myths, fables, folk tales and fairy tales. It should be remembered that until recently, fantasies were called 'invented fairy tales' or 'modern fairy tales'. Thus Lillian Smith writes, in *The Unreluctant Years*:

A child of today asks 'why' and 'how' as he wonders about the natural world which he does not understand. So, in the childhood of the race, without knowledge of the discoveries with which science has enlarged our understanding, primitive peoples made their own explanations of the physical world in terms of themselves.[24]

And Elizabeth Cook documents the 'natural afinity [*sic, passim*] between the childhood of the race and the childhood of the individual human being' in matters of taste:

They expect a story to be a good yarn, in which the action is swift and the characters are clearly and simply defined. And legends and fairy tales are just like that. Playground games show that children like catastrophes and exhibitions of speed and power, and a clear differentiation between cowboys, cops and spacemen who are good, and Indians, robbers and space-monsters who are bad.[25]

This 'natural afinity' is brought forward to explain why fantasy appeals to children, but it is not taken as a sufficient explanation as to why fantasy is *good* for children. The Romantic version of the recapitulation theory was inclined to rate the child's and primitive's view of the world highly and to regard growing up as a process of losing touch with essentials. Since that time other theories of development have prevailed, the one most in point here being that which views growing up as a progress towards maturity and that people, as part of that process, gradually acquire a grip of reality in the course of their childhood; that to do so is a vital advance in child development, and that anything which interferes with a child's acquisition of a sense of reality is harmful to his development. Fantasy might according to this theory, constitute just such a hazard to a child's healthy acquisition of a sense of reality. Indeed, the eighteenth century Rousseauists who held an analogous theory about the acquisition of reason, acted consistently with it in banning all fairy tales (thus annoying Lamb and Coleridge). Mrs Barbauld, for instance, supported a programme almost the reverse of the modern, namely that children should be offered informative, factual material about the actual world and that only the most highly educated and developed tastes would reach the 'pure poetry' of, say, Collins, the literature least concerned with actuality.

The inconsistencies in our position lead to an anxiety about children reading 'too much' fantasy and the advocacy of a 'balanced diet'. The range of critical opinion on the issue includes those who, like W. J. Scott, are inclined to place severe limits on the reading of fantasy:

An acceptance with such enthusiasm of a representation of human beings in action that is so patently false must tend to create some misunderstanding in the mind of the young reader of the nature and motives of human behaviour. Further it compels him to lead a dual existence, using part of his energy in an excessive emotional participation in a life of fantasy at a time when he needs so much to grapple with the real world. Granted that it is still necessary for him to withdraw sometimes from the real world into one of fantasy, it is of great importance that the experience given in fantasy should be of good quality, indirectly extending his understanding of reality.[26]

and those who, like Lillian Smith, are prepared to adopt the Romantic position:

> A child's acceptance of fantasy is based on imagination and wonder. An adult lacking these universal attributes of childhood is often at a loss when he is asked to consider seriously a work of purely imaginative content, far removed from the reality of his experience of life. Before the adult can feel at ease in this different world of fantasy he must discover a means of approach. There is an interesting discussion of fantasy by E. M. Forster in his *Aspects of the Novel*, in which he says 'What does fantasy ask us? It asks us to pay something extra.' That is to say that over and above what we ordinarily bring to the reading of a story, fantasy demands something extra, perhaps a kind of sixth sense. All children have it, but most adults leave it behind with their cast off childhood.[27]

Lillian Smith's misinterpretations of Forster's remarks is a clear example of the way that such apologists for fantasy have had to close their eyes to the manifest change in the critical climate, in order to feel justified in what they are doing.

Obviously, the whole issue is distorted by the almost universal assumption that fantasy appeals to children because they believe it is true or at least don't know that it is false, and that adults reject it because they know it is not true. The question as to whether any art produces belief in any reader of any age is too big to go into here. I merely point out that confusions and disagreements on that question add to the confusions on this one. The issue of belief is introduced in an attempt to answer an irrelevant question on to which critics have allowed themselves to be diverted, namely, 'why does fantasy appeal to children and not to adults?' They have discussed that question because they were unwilling to face the fact that fantasy had been merely abandoned to the child reader. Even where critics have avoided the distracting question, they have found themselves ill-equipped to deal with fantasy properly, perhaps because they have only second-hand equipment of the Forster design.

The theory of children's literature has been for some time in a state of confusion. The achievements of the writers, in particular the fantasists, in spite of the lack of critical and theoretical support has been remarkable and provided a challenge to the critic which should be taken up.

NOTES

1 Donald David Stone, *Novelists in a Changing World* (Cambridge, Mass., 1972), p. 1.

2 John Goode, 'The Art of Fiction: Walter Besant and Henry James' in David Howard, John Lucas, John Goode (eds), *Tradition and Tolerance in Nineteenth-Century Fiction: Critical Essays on some English and American Novels* (London, 1966), p. 245.

3 Walter Allen, *The English Novel: A Short Critical History* (London, 1954), p. 249.

4 (London, 1970).

5 George Moore, *Literature at Nurse or Circulating Morals* (London, 1885), p. 18.

6 Allen Tate, 'Techniques of Fiction', *Sewanee Review*, 53 (1944), p. 225.

7 First published 1884. From Henry James, *Selected Literary Criticism*, ed. Morris Shapiro (London, 1963), p. 49.

8 'A Humble Remonstrance', first published 1884. In *Works*, ed. Swanson (London, 1911–12), IX, p. 148.

9 First published 1882. In *Works*, IX, p. 134.

10 S. Colvin (ed.), *Letters of Robert Louis Stevenson* (London, 1901), II, p. 20.

11 This essay was discovered 'long buried' by Leon Edel and given pride of place in *Henry James: The Future of the Novel. Essays on the Art of Fiction* (New York, 1956). It was not completely unknown before that time, however, and seems to have influenced Walter Allen. See below n. 19.

12 George Moore, p. 21.

13 Introduction, p. 17.

14 Wayne Booth, *The Rhetoric of Fiction* (Chicago, 1961), p. 284.

15 Cornelia Meigs (and others), *A Critical History of Children's Literature* (New York, 1969), p. 3 (my emphasis).

16 Dated 5 May 1925. Quoted in Morton Cohen, *Rider Haggard, His Life and Work*, 2nd edn (London, 1968), p. 281.

17 H. Rider Haggard, *The Days of My Life*, ed. C. J. Longman, II, 92. Quoted in Cohen, pp. 284–5.

18 John Rowe Townsend, *A Sense of Story: Essays on Contemporary Writers for Children* (London, 1971). The book however advocates and offers proper, serious criticism.

19 Walter Allen, p. 249.

20 E. M. Forster, *Aspects of the Novel* (London, 1927), chapters 6 and 7.

21 E. Nesbit, *Five Children and It* (London, 1902), p. 18.

22 The place of publication of novels mentioned in the preceding paragraphs is London except where otherwise stated.

23 Robert Scholes and Robert Kellogg, *The Nature of Narrative* (New York, 1966), p. 232.

24 Lillian Smith, *The Unreluctant Years* (Chicago, 1953), p. 65.

25 Elizabeth Cook, *The Ordinary and the Fabulous* (Cambridge, 1969), p. 7.

26 W. J. Scott, quoted, without reference, in Geoffrey Trease, *Tales Out of School*, 2nd edn (London, 1964), p. 73.

27 Lillian Smith, p. 152.

Felicity Hughes' criticism suffers from the critical and theoretical limitations of its day, and, thus far, we have seen children's literature approached from a point of view recognizable to generations of critics rooted in the twin educational strands of Leavisite liberal-humanism, and the 'New Criticism'. These are often portrayed as being in opposition, but both have been absorbed into the thinking of a generation of teachers, one as a set of assumptions, the other as a methodology.

One of the earliest articles to make a positive break from this tradition, to acknowledge the developments in critical theory, and to translate them into a form which could be used by readers, is reprinted below. Aidan Chambers has a distinguished reputation in what might be called the central ground of children's book criticism. His initial work was in education, with The Reluctant Reader *(Pergamon, 1969), and* Introducing Books to Children *(Heinemann Educational, 1973), and his work as editor of series designed for specific types of reader has been eclectic and pragmatic.*

But the central concern with the reader, which has led him, like Michael Benton, into innovative areas of encouraging criticism by children (once dismissed as a contradiction in terms), has been balanced by his own experimental work in fiction, pushing at the boundaries of text, with Breaktime *(Bodley Head, 1978),* Dance on My Grave *(Bodley Head, 1982), and* Now I Know *(Bodley Head, 1987). In these books, he has turned to critical theory both to elucidate and formulate what he is doing, and so has brought a remarkable change in direction in critical thinking. This has, of course been paralleled elsewhere, but Chambers, both in this article, and in his involvement in the publication of* Signal, *has had a massive international influence.*

'The Reader in the Book' was written, of course, in the relatively early days of response/reception criticism – at least in terms of its availability to a general audience. In that sense, the article has some limitations, and Chambers has taken his arguments further since then. However, this remains a distinctive landmark in criticism.

Aidan Chambers
'The Reader in the Book', in
Booktalk; Occasional Writing on Literature and Children,
Bodley Head, 1985, pp. 34–58

I

1. Two to say a thing . . .

There is constant squabble about whether particular books are children's books or not. Indeed, some people argue that there is no such thing as books for children but only books which children happen to read. And unless one wants to be partisan and dogmatic – which I do not, having had my fill of both – one has to agree that there is some truth on both sides and the whole truth in neither.

The fact is that some books are clearly *for* children in a specific sense – they were written by their authors deliberately for children – and some books, never specifically intended for children, have qualities which attract children to them.

But we must go further into that truism, which helps us very little to deal critically with books or to mediate them intelligently and effectively. We need a critical method which will take account of the child-as-reader; which will include him rather than exclude him; which will help us to understand a book better and to discover the reader it seeks. We need a critical method which will tell us about the reader in the book.

For it seems to me that all literature is a form of communication, a way of saying something. Samuel Butler once observed that it takes two to say a thing, a sayee as well as a sayer – a hearer as well as a speaker. Thus, if literature is a way of saying something, it requires a reader to complete the work. And if this is so, as I am convinced it is, it must also be true that an author addresses someone as he writes. That someone has come to be called 'the implied reader'.

2. The implied reader

Let me defend myself against an obvious objection. I am not suggesting that, as an author writes, he necessarily has in the front of his mind a particular reader. F. H. Langman in a useful article, 'The Idea of the Reader in Literary Criticism', puts it this way:

I do not say we need to know what readers the author had in

mind. An author may write for a single person or a large public, for himself or for nobody. But the work itself implies the kind of reader to whom it is addressed and this may or may not coincide with the author's private view of his audience. What matters for the literary critic is to recognize the idea of the reader implied by the work. Not only correct understanding but also evaluation often depends principally upon correct recognition of the implied reader (*British Journal of Aesthetics*, January, 1967, p. 84).

I would go further. I would say that, until we discover how to take account of the implied reader, we shall call fruitlessly for serious attention to be paid to books for children, and to children as readers by others than that small number of us who have come to recognize their importance. What has bedevilled criticism of children's books in the past is the rejection of any concept of the child-reader-in-the-book by those people who have sought most earnestly for critical respectability. And they have done this, have set aside the reader-in-the-book, in the belief that mainstream criticism requires them to do so, when in fact literary criticism has for years now been moving more and more towards a method that examines this very aspect of literature. If children's book critics look for parity with their colleagues outside the study of children's books, they must – if for no other more valuable reason – show how the concept of the implied reader relates to children as readers and to the books they read.

The idea of the implied reader derives from the understanding that it takes two to say a thing. In effect it suggests that in his book an author creates a relationship with a reader in order to discover the meaning of the text. Wolfgang Iser, in *The Implied Reader* (Johns Hopkins, 1974), puts it this way: he says that such a critical method 'is concerned primarily with the form of a work, in so far as one defines form basically as a means of communication or as a negotiation of insight' (p. 57).[1]

To achieve this, an author, sometimes consciously sometimes not, creates, in Wayne C. Booth's words: 'an image of himself and another image of his reader; he makes his reader, as he makes his second self, and the most successful reading is one in which the created selves, author and reader, can find complete agreement' (*The Rhetoric of Fiction*, University of Chicago Press, 1961, p. 138).

The author's second self[2] is created by his use of various techniques: by the way, for example, he puts himself into the narrator – whether that be a third-person godlike all-seer or a first person child character;

by the way he comments on the events in the story; and by the attitude he adopts towards his characters and their actions, which he communicates in various ways, both subtle and obvious.

In the same way (and let me stress again, deliberately or otherwise) the reader's second self – the reader-in-the-book – is given certain attributes, a certain persona, created by the use of techniques and devices which help form the narrative. And this persona is guided by the author towards the book's potential meanings.

Booth points out that a distinction must be made 'between myself as reader and the often very different self who goes about paying bills, repairing leaky faucets, and failing in generosity and wisdom. It is only as I read that I become the self whose beliefs most coincide with the author's. Regardless of my real beliefs and practices, I must subordinate my mind and heart to the book if I am to enjoy it to the full.' (p. 137)

3. *The unyielding child reader*

Booth expresses something mature literary readers have always understood: that a requirement of fulfilled readership is a willingness to give oneself up to the book. They have learned how to do this: how to lay aside their own prejudices and take on the prejudices of the text, how to enter into the book, becoming part of it while at the same time never abandoning their own being. In C. S. Lewis's words, literature allowed him 'to become a thousand people and yet remain myself.'

Children, of course, have not completely learned how to do this; they have not discovered how to shift the gears of their personality according to the invitations offered by the book. In this respect they are unyielding readers. They want the book to suit them, tending to expect an author to take them as he finds them rather than they taking the book as they find it. One of the valuable possibilities offered by the critical method I look for is that it would make more intelligently understandable those books which take a child as he is but then draw him into the text; the books which help the child reader to negotiate meaning, help him develop the ability to receive a text as a literary reader does rather than making use of it for non-literary purposes.

The concept of the implied reader and the critical method that follows from it help us to do just that. They help us establish the author's relationship with the (child) reader implied in the story, to see how he creates that relationship, and to discover the meaning(s) he seeks to negotiate. Clearly, such understanding will lead us beyond a critical appreciation of the text towards that other essential activity of those concerned with children's books: how to mediate the books to their readers so that not only are individual books better appreciated by children but children are helped also to become literary readers.

II

We must examine one book closely in an attempt to reveal its implied reader. But before we come to that, it may be useful to consider some of the principal techniques by which an author can establish his tone – his relationship with his desired reader – and, of particular importance in children's books, by which he can draw the reader into the text in such a way that the reader accepts the role offered and enters into the demands of the book.

4. Style

Style is the term we use for the way a writer employs language to make his second self and his implied reader and to communicate his meaning. It is far too simplistic to suppose that this is just a matter of sentence structure and choice of vocabulary. It encompasses an author's use of image, his deliberate and unaware references, the assumptions he makes about what a reader will understand without explication or description, his attitude to beliefs, customs, characters in his narrative – all as revealed by the way he writes about them.

A simple example which allows a comparison between the style a writer employed when writing for adults and the alterations he made when rewriting the story for children is provided by Roald Dahl. 'The Champion of the World' is a short story first published in *The New Yorker* and now included in *Kiss Kiss* (Penguin, 1962). Some years afterwards Dahl rewrote the story for children under the title *Danny: The Champion of the World* (Cape, 1975). The original version could hardly be called difficult in subject or language. A ten-year-old of average reading ability could manage it without too much bother, should any child want to. Both versions are told in the first person; the adult narrator of the original is in some respects highly ingenuous, a device Dahl employs (following *New Yorker*-Thurber tradition) as a foil for the narrator's friend Claud, a worldly wise, unfazable character, and as a device to exaggerate into comic extravagance the otherwise only mildly amusing events of a fairly plain tale.

Because the original is written in the first-person, easily read narrative, which is naive even in its emotional pitch, Dahl could transfer parts with minimal alterations straight from the original into the children's version. Yet even so, he made some interesting and significant changes. Here, for example, is the original decription of the entry into the story of its arch-villain, Victor Hazel (differently spelt in the two tellings), whose unforgivable snobbery and unscrupulous selfishness are justification enough in the narrator's eyes to warrant poaching his pheasants:

> I wasn't sure about this, but I had a suspicion that it was none other than the famous Mr. Victor Hazel himself, the owner of the land and the pheasants. Mr. Hazel was a local brewer with an unbelievably arrogant manner. He was rich beyond words, and his property stretched for miles along either side of the valley. He was a self-made man with no charm at all and precious few virtues. He loathed all persons of humble station, having once been one of them himself, and he strove desperately to mingle with what he believed were the right kind of folk. He rode to hounds and gave shooting-parties and wore fancy waistcoats, and every weekday he drove an enormous black Rolls-Royce past the filling-station on his way to the brewery. As he flashed by, we would sometimes catch a glimpse of the great glistening brewer's face above the wheel, pink as a ham, all soft and inflamed from drinking too much beer. (p. 209)

Here is the recast version for the children's telling:

> I must pause here to tell you something about Mr. Victor Hazell. He was a brewer of beer and he owned a huge brewery. He was rich beyond words, and his property stretched for miles along either side of the valley. All the land around us belonged to him, everything on both sides of the road, everything except the small patch of ground on which our filling-station stood. That patch belonged to my father. It was a little island in the middle of the vast ocean of Mr. Hazell's estate.
>
> Mr. Victor Hazell was a roaring snob and he tried desperately to get in with what he believed were the right king of people. He hunted with the hounds and gave shooting parties and wore fancy waistcoats. Every week-day he drove his enormous silver Rolls-Royce past our filling-station on his way to the brewery. As he flashed by we would sometimes catch a glimpse of the great glistening beery face above the wheel, pink as a ham, all soft and inflamed from drinking too much beer. (pp. 49–50)

Dahl has simplified some of his sentences by chopping up the longer ones with full stops where commas are used in the adult version. And he does some cutting: he takes out the abstractions such as the comment about Hazel loathing people of humble station because he had once been one of them himself. Presumably Dahl felt children would not be able (or want) to cope either with the stylistic complexities of his first version or with the motivation ascribed to Hazel's behaviour. Whatever we may think about this, it certainly reveals Dahl's assumptions about his implied reader.

What he aims to achieve – and does – is a tone of voice which is clear, uncluttered, unobtrusive, not very demanding linguistically, and which sets up a sense of intimate, yet adult-controlled, relationship between his second self and his implied child reader. It is a voice often heard in children's books of the kind deliberately written for them: it is the voice of speech rather than of interior monologue or no-holds-barred private confession. It is, in fact, the tone of a friendly adult storyteller who knows how to entertain children while at the same time keeping them in their place. Even when speaking outrageously about child-adult taboo subjects (theft by poaching in *Danny* and, in this extract, harsh words about a grown-up), the text evinces a kind of drawing-room politeness. At its most typical the style speaks of 'the children' in the tale. Arthur Ransome marks a high point in that traditional manner:

So the letters had been written and posted, and day after day the children had been camping on the Peak of Darien by day, and sleeping in the farmhouse by night. They had been out in the rowing-boat with their mother, but they had always rowed the other way so as not to spoil the voyage of discovery by going to the island first. But with each day after the sending of the letters it had somehow seemed less and less likely that there would ever be an answer. The island had come to seem one of those places seen from the train that belong to a life in which we shall never take part. And now, suddenly, it was real. It was to be their island after all. They were to be allowed to sail out from the little sheltered bay, and round the point, and down the lake to the island. They were allowed to land on the island, and to live there until it was time to pack up again and go home to town and school and lessons. The news was so good that it made them solemn. They ate their bread and marmalade in silence. The prospect before them was too vast for chatter. John was thinking of the sailing, wondering whether he really remembered all that he had learnt last year. Susan was thinking of the stores and the cooking. Titty was thinking of the island itself, of coral, treasure, and footprints in the sand. Roger was thinking of the fact that he was not to be left behind. He saw for the first time that it was a good thing to be no longer the baby of the family. Vicky was the youngest now. Vicky would stay at home, and Roger, one of the crew of a ship, was to sail away into the unknown world.

Ransome achieves precisely the same relationship with his reader as Dahl, and by pretty much the same stylistic qualities. Ransome's style is more fluid than Dahl's, gentler on the ear, better balanced and more tuneful. But it is essentially writing for children; no one, surely, can believe that, had Ransome been writing for adults - in the sense of an implied adult reader - he would have adopted the tone of voice so evident and so well created in *Swallows and Amazons* (Cape), from which the extract is taken (pp. 16–17 in the Puffin edition).

Style can, as I say, work in a much more complex and subtly effective way than these two extracts suggests - or rather than my use of them here suggests. And we will look further into this aspect of the writer–reader relationship when we come to examine a major text.

5. Intermission: What the writers say . . .

Mention of Ransome calls to mind his much-quoted words about writing for children: 'You write not FOR children but for yourself, and if, by good fortune, children enjoy what you enjoy, why then you are a writer of children's books.'

All very well and, obviously, what Ransome believed about himself. But it is difficult to believe on the evidence of Ransome's books that, had he really thought he was speaking to an adult audience primarily, he would have adopted the same tone of voice or would have treated his stories in the ways he does. Even a traditional critical examination of his books, eschewing all thought of the reader, implied or otherwise (excepting of course the critic, who never considers himself anything but an objective, and therefore somehow never a specific, reader - a matter Langman in the article already mentioned deals with very effectively), must surely reveal that Ransome's books are for children in quite specific ways, whatever Ransome himself said. Which is not to suggest that he, or any other writer who adopts this idea about himself as a writer, is dissembling. Rather, I want simply to reinforce Langman's observation: 'An author may write for a single person or a large public, for himself or for nobody. But the work itself implies the kind of reader to whom it is addressed and this may not coincide with the author's private view of his audience.'

Which proves one thing, if anything at all: we must be wary of using as evidence in criticism what an author says about himself, publicly or privately: a caution we have not sufficiently taken to heart in talking about children's books. Over the past five or six years there has been a fashion for calling the authors on stage to explicate themselves and their work in public and to defend it against the worst ravages of pedagogy and off-the-cuff criticism. That has been beneficial neither for the authors nor for their audiences.

6. Point of view

Tone of voice, style as a whole, very quickly establishes a relationship between author and reader; very quickly creates the image of the implied reader. In books where the implied reader is a child, authors tend to reinforce the relationship by adopting in their second self – giving the book, if you prefer – a very sharply focused point of view. They tend to achieve that focus by putting at the centre of the story a child through whose being everything is seen and felt.

This is more than simply a device. If literature for children is to have any meaning at all, it must primarily be concerned with the nature of childhood, not just the nature commonly shared by most children but the diversity of childhood nature too. For, like all literature, children's literature at its best attempts 'to explore, re-create and seek for meanings in human experience' (the phrase is Richard Hoggart's); this attempt is made with specific reference to children and their lives through the unique relationship between language and form.

But, at the level of creating the implied reader and of an author's need to draw a child reader into his book, this narrowing of focus by the adoption of a child point of view helps keep the author's second self – himself in the book – within the perceptual scope of his child reader. And the child, finding within the book an implied author whom he can befriend because he is of the tribe of childhood as well, is thus wooed into the book. He adopts the image of the implied child reader and is then willing, may even desire, to give himself up to the author and the book and be led through whatever experience is offered.

Thus the book's point of view not only acts as a means of creating the author–reader relationship but works powerfully as a solvent, melting away a child's non-literary approach to reading and re-forming him into the kind of reader the book demands.

Some authors, feeling constricted by a too narrowly child-focusing viewpoint, try to find ways of presenting a fuller picture of adulthood without losing the child-attracting quality of the narrower focus. A few have tried to do this directly, using adult characters and a point of view that shifts between a child-focus and an adult-focus, but very few of the few who have tried have succeeded. It remains one of the major problems for children's writers now. *Carrie's War*, by Nina Bawden, is well worth critical consideration as a very fine example of how an author creates an implied reader, and how adult characters can be revealed in much of their complexity without loss of definition for young readers.

Most writers approach the problem of adult-portrayal less directly. They tend to cast their tales in the form of fantasy, usually with animal-human characters. Robert C. O'Brien's *Mrs. Frisby and the Rats of NIMH* provides a much enjoyed modern example; Kenneth Grahame's *Wind in the Willows* probably the best known and most affectionately regarded; and Russell Hoban's *The Mouse and His Child* one of the most complexly layered and handled (for which reasons, no doubt, it is finding its most responsive audience not among children but among adolescents).

But if I wanted to select, in the context of my theme, two superlative examples that encompass a possible readership of about seven years old right on to adulthood, I would choose Alan Garner's *The Stone Book* to demonstrate the direct approach and Ted Hughes' *The Iron Man* as an example of the solution through fantasy.

7. *Taking sides*

It does not follow, of course, that a writer who places a child at the narrative centre of his tale necessarily or even intentionally forges an alliance with children. *Lord of the Flies* is entirely peopled by children, but no one would call it a book for children in any sense. (Adolescents enjoy it – or at least their teachers have decided they shall study it; but adolescents are not children, an understanding I have so far taken for granted). Even the point of view of William Golding's book, though the narrative restricts itself to the child characters' points of view, is in fact profoundly adult in range and perceptions. And this is to say nothing about the style and the implied reader it helps create.

William Mayne, always published as a children's author but

notoriously little read by children and much read by adults, may, for all I know, intend to be a writer for children. But what the tone of his books actually achieves, as Charles Sarland brilliantly uncovered in his article, 'Chorister Quartet' (*Signal*, 18, September, 1975), is an implied author who is an observer of children and the narrative: a watcher rather than an ally. Even his dramatic technique seems deliberately designed to alienate the reader from the events and from the people described. This attitude to story is so little to be found in children's books that even children who have grown up as frequent and thoughtful readers find Mayne at his densest very difficult to negotiate. He wants his reader to stand back and examine what he, Mayne, offers in the same way that, as nearly as I can understand it, Brecht wanted his audiences to stand back from and contemplate the events enacted on stage.

As Sarland says, Mayne 'requires a degree of sophistication in the reader that would not normally be found in children of the same age as his characters. It is clear from the way he uses pace, dialogue, causal relationships, puns and wordplay that the last thing he wants is that the reader should be carried along on the tide of the narrative' (p. 113).

There is, in other words, an ambivalence about Mayne's work that disturbs his relationship with his child reader. And this is made more unnerving by a fracture between a narrative point of view that seems to want to ally the book with children, and narrative techniques that require the reader to disassociate from the story – to retreat and examine it dispassionately.

What Mayne may be trying to do – I say 'may be' because I am not sure that he *is* trying for it – is not impossible to achieve, though it is very difficult indeed to achieve for children. I have no space to delve into the matter here, fascinating though I find it, except to say as a pointer to those who want to follow this direction for themselves: Alan Garner's *The Stone Book*, besides the other extraordinary qualities it possesses, manages to balance these paradoxical demands, involving the reader with the narrative while at the same time helping him to stand back and contemplate it. And Garner makes it possible for children to participate like this at even quite an early time in their growth as readers, though the younger ones may require the mediation of an adult alongside them in order to enter into such a profound experience.

Taking sides can be crudely worked for, simply as a way of 'getting the child reader on your side'. Enid Blyton provides the obvious example. She quite literally places her second self on the side of the children in her stories and her readers she deliberately looks for. Her allegiance becomes collusion in a game of 'us kids against them adults'. Nothing reveals this more completely than her treatment of adult characters like the policeman Mr Goon in *The Mystery of the Strange Bundle*. The unfortunate constable's name itself – chosen by the author, remember – indicates Blyton's attitude to the man, to his office, and her stance as one of the gang, one of the children in the story. Let's play this game together, she says openly and without embarrassment; let's have fun at the expense of the grown-ups; let's show them who's best; let's solve a mystery and have an adventure.

The very titles of her books reinforce this taking of sides. They act as an attraction to the book, raising in the reader expectations about the nature of the story to come that she never fails to satisfy. There are ten books in the *Mystery of . . .* series, eight in the Adventure series, and twelve 'about the Five Finder-Outers and Dog'.

Incident by incident Blyton sustains her collusion with her implied reader, sometimes letting him have the edge on the characters by telling him what they don't yet know, sometimes letting the characters have the edge on the reader by withholding details it later turns out the characters knew all the time. And adults get the edge only so that they can be done down later by the narrator, her characters and her readers.

There is about her stories a sense of secrets being told in whispers just out of earshot of the grown-ups, a subversive charm made all the more potent for being couched in a narrative style that sounds no more disturbing than the voice of a polite maiden aunt telling a bedtime story over cocoa and biscuits. Ultimately Blyton so allies herself with her desired readers that she fails them because she never takes them further than they are. She is a female Peter Pan, the kind of suffocating adult who prefers children never to grow up, because then she can enjoy their petty foibles and dominate them by her adult superiority. This betrayal of childhood seeps through her stories; we see it as the underlying characteristic of her children who all really want to dominate each other as well as the adults.

Richmal Crompton is quite as canny: she too allies herself strongly with her child reader.[3] But her work has a redeeming quality – one among others: her ironic treatment of William, the Outlaws and their adventures. A skilled short-story writer, she structures her tales with an elegance outstanding in its craftsmanship and finish. But above all she brings to children's reading that essential element they must discover if they are to grow beyond the kind of writing Blyton's epitomizes. For without an understanding of irony, literature –

beyond the merely plotful level – will never provide much pleasure and certainly cannot yield up its deepest meanings.

Once an author has forged an alliance and a point of view that engages a child, he can then manipulate that alliance as a device to guide the reader towards the meanings he wishes to negotiate. Wolfgang Iser provides a useful example, not from a specifically children's book, where such a manoeuvre is too rarely used, but from *Oliver Twist*. Iser cites the scene in which the hungry Oliver

> has the effrontery (as the narrator sees it) to ask for another plate of soup. In the presentation of this daring exploit, Oliver's inner feelings are deliberately excluded in order to give greater emphasis to the indignation of the authorities at such an unreasonable request. The narrator comes down heavily on the side of authority, and can thus be quite sure that his hard-hearted attitude will arouse a flood of sympathy in his readers for the poor starving child. (p. 116)

What such manipulation of the reader's expectation, allegiances, and author-guided desires leads to is the further development of the implied reader into an implicated reader: one so intellectually and emotionally given to the book, not just its plot and characters but its negotiation between author and reader of potential meanings, that the reader is totally involved. The last thing he wants is to stop reading, and what he wants above all is to milk the book dry of all it has to offer, and to do so in the kind of way the author wishes. He finally becomes a participant in the making of the book. He has become aware of the 'tell-tale gaps'.

8. *Tell-tale gaps*

As a tale unfolds, the reader discovers its meaning. Authors can strive, as some do, to make their meaning plain, leaving little room for the reader to negotiate with them. Other authors leave gaps which the reader must fill before the meaning can be complete. A skilful author wishing to do this is somewhat like a play-leader: he structures his narrative so as to direct it in a dramatic pattern that leads the reader towards possible meaning(s); and he stage-manages the reader's involvement by bringing into play various techniques which he knows influence the reader's responses and expectations, in the way that Iser, for example, described Dickens doing in *Oliver Twist* (7). Literature can be studied so as to uncover the gaps an author leaves for his reader to fill, and these gaps take two general forms.

The first is the more superficial. These gaps have to do with an author's assumptions, whether knowingly made or not, about his readers. Just as we saw in the Dahl extracts (4) how a writer's style revealed his assumptions about the implied reader's ability to cope with language and syntax, so we can also detect from a writer's references to a variety of things just what he assumes about his implied reader's beliefs, politics, social customs, and the like. Richmal Crompton in common with Enid Blyton, A. A. Milne, Edith Nesbit and many more children's authors assumed a reader who would not only be aware of housemaids and cooks, nannies and gardeners but would also be used to living in homes attended by such household servants. That assumption was as unconsciously made as the adoption of a tone of voice current among people who employed servants at the time the authors were writing.

These referential gaps, these assumptions of commonality, are relatively unimportant until they become so dominant in the text that people who do not – or do not wish to – make the same assumptions feel alienated by them as they read. And this alienation, this feeling of repugnance, affects the child just as much as the adult, once the referential gaps become significant.

Far more important, however, is another form of tell-tale gap: these are the ones that challenge the reader to participate in making meaning. Making meaning is a vital concept in literary reading. Laurence Sterne refers to it directly in *Tristram Shandy*:

> No author who understands the just boundaries of decorum and good breeding would presume to think all: The truest respect which you can pay to the reader's understanding is to halve this matter amicably, and leave him something to imagine, in his turn, as well as yourself. For my own part, I am eternally paying him compliments of this kind, and do all that lies in my power to keep his imagination as busy as my own. (Penguin, 1967, p. 127)

Of course, it doesn't all depend on the author: he can deploy his narrative skills brilliantly, 'halving the matter amicably' with his reader. But unless a reader accepts the challenge, no relationship that seeks to discover meaning is possible. It is one of the responsibilities of children's writers, and a privileged one, so to write that children are led to understand how to read: how to accept the challenge.

Let me offer the crucial gap in Sendak's *Where the Wild Things Are* as example. In its pictorial as well as its textual art this

103

extraordinary masterpiece is compactly authored. One might be forgiven for supposing at first sight that there are no gaps of any kind for the reader to enter. But not so; there is one so vital that, unless the reader fills it, the profound meaning of the book cannot be discovered. It is the gap which demands that the child reader supply the understanding that Max has dreamt his journey to the Wild Things, that in fact the Wild Things are Max's own creation. Once understood, that meaning having been made, the book opens itself to all sorts of other pleasurable discoveries which actually were clues to the meaning all along and which, once realized, present themselves as clues to yet further meaning. There is, for instance, in the first picture in the book, the Wild-Thingish doll hanging from a coathanger; and then, in the very next picture, there is the portrait of a Wild Thing framed and hung on the wall and signed 'by Max'.

Such guides to the reader may seem obvious to an adult, but children of four and five and six, who are the book's implied readers, make such a significant contribution and discover such details only if they give the book a willing attention of the same order as adults must give to filling the gaps in, say, Joyce's *Ulysses*.

Alan Garner's *The Stone Book* is built around three main images, each placed in precise relationship to each other so that they create two vital gaps which the reader must enter and fill before the potential meanings of the book become plain. Reiner Zimnik's *The Crane* is as halved as Sterne could wish; Zimnik's tone of voice is so sensible, so matter of fact, so gentle and everyday, you can suppose the meaning(s) of his story must be so too. But in fact the book is heavy with possibilities and is not at all easy to plumb intellectually, though emotionally – as an increasing number of teachers are finding after introducing it to their nine- to twelve-year-olds – it is powerfully attractive.

9. In sum . . .

. . . and before we begin an exploration of one text.

I am suggesting that the concept of the implied reader, far from unattended to by literary critics in Europe and America, offers us a critical approach which concerns itself less with the subjects portrayed in a book than with the means of communication by which the reader is brought into contact with the reality presented by an author. It is a method which could help us determine whether a book is for children or not, what kind of book it is, and what kind of reader (or, to put it another way, what kind of reading) it demands. Knowing this will help us to understand better how to teach not just a particular book but particular books to particular children.

I have been trying to sketch in some of the more significant ways in which specific responses are provoked in a reader, the techniques that make up what Kenneth Burke in *The Philosophy of Literary Form* has called 'the strategy of communication'. This is achieved by major techniques such as I have described and by a variety of other devices such as what an author discloses to his reader and what he conceals, the way he signals his intentions, his evocation of suspense, the introduction of the unexpected, and the way he can play about with the reader's expected responses to the narrative.

All these create a relationship between author and reader, which I have used the word 'tone' to denote; and an author, consciously or otherwise, reveals in his narrative, through the way he uses all these techniques and by other signals too, what he wants from his reader, what kind of relationship he looks for.

Now I want to examine some of these matters at work in one book, Lucy Boston's *The Children of Green Knowe*.

III

10. Why 'The Children of Green Knowe'?

For three reasons:

Mrs Boston is a much admired and respected writer; her first children's book lends itself to my critical needs here.

Not only is she much respected, but she is historically important. *The Children of Green Knowe* appeared in 1954 and was one of the first of the new wave of children's books that marks the out-cropping since the Second World War. I think it intelligently arguable that this book directly influenced a number of writers who began work in the 50s and 60s. (Philippa Pearce's *Tom's Midnight Garden*, Alan Garner's *The Weirdstone of Brisingamen* and the work of William Mayne owe a considerable debt to Lucy Boston. Discuss.)

Mrs Boston has said publicly some interesting things about her work, which provide an example of the kind of authorial self-comment I warned against earlier. During a talk given in November 1968 to the Children's Book Circle (a gathering of children's book editors in London who meet to discuss their professional concerns) Mrs Boston said:

> Is there a conscious difference in the way I write for grown-ups and children? No, there is no difference of approach, style,

vocabulary or standard. I could pick out passages from any of the books and you would not be able to tell what age it was aimed at.[4]

Let's see. The opening of *Yew Hall* (Bodley Head, 1972), Lucy Boston's first book, and written for adults (or, to use her word, grown-ups):

Possibly it was their voices that made me decide that I could share my house with them, so that after having once refused, I repented and told them that they could come. He was a huge man, handsome like a statue in St. Paul's. His martial features and great neck suggest at once to the imagination the folds of a marble cloak drawn back across a superlative torso and looped over an arm to free the incredible giant legs in their marble tights. He was so near to the type classified as admirable at the turn of the eighteenth century that his own personality might have escaped my notice if it had not been that his voice was as soft and warm in quality as a man's voice could possibly be. There was nothing feminine about it. It was like a breeze in the tops of a forest, and he gave the impression, that afterwards was amply confirmed, of having so much space to live in that he need never knock elbows with or trip over anyone else. Well might he be self-satisfied - like America he has no need of imports. A general comfort radiated from his bigness - a big heart, a big fire, a big meal, a big bed, a big pair of shoes; and, I suppose, we must also think of a big stick, a big clap of thunder. (pp. 9–10)

Compare the opening passage of her first children's book, published the same year (see extract in (11) below): there are unmistakable differences in approach, style and vocabulary. The urbanity of *Yew Hall* establishes very quickly a tone that implies a literate adult reader. The handsome statues of St Paul's, the martial features and superlative torso, the type classified as admirable at the turn of the eighteenth century, America having no need of imports: this one paragraph is littered with references that expect a reader who can match the author's cultural and social background: the educated English middle class. The writing is confident, witty, slightly superior ('Possibly it was their voices that made me decide that I could share my house with them . . .'), the kind of writing one would not be ashamed to be caught reading by one's butler.

What of *The Children of Green Knowe?* Who is its implied reader? Let's look at it under the headings suggested in section II.

11. Style

Here are the opening paragraphs of *The Children of Green Knowe* (Faber, 1954):

> A little boy was sitting in the corner of a railway carriage looking out at the rain, which was splashing against the windows and blotching downward in an ugly, dirty way. He was not the only person in the carriage, but the others were strangers to him. He was alone as usual. There were two women opposite him, a fat one and a thin one, and they talked without stopping, smacking their lips in between sentences and seeming to enjoy what they said as much as if it were something to eat. They were knitting all the time, and whenever the train stopped the click-clack of their needles was loud and clear like two clocks. It was a stopping train – more stop than go – and it had been crawling along through flat flooded country for a long time. Everywhere there was water – not sea or rivers or lakes, but just senseless flood water with the rain splashing into it. Sometimes the railway lines were covered by it, and then the train-noise was quite different, softer than a boat.
>
> 'I wish it was *the* Flood', thought the boy, 'and that I was going to the Ark. That would be fun! Like the circus. Perhaps Noah had a whip and made all the animals go round and round for exercise. What a noise there would be, with the lions roaring, elephants trumpeting, pigs squealing, donkeys braying, horses whinnying, bulls bellowing, and cocks and hens always thinking they were going to be trodden on but unable to fly up on to the roof where all the other birds were singing, screaming, twittering, squawking and cooing. What must it have sounded like, coming along on the tide? And did Mrs. Noah just knit, knit and take no notice?'
>
> The two women opposite him were getting ready for the next station. They packed up their knitting and collected their parcels and then sat staring at the little boy. He had a thin face and very large eyes; he looked patient and rather sad. They seemed to notice him for the first time. (pp. 9–10)

The language in *Yew Hall* tends towards the Latinate. *Green Knowe* is much more firmly Anglo-Saxon. Rain is splashing and blotching, lips are smacking, knitting needles click-clack, not to mention Tolly's own list of participial verbs describing Noah's animals. This makes for a style not only simpler to read but far more active then a Latinate one, far more concrete in an everyday and child-appealing sense.

There is, however, as Mrs Boston claims, no lowering of standard between the two books. *Green Knowe* is just as densely and richly textured – perhaps is even more richly textured – than *Yew Hall*. But the images and the words used to communicate them are quite different in the experiential demands made on the reader. At the crudest level *Yew Hall* requires familiarity with St Paul's Cathedral, the late eighteenth century and the economy of the United States if one is to enjoy all Mrs Boston has to offer. *Green Knowe* requires no such sophistication. You need only to have seen some rain, have been on a train, know something about the story of Noah and the Flood, and to have observed women knitting for the text to be completely open to you. After that you need only put at Mrs Boston's disposal a sympathetic imagination and she leads you off in a very clearly signposted direction. Even from these three opening paragraphs we can see she is busy with sensual experience: the sight, sound, feel, and sense of things. It is a direction in which her story will take young readers a very long way.

For sure, then, the style of *The Children of Green Knowe* is much more accessible to a child reader, and comparison with the style of *Yew Hall*, which seems so much more confidently natural to Mrs Boston – one feels it is closer to her own thinking voice – leads one to suppose its implied reader is a child. At the very least the style appeals to the child-in-the-adult, possessing that very tone of voice I earlier suggested is traditionally the English tone used in telling stories to children: direct, clear, polite, firm, uncluttered. And Mrs Boston achieves it admirably.

We must discover whether or not the other aspects of her book reinforce the impression given by her style.

12. Point of view

Tolly is seven; remarkable for his age, a child of a very particular class. His father and stepmother are in Burma, the boy has been put into boarding school, left for the holidays with the headmistress and her old father, and then sent alone on a train journey to visit his great-grandmother, Mrs Oldknow, who lives in a large old house. Throughout, the story is told from Tolly's point of view. Only occasionally is there a brief shift for some narrative purpose, as when the two women in the train 'sat staring at the little boy. He had a thin face and very large eyes; he looked patient and rather sad. They seemed to notice him for the first time.' Otherwise, the perceptions are all the boy's.

Even Mrs Oldknow, so central a character in the story, is seen only from the outside. Her private thoughts and perceptions remain enigmatic, and influentially so: she occupies a somewhat mysteriously attractive place in the book. One wonders about her, and feels too a little daunted by her, a little afraid of her secret knowingness. The reader gets that impression from a subtly handled feature of the book. All along one cannot help feeling that it is Mrs Oldknow who is telling the story. And probably the feeling would not be so strong were it not for the stories Mrs Oldknow tells Tolly at night. They are about the children who lived in the house and died in the Plague of 1665. But then, the rest of the book is also about a boy in the house. Isn't the whole book therefore a story by Mrs Oldknow? Has she, in fact, invented Tolly? Or isn't she, at the very least, telling his story, and doing it so well because she *knows* - can see into children's minds, as children so often believe some adults can, and tell what is going on in them?

So, though the story is told from Tolly's point of view - apart, of course, from Mrs Oldknow's stories about the other, long-ago children - Mrs Oldknow herself seems in control of it. These two things together stimulate a strong sense of alliance between Mrs Oldknow, Tolly and the reader, thus placing the author unmistakably on the reader's side.

13. Taking sides

Before the story has gone far enough to establish the strong relationship I've just described, Mrs Boston is signalling her allegiance. The opening paragraphs of the book reveal her sympathetic understanding of a small boy's response to the world about him, and in particular the world as it surrounds Tolly at that moment on the train. Every slight detail serves this end, from the clacking needles and the train being more stop than go, to the child-accurate observation of the rain and the flood and the train noise.

Then the two women take notice, and their conversation with Tolly sets him thinking about his circumstances. Now Mrs Boston reveals unequivocally whose side she is on: Tolly being miserably shy of his headmistress, the kind Miss Spudd, who yet always calls him 'dear'.

When Tolly at last meets his great-grandmother, wondering if she is a witch and whether he will be afraid of her (the terrible business of meeting strange relatives), Mrs Boston–Oldknow (for Mrs Boston's second self must surely be Mrs Oldknow) declares her allegiance openly: 'What does one generation more or less matter? I'm glad you have come. It will seem lovely to me. How many years of you have I wasted?' A declaration of friendship, if not of love, which is reinforced by a further shift from adult-child allegiance to collusion no more than a page later:

> At that moment the fire went *pop!* and shot a piece of wood out into the room. *Pop!* again.
> 'Buttons! Who said buttons? Poor Mrs Noah.' Tolly chased the sparks and trod on them to put them out.
> 'Why do you live in a castle?' he said, looking round.
> 'Why not? Castles were meant to live in.'
> 'I thought that was only in fairy tales. Is it a real castle?'
> 'Of course.'
> 'I mean, do things happen in it, like the castles in the books?'
> 'Oh yes, things happen in it.'
> 'What sort of things?'
> 'Wait and see! I'm waiting too, to see what happens now that you are here. Something will, I'm sure.' (p. 20)

Something is being proposed here: at the least a game, at the most something more mysteriously magical, and it is to be an adventure enacted between Tolly and Mrs Oldknow.

Next morning, the adventure begins: it involves Tolly's long-ago child relatives – whether as ghosts or not we hope to discover – household toys, garden animals, and Mrs Oldknow. Being cut off by the flood simply asserts actually and symbolically the private collusive world inhabited by the boy and the old woman.

But the collusion is not just a means of disposing the reader to the book: its profoundest meaning depends upon the nature of the relationship.

14. Tell-tale gaps

Game or ghost story? More than a game and not just a ghost story. Each time we think that at last Tolly is indisputably seeing apparitions of Toby, Alexander and Linnet, Mrs Boston withdraws confirmation.

A crucial scene comes after the snowfall. A tree's branches form a

cave, which Tolly enters, and there seems to meet and hear speaking
the three ghosts; Alexander even plays his flute. But the scene ends:
'Had he been dreaming?' And when Tolly creeps out of his snow-cave,
'Somewhere in the garden a thrush was trying to whistle Alexander's
tune.' We are left wondering still.

Later Mrs Oldknow leaves Tolly alone in the house, and Boggis too
is gone. Surely now the ghosts will emerge and they, Tolly and the
reader can meet undeniably. But no. Despite the house being empty of
others and dark coming on, so that the stage is set for a final exciting
ghost-drama, our expectations raised for a climax (how many other
writers have prepared us so before) Mrs Boston will not satisfy us:
'For some reason [Tolly] felt convinced that, until his great-grandmother returned, not so much as a marble would move in the house.'
She has employed a device similar to Dickens's in *Oliver Twist*:
reader's expectations raised, and deliberately dashed. We are forced to
wonder why.

Here is the amicable halving of this book; here is a tell-tale gap
which the reader must enter if the book's true meaning is to be
negotiated. Whatever is going on in the story can only be enacted
between Mrs Oldknow and Tolly. Nothing happens when they are
apart. Together, their lives have followed a pattern. During the day,
Tolly explores and plays, sometimes on his own, sometimes with Mrs
Oldknow, sometimes with Boggis, but always, however gently and
subtly suggested, at the instigation of his great-grandmother. She, like
a superlatively wise play leader, offers opportunities for Tolly to
enjoy himself through experiences that enliven the world to him. He
is led to look closely, hear clearly, touch sensitively, think imaginatively. The book is laden with instances in which Tolly encounters
objects and, by sensing them and playing with them, imaginatively
perceives the life in them.

These moments extend from the purely sensational –

In the fire the snow drifting down the chimney was making the
only noise it ever can – a sound like the striking of fairy
matches; though sometimes when the wind blows you can hear
the snow like a gloved hand laid against the window. (p. 64)

– to lengthy passages in which Tolly's exploration of a room or a part
of the garden or of a toybox is described in close and carefully imaged
detail. The walk through the snow that leads to the snow-cave scene is
one such.

Punctuating these descriptions of the day-to-day activities are four
stories told by Mrs Oldknow to Tolly at bedtime. This device suits the

apparently naturalistic plot: Tolly is on holiday with his great-grandmother: the house and gardens provide his daily adventures; before bed he is given his fictional adventure. But these four stories are not just any stories: they are about the three long-ago children and their horse Feste, one story for each. Some critics – John Rowe Townsend in *A Sense of Story*, for instance – have felt this an awkward construction. To my mind it is not only a pattern that creates a satisfying rhythm in the book – entirely suited, as I say, to the plot's boy-on-holiday structure – but it actually makes the book's true meaning possible.

We are led to see things this way: Tolly and Mrs Oldknow fantasize about Toby and Alexander and Linnet. Tolly may or may not actually see their ghosts, and enjoys the game. But the three long-ago children have undeniable reality only in the stories Mrs Oldknow tells about them. There they live in their own right, not as spectres raised by Tolly and his great-grandmother, just as Tolly and Mrs Oldknow have a reality in their own right only as characters in Mrs Boston's story about them. Stories, Mrs Boston is telling us, are the means by which we give life to ourselves and the objects around us. Stories, in fact, create meaning.

Strangely enough, in the very talk to the Children's Book Circle in which she claimed no difference between her writing for adults and her writing for children, Mrs Boston also said:

> My approach has always been to explore reality as it appears, and from within to see how far imagination can properly expand it. Reality, after all, has no outside edge. I never start with a fantasy and look for a peg to hang it on. As far as I deliberately try to do anything other than to write a book that pleases me, I would like to remind adults of joy, now considered obsolete – and would like to encourage children to use and trust their senses for themselves at first hand – their ears, eyes and noses, their fingers and the soles of their feet, their skins and their breathing, their muscular joy and rhythms and heartbeats, their instinctive loves and pity and their awe of the unknown. This, not the telly, is the primary material of thought. It is from direct sense stimulus that imagination is born . . . (p. 36)

Nowhere has an author so exactly stated her aims, and in few books has an author achieved her highest aims so certainly as Mrs Boston does in *The Children of Green Knowe*. Through Tolly, guided by Mrs Boston's second self, her implied reader is brought to grips with the direct sense stimulus that gives birth to life-expanding imagination.

By any standard this is a fine achievement, all the more remarkable for the simplicity with which it is executed.

15. Lucy Boston's implied reader

Mrs Boston makes no impossible demands on her child reader's ability to construct meaning from words. Her style is approachable, uncomplicated, specific rather than abstract. The first Green Knowe book is not long; its episodic and day-to-day rhythm punctuated by the stories-within-the-story makes it easy to read in unexhausting parts. Her alliance with her young reader is persuasive. The now almost old-fashioned middle-classness of Tolly's and Mrs Oldknow's life (and Mrs Boston's preference for it) is strong but not so dominantly obtrusive as to be a disadvantage. (The polite formality of the collusion between Mrs Oldknow and Tolly is nowadays amusing. Even though they are playing a game, Tolly must always behave impeccably; he commits only one naughty act throughout the whole book: he writes on the newly whitewashed wall in Boggis's room, a wickedness allowed to pass without censure, of course, because it is done in a servant's room, not in the main house. Even Boggis, old retainer, wants to perserve the benevolent hierarchical social tradition, to the point of tolerating his daughter's indiscretion because it provides him with a male heir to his post. The book is deeply conservative and traditionalist: a political attitude which disposes children all the more readily to the story, for most children prefer things to remains as they always have been.)

All Mrs Boston requires of her reader is a willingness to enter into the spirit of sensuous discovery. Given this, she deploys her craft subtly indeed towards her stated aims. And that she is speaking primarily to children I have no doubt.

NOTES

1. Iser has enlarged and refined his ideas in *The Act of Reading* (Baltimore, MD, Johns Hopkins, 1979).
2. The term was revived by Kathleen Tillotson in her inaugural lecture at the University of London, published under the title *The Tale and the Teller* (Athlone Press, 1959): 'Writing on George Eliot in 1877 Dowden said that the form that most persists in the mind after reading her novels is not any of the characters, but "one who, if not the real George Eliot, is that second self who writes her books, and lives and speaks through them".

The "second self", he goes on, is "more substantial than any mere human personality" and has "fewer reserves"; while "behind it, lurks well pleased the veritable historical self secure from impertinent observation and criticism".' (p. 15)

3. Of course, the William stories were first written for adults. But children soon adopted them, after which Richmal Crompton was never in doubt about her true audience.

4. Quoted from an extract published in John Rowe Townsend's *A Sense of Story* (Kestrel, p. 36).

3

Specialist areas of criticism

A landmark article in the field of reception-response criticism was Michael Benton's 'Children's Responses to the Text' first delivered at the Fourth Symposium of the International Research Society for Children's Literature at Exeter in 1978 and published in *Responses to Children's Literature* (ed. Geoff Fox *et al.*, Munich, K. G. Saur, 1983). Benton's work is firmly in the orbit of teaching, and his book, with Geoff Fox, *Teaching Literature, Nine to Fourteen* (OUP, 1985) takes the theory of narrative, reading, and reception, and translates it into classroom practice.

'The subject of "the reader's response" ', Benton notes, 'is the Loch Ness monster of literary studies', and to answer the question, 'what is going on in that child's head as he reads?' he suggests that 'the reading state' has four attributes:

(a) *It is active.* It is a commonplace in any reader's experience (and in books about reading) that the mental activity set going when reading a story involves the reader in making meaning from signs. When we are engrossed in a book, we are conscious not of words on the page, but of meanings made. It is necessary to underline this truism for, though there are few who describe the reading of fiction as mere *passive* time-filling, there are, equally, few of us who have not felt unnerved at some time by the fact that when children read stories there is no observable outcome, no finished product for us to examine. The story has happened inside the child's head. The activity of 'storying' from the printed pages of a book lies within; it is over before it can be articulated. The nearest we can get to it is introspective recall. If we want to fathom the process of 'storying', we need to develop new methodologies which genuinely take account of the insubstantial nature of the fictions we construct in imagination as we read.

(b) *It is creative.* Tolkien's oft-quoted statement about the

115

writer as a 'sub-creator' of a 'secondary world' has implications for the reader too (J. R. R. Tolkien, 'On Fairy
Stories', p. 36). For, in remaking a story from a text, the
reader generates a 'secondary world' in his own imagination, his 'novel within the novel'. He recreates something
which approximates to the original conception of the
author. In this sense, he is a performer, an interpreter of a
text. Granted he does not have the expressive outlet of a
stage and an audience but, instead, he builds a mental stage
and fills it with the people and scenes and events that the
text offers him and, as I shall argue later, with other images
generated by his own individual inclinations and limitations. Reading is a sort of 'armchair acting' in which, to
quote Wayne Booth, 'there is an implied dialogue among
author, narrator, the other characters and the reader'
(Wayne C. Booth, *The Rhetoric of Fiction*, Chicago,
University of Chicago Press, 1961, p. 302). Books are
embalmed voices. The reader's job is to disinter them and to
breathe life into them.

(c) *It is unique*. As with the performance of a play or a
symphony, each 'reading' is a unique experience. To take an
extreme example, this includes re-readings of the same text
by the same person. Most people have had the experience
of finding different things in the story world on reading a
book for the second time. The book has not changed: the
same words are in the same order. It is the reader who has
changed or, more precisely, the nature of his imaginative
participation has changed – and will change every time he
reads. The idea of participation suggests my fourth point.

(d) *It is co-operative*. The experience of reading fiction is a
compound of what the text offers and what the reader
brings. If writing is a 'one-headed' job (the author with his
pen and blank sheet of paper), reading is a 'two-headed'
experience. The reader creates with the products of two
imaginations, his own and the writer's. Now, given that no
two readers recreate the same story and no one reader can
ever repeat his experience a second time, this leaves what
we can call each unique 'textual performance' in a curious
limbo, for it belongs wholly neither to the author nor to the
reader but hovers somewhere between them, partaking of
both. Whether looked at through the author's or the

reader's inward eye, its status is that of a 'virtual experience'. (pp. 19–20)

Benton's conclusions, and the work that he has subsequently developed from them have produced a distinctive brand of empiricism which may have a decisive influence, in educational terms, within the map of modern criticism. (See, for example, Michael Benton *et al.*, *Young Readers Responding to Poems*, Routledge, 1989.)

> In conclusion, the approach I have outlined to children's responses to the text has sought to do three things:
>> to build upon the knowledge available to us from different disciplines;
>> to offer a conceptual model that accounts for the nature and dimensions of the Secondary World; and
>> to argue that children's responses to stories can be most satisfactorily described in relation to this model rather than in terms of classificatory systems or psychoanalytic theory.
>
> As readers, we make a mole-like progress through a novel, shovelling mounds of textual information behind us while simultaneously anticipating light at the end of the fictional tunnel. Like the mole, too, we are all but blind to the processes we undergo. It is the lot of moles and readers to work in the half-light of other worlds.
>
> As researchers, we find this especially irksome for we tend to prize the clear light of the tidily explained rather than the twilight of the dimly apprehended. Yet, in the area of reader response, above all, we must be prepared to work with untidy, uncertain data: fleeting images, half-formed notions, inadequately articulated ideas, partially glimpsed meanings are the yield of the introspective recall. Whether or not other enquiries adopt the approach suggested here, clearly there is much detailed work needed with individual child readers before we can develop a convincing picture of what it means to be inside the Secondary World of story. (Benton 1983, p. 31)

Thus Benton's views can be usefully read alongside those of Margaret Meek in *The Cool Web*; Robert Protherough, in *Developing Responses to Fiction* (Open University Press, 1983); articles such as 'How Children Judge Stories' (*Children's Literature in Education*, vol. 14, no. 1, 1983); and the work of Arthur Applebee in *The Child's Concept of Story: Ages Two to Seventeen* (Chicago, Chicago University Press, 1978). Aidan Chambers and his colleagues have also developed subtle ways of analysing child responses, reported in 'Tell Me: Are Children Critics?', in *Booktalk*, pp. 138–74.

One of the most interesting of writers involved in this area is Hugh Crago, whose shift of interest from literary criticism to psychotherapy has been reflected in a long series of articles exploring, at first, the socio-cultural axes of children's books, through, with his wife, Maureen, a longitudinal study of the story experience of one of their daughters and so to some fascinating results and speculations on the nature of the act of reading for the child.

To some readers, the inclusion of this article may seem to be a long way from 'children's literature', dealing, as it does, primarily with the reading processes of the young child, and with a whole category of texts for which the critical world has had little time, and has thus scant critical vocabulary. Nevertheless, it illustrates the way in which research in children's literature often, by its necessary pragmatism, shows the way to more academic studies.

As some indication of the respectability of the subject, 'The Roots of Response' was first presented as a paper at the 100th Convention of the Modern Language Association of America, at Washington, D.C., in December 1984.

Hugh Crago
'The Roots of Response',
Children's Literature Association Quarterly, vol. 10, no. 3
(Fall, 1985), pp. 100–4

Fortunately, I need not begin by justifying my topic: if some of us did not consider the literary experience in early childhood worth studying, then a special section under this title could hardly have been included in MLA 100. I do however need to define some terms. In common with most others who have observed the interaction between young children and books, I have taken 'literary experience' to mean the experience of visual as well as verbal texts, and you will see me use 'text', 'fiction' and 'literature' all in this extended sense. Secondly the word 'response' in the title of this paper is there in deference to established usage, rather than because it carries the best range of implications. Child-book interaction is a complex, *systemic* process which is inadequately and even misleadingly represented in the linear language of stimulus and response. More of that shortly.

I may be known to some of you as the co-author of *Prelude to Literacy*. *Prelude* is the published report of five years' observation and recording (undertaken primarily by my wife, Maureen Crago) of our daughter's experience of fiction prior to her learning to read. If you have read our book, you may well have shared the disappointment expressed by reviewers like Bonnie Lass and Grant Noble at the way we focussed on the particular rather than the general. It's as if Maureen and I wandered through a forest, exclaiming over individual trees and clumps of trees, but rarely indicating that we knew anything about the shape and composition of the forest as a whole. Only in the final chapter, which our publishers (for reasons best known to themselves) retitled 'Epilogue', thereby suggesting that it was a set of afterthoughts rather than a proper conclusion, did we give a sketchy aerial map of that forest. Maureen reminds me that to an extent this was quite deliberate. We wanted our readers to share our own experience of seeing shape and pattern emerge only gradually from a mass of detail. It's also true to say that as we have gained distance from our material, we have likewise gained skill in discerning the general, in guessing the generalisable. So in this paper I have tried to supplement *Prelude* with some thoughts on the *kind* of data that we and others have so far gathered on the literary experience in early childhood – what the inbuilt limitations of our methodology and our data might be, and what wider questions are raised by our reliance on them. Having done that, I then summarise some of the patterns that we ourselves found in our data, those patterns that seem most likely to correlate with the ones discovered by other investigators working in this field. In other words, I am asking first, 'what are the risks in generalising?' and second, 'given those risks, what can we tentatively say that *might* be generalisable?'

The best evidence we yet have of the experience of literature in early childhood has been provided by one particular form of research, the participant–observer case study, based on 'parent diaries'. Parent diaries record observations of one or two children (occasionally more) listening to stories read or told by a parent (most often, the mother) in a home setting. The suitability (indeed, the virtual necessity) of this method for the preschool age group is obvious. Children of elementary-school age have of course been studied by methods more generally favored in this century by behavioural psychology (structured tests, questionnaire, interview) but clearly, such techniques for gaining information would be difficult or impossible to utilize with children whose linguistic competence is far less developed, and whose utterances depend far more on a domestic context than those of school age children.

Now it will be immediately clear that parent diaries, including our own, arise from, and are limited by, a very specialized socio-economic and gender context. To my knowledge, all the parents involved were professional people, and almost all were women. We are looking at what appears to be a middle-class phenomenon, and at a product of traditional gender-role dispositions in which it is the *mother* who is assumed to have the closest contact with, and the greatest interest in, the young child. Chapter 4 of Carolyn Steedman's *The Tidy House* (1982) makes it obvious that the parent diaries to which I have been referring are in fact part of a wider tradition of parent–observers going back to 1800, and that these are almost without exception of middle-class origin.

Then again, no mother would bother to read aloud extensively to her children if she were not already convinced of the value of literary experience, and of the determining power of early childhood experience. No parent would undertake the onerous task of recording her child's words and actions unless she already saw her child as an individual person whose actions, thoughts and feelings were interesting and important for their own sake. The communication system set up between parent and child in such cases would be typical of what Bernstein calls the 'person-oriented family' rather than the 'positional' family: '. . . the parents would be very sensitive towards the unique characteristics of the children . . . thus there would develop an 'open' communication system which would foster and provide the linguistic means and role learning for the verbal signalling and making explicit of individual differences, together with the explication of judgements, their bases and consequences. (p. 178)

There are two conclusions that I would draw from these facts about parent diaries: first, that in terms of the ideology of parenting, all of our case-studies are products of the most recent stage in De Mause's model of the history of attitudes to children. De Mause calls this stage the 'helping mode', meaning by that a 'child-centered' or empathic stance on the part of the parent. Our studies are thus products of the growing edge of child-parent relationships in our culture. Second, if we consider our case-studies in pedagogical terms (as indeed some of the parent–observers themselves have done), then all of them were conducted under conditions that maximized the chance of a successful outcome. Books were introduced in the context of an individualized, caring relationship with a loved adult, herself fully committed to the value of story as well as to the value of the child. In such circumstances, it would have been most surprising if the children concerned had not responded with reciprocal enthusiasm!

In other words, we have been privileged to witness young children interacting with literature *under the most favorable possible conditions*. Immediately, then we need to ask ourselves:

1. Would the sequence of behavior patterns that our studies revealed be displayed by children of similar ages, but in less supportive educational environments? Would the same sequence be displayed by older children, whose introduction to literature had been delayed until they were well beyond the chronological stage evinced by the subjects of our case studies? How close are the ties between stages of cognitive/emotional development and stages of socialization into literary conventions?

2. Extensive reading-aloud or storytelling being presently practiced only by a small segment of the population, what is the relationship between our findings and the processes by which children are socialized into the iconic language of television? Would the same developmental stages apply? To find out we would, I think, need a new kind of study of TV viewing, a home-based naturalistic study that would utilize the same methods as Jules Henry and his associates employed for their impressive anthropological study, *Pathways to Madness*.

Having posed these questions, I must confess that at this stage I have little to offer by way of answers to them. But I think that they need to be in the backs of our minds as we pursue research in this field. Let's now turn back to the evidence afforded by our parent diaries, and consider some things that we need to keep in mind while interpreting them.

First, *observed response to literature is not equivalent to internal experience of literature*, though we all often talk and think as if it is. We can *never* know exactly how an individual experiences that particular body of organized stimuli that we call a 'story' or a 'picture book'. All we can trace, measure, analyze, is what individuals *show* us of their experience through speech, facial expression, or gesture. Here is the best analogy that I have so far been able to come up with for the relationship between response and inner experience: the relationship is like the one between those worms that live in the soft sand at the edge of the sea, and the visible trails that they leave behind them on the surface of the sand. The worm itself is completely buried; only the trails appear, and they, being in sand so wet that it will not hold the shape, are constantly vanishing even as one watches. The trail is evidence of the worm's presence, but it doesn't tell us much about what the worm looks like, only where it has been.

Secondly, *the act of articulating one's inner experience changes that experience*. When I experimented with recording my own response to a novel as it was actually occurring (or at any rate, as soon as possible after), I discovered that as soon as I ceased reading and allowed my mind to dwell on the mental images, the inner conversations and the feelings that I had been dimly aware of previously, all of those internal events began to 'expand', to lead off in all directions at once: I had the sense of tightly-furled buds filmed with a time-exposure, and then speeded up, so that the buds bloomed in seconds. As I suggest in 'The Readers in the Reader', trying to film the buds at all led inevitably to this surge into expanded meaning – meaning which was not present except embryonically while the novel itself was being read. If that is true when one is alone, and seeking to articulate one's experience of reading, how much more true it must be when there is an audience of other people present for whom the articulation is being shaped. *Interpersonal contexts cannot but affect the form and the content of what we choose to report from our inner worlds.* When parent diaries are in question, the fact that the 'other person' to whom the child's response is directed happens to be extremely interested in what the child says, and may even be observed to write it down or tape it, must also affect what the child selects to report. I recognize, of course, that a preschool child is probably far less likely to be worried by a parent's serious interest than an older child might be. The child will not clam up (not usually, anyway) and is less likely to censor, or to offer only what the adult will approve of. But a measure of influence is bound to be there, nonetheless.

What is in question is a powerful 'positive feedback loop' (to use the language of general systems theory): adult enthusiasm for story, adult perception of story (embodied in the way it is read, the emphases that are given) elicits a pattern of response from the child listener in which the child's perceptions are focussed and the child's enthusiasm is maximized. The child's response, in turn, will feed back into the adult's performance. In *Prelude to Literacy*, Maureen reports how Anna pinched the bridge of her nose while asking me the meaning of the word, 'brass' in Charles Keeping's *Black Dolly* (1966). In fact, the nose-pinching gesture derived from Maureen's own response to being asked the same question by Anna in an earlier reading; Maureen characteristically pinches the bridge of her nose when considering knotty questions! To this vignette I could add that my puzzlement at seeing Anna pinch *her* nose (we did not recognize the source of the behaviour until much later) led to my dwelling on her question, and affording it time and energy that I would not have given had her gesture not surprised me. And so on.

Perhaps I should hasten to say that in no way am I claiming that a child's response is simply a carbon copy of the mediating adult's, or that the child is not free to find centers of interest that may differ very markedly from the adult's (as all of us who have read to very small children know), or indeed to reject the book entirely. But the harder we look at the nuances of the mediating adult's performance, her framing comments, glosses, and answers to the child's questions, the harder it is to see the child's reactions as coming solely from within itself. *Story and mediating performance are one and the same for the preschool children observed by our parent diarists.* This was incompletely recognized by Dorothy White in her pioneering *Books before Five* (originally published in 1954) and by some who have followed her (notably Dorothy Butler, in *Cushla and her Books*). This is hardly surprising. We ourselves came to understand it only late in our work, when we began recording parental input preceding and following the places Anna commented or questioned. It is easy enough now to look back and say how inadequate this was to deal with the interactive process, to say how differently we would do it if we were doing it again! (In recent follow-up work with Anna and her sister, such as I report in 'The Opening Door', my transcripts include *everything said by everyone*, whether 'relevant to the reading' or not.)

Just as our awareness of the mediating performance changes our perception of how much of the response 'belongs' to the child, so it alters our perception of the text, since that text is realized only in performance. Maureen and I read rather dramatically, assigning distinctive 'voices' to all chief characters: so the text our child experiences is going to be a different one from that experienced by a child whose parents read with fewer histrionics and with no clear differentiation of dialogue from narrative. Our investment in a particular text, as realized in our performance of it, is going to be one (not the only one, but one) of the factors that influence the degree of the child's investment in it. Butler, seeking evidence of Cushla's 'natural good taste', finds specious evidence of it when Cushla's enthusiams coincide with her own, disregarding the strong possibility that she or Cushla's mother may have helped to produce it. Most of us, I guess, were educated to see texts as quite independent of performance, just as New Criticism (still the reigning orthodoxy when I was an undergraduate) encouraged us to treat texts as largely independent of the author who had created them and of the society in which they were created. Such a view is not totally inappropriate, perhaps, to texts read silently and privately by literate people, but clearly it does not fit the literary experience of preschool children.

I have deliberately emphasized this matter of how a young child's 'taste' is embedded in a context of relationship and performance; does that mean, then, that we can say nothing useful about the child's aesthetic, nothing that is not totally dependent on the individual performance and the individual mother–child relationship? No, I think we *can* begin to formulate some generalizations at this point, even though they may not be of the 'little kids like . . . ' type, which have been peddled for years.

First, on the basis of our own work, we would guess that taste or preference patterns are determined very, very early. In *Prelude* (pp. 179–82), we trace the roots of Anna's preference for particular colors and for a particular composition structure to a single preferred opening in Janet Aitchison and Jill McDonald's *The Pirates' Tale*, a book Anna received at age 11 months. But we have subsequently remembered that at least one element of that preferred set (luminous colors against a black or very dark background) is in fact traceable to a cloth that we hung over Anna's basket in infancy, months before she had any books at all! What she explicitly *preferred* seemed to be what she *knew*, what she recognized. When you think about it, that isn't really very epoch-making. Surely it is true that most adults *like* what they *know*. But why Anna preferred the black ground and bright colors of that cloth to the blue of her 'special blanket' (equally part of her early experience) remains a mystery. At all events, the point is the extreme earliness of the key aesthetic experience that seemed to underlie later response-patterns. Of course we are talking here of a purely visual experience; Anna did not, until very late in the period we studied her, express preferences for purely verbal art in the same explicit way that she did for pictures, but there seems no reason to doubt that the same conditioning of later response-patterns by very early experience was in question. Certainly, there is plenty of evidence in our own work and that of others for long-term verbal *recall*.

At this point it may be important to state that:

1. by emphasizing the power of earliest aesthetic experience to underlie and shape later preferences, we are not being as deterministic as may appear. Apart from their appetite for the tried and true, all the preschool children studied by our diarists also display a vast willingness to embrace the new and strange. Like all of us, they could *learn* to like what they did not already know.

2. patterns of preference (which we should perhaps call 'expressed preference', to distinguish it from preference that was *implied* – for example by requests for repeated re-readings of a given text) are really only a sub-set of patterns of response; that is, in saying that a given child expressed such-and-such a preference, we are simply

describing one aspect of his or her overall pattern of behaviour in relation to literary experience in general. And in saying that preference-patterns are laid down very early, we are also saying that response patterns themselves are laid down early, and can persist with remarkable stability for years thereafter; in 'The Opening Door', Molly Travers and I report instances of Anna's questioning at age nine parelleling her questioning at age three and four.

If it could be shown that for other children besides Anna the earliest-experienced texts were crucial in the formation of preferences, would it then be true to say that therefore the *quality* of those first texts would be of paramount importance if one wished to 'form taste'? Well, not exactly. There would perhaps be grounds for ensuring that first books be aesthetically 'good', but the facts in Anna's case seem to show that what she *abstracted* from those first books – the selection of configurations and colors that underlay later preferences – was abstracted at a level where adult-formulated judgements of 'quality' were largely irrelevant. In other words, *the younger the child, the less 'quality' might matter*. At that level I would guess, configuration of characters, facial expressions, bits of dialogue, might be where Anna's attention was focussed, rather than on the sorts of things we as critics might look for. Hence 'Who Does Snow White Look At?' my attempt to examine four picturebook versions of 'Snow-White' at a level where Walt Disney and Nancy Ekholm Burkert are equal, and so to reach the variables that might be significant for a naive viewer.

As with 'quality', so with 'difficulty'. Here again I can generalize with some confidence: the more inexperienced the child in the ways of books, the less adult measures of difficulty will be relevant. ('Inexperienced in the ways of books' is in fact a more accurate term than 'young', since chronological age is less in question than degree of acquaintance with fiction). At age two, virtually any book offers Anna new, interesting and challenging experiences to master; by four, she has knowledge of so many visual and verbal conventions that books which fail to offer either the gratifying (in the sense of the preferred-familiar of which we have spoken above) or the challenging and new, will be heard in silence and returned to the library without comment: they are, we might say, 'too easy' for her. Clearly what will be 'simple' or 'complex' for any particular child will vary enormously with that child's prior experience, and with how much she has been expected to stretch herself in accommodating to new texts in the past.

Here I can agree with Virginia Lowe. Where Dorothy Butler was puzzled by Cushla's fondness at 2.11 for Joyce Woods and Frank

Francis' *Grandmother Lucy and her Hats*, a long and liguistically complex story, Lowe suggests that it was precisely the length and difficulty of *Grandmother Lucy* that elicited such a significant response. Our own work multiplies instances of the principle that *the richer and more ambiguous the text, the more wide-ranging and interesting the evoked response*. Notice that this is a different thing from saying that more ambiguous texts were *explicitly preferred*, or were 'favourites', just as *lack* of verbal response at the time of first reading is not always to be equated with a book's having been 'too easy' or having had 'no impact'. In both these instances, it seems to me that the presence of powerful affect had a great deal to do with the response pattern in question. Our records indicate that certain books which seemed at the time to be 'failures' (in the sense that Anna said little in response to them and did not request re-reading) were revealed by much later, 'delayed' responses to have elicited disturbing feelings when first heard, and that these feelings had accounted for the silence in which the book had been received.

Similarly, in the case of Anna's reaction to *Grandmother Lucy and her Hats* (for it was a significant text for her too) it was not simply the length or complexity of the book that elicited a rich response, but the presence of the apparent threat to Anna's own identity (at age 3.7) contained in its first-person narrative. In this sense, affect could catalyse new cognitive concerns or breakthroughs, just as increasing cognitive mastery of a particular concept might lead to increased emotional maturity.

Nina Mikkelsen asks, 'What . . . causes four year old Lolly to ask repeatedly to hear 'Snow White' and to reach for Sendak's *Outside Over There, Where the Wild Things Are* and *In the Night Kitchen* over and over again?' On the basis of her analysis and our own (and there are many correspondences in details as well as in general) I think we can begin to guess at an answer. An obsession with a particular story, a wish to revisit it again and again, and especially a wish to re-create it (in a play or storytelling) does not spring simply from a failure to *understand* at a cognitive level, even though frequent requests for re-reading are one of the main ways preschool children do extend their cognitive grasp of new information. Rather, I would suggest that three interlocking and mutually reinforcing factors must be present, some 'originating' in the child and some in the text:

1. The child listener needs to have reached a developmental stage where he or she is able to make a *secure self/other distinction*. (See *Prelude*, pp. 254–6.) This in turn permits the child to experience itself as two separate, complementary characters in the story, and to

recreate or re-enact both of these roles in play or storytelling.

2. The story in question needs to *embody* two such complementary roles. Most probably (as in 'Snow-White' or *In the Night Kitchen*) they will be strongly contrasted, and it is likely that one will be child/victim and the other, adult/aggressor/protector (the latter can be, and often is, split up into two separate characters: Red Riding Hood/Wolf/Woodcutter; Snow-White/Queen/Dwarfs (or Prince)). The story thus offers a situation where strong identification is possible for the young child.

3. The story in question needs to have *an underlying narrative structure that is easily grasped in terms of paired opposites* (harm done/harm righted; victim stolen/victim returned, etc.)

To these we might add a fourth, that the central situation presented by the story needs to match closely with a central emotional issue for the child – but it is probably safe to say that for most preschool children, *the* central issue is going to be some variant of the relationship between themselves (as small, vulnerable people) and a parent or parent-figure (perceived as a large, powerful person who may be either loving or rejecting, or, most usually, both).

If all of these factors are present, as they were for Lolly in 'Snow-White' and the Sendak texts, then what develops is an intense relationship between child and story, in which the story functions as a sort of extension of the child's own self: Lolly tells the truth when she tells Mikkelsen, 'I like it . . . because I want it.' She *does* want it: she wants to incorporate its truth into herself, to make it part of her, and that is what she proceeds, over several re-readings and recreations, to do.

On many occasions, we would do best not to separate the affective and the cognitive in discussing the literary response of preschool children: they are better viewed as two sides of one coin. And that is only one of several re-thinkings of our current terminology that I think we should carry out on the basis of the sort of evidence we've been considering here. Implicit in what I have said about 'quality' is the suggestion that we might well think in terms of 'richness' and 'poverty' of texts, rather than 'goodness' or 'badness' (always bearing in mind the qualifications about the relativity of 'complexity' and 'difficulty' for particular children). Or, better still, *perceived ambiguity* might be the most sensible criterion for appraising responses to a given text, rather than quality, difficulty, or even richness. Peter Hunt expresses a similar idea: 'In short, rather than saying "better/worse" or "suitable/unsuitable", criticism should say "this text has certain potentials for interaction, certain possibilities for meaning" ' (p. 194).

Preference, what is explicitly liked, is we've seen, better considered as a sub-set of each individual's overall response pattern than as a thing in itself. And (though I've had no time to develop evidence for it here) I would also maintain that traditional categories like 'plot', 'character', 'theme' are often less than useful in discussing the literary experience of young children: the categories that matter, so far as I can discern, are chunks like 'two opposed characters dialoguing', or 'protagonist-acting' (on this, see chapters nine and fifteen in *Prelude*). And finally, text-as-mediated is the crucial variable more often than text in itself.

All of these suggested rethinkings make the whole subject a great deal less neat and a good deal more confusing. I would like to hope that they would also make it more real – and more exciting.

REFERENCES

Aitchison, Janet and McDonald, Jill, *The Pirates' Tale*, Harmondsworth, Penguin, 1970.

Bernstein, Basil, *Class, Codes and Control*, London, Paladin (repr.), 1973. First published 1971.

Butler, Dorothy, *Cushla and her Books*, 1954; repr. Boston, Horn Book, 1980.

Cochrane-Smith, Marilyn, *The Making of a Reader*, NJ, Ablex, 1984.

Crago, Hugh, 'The Readers in the Reader', *Signal*, 39, 1982.

——'Who does Snow White Look At?', *Signal*, 45, 1984.

Crago, Hugh, with Travers, Molly, 'The Opening Door: Reader, Text and Child Listeners as a Novel Begins', *Developments in English Teaching* (Australia) 3, 1984.

Crago, Maureen and Hugh, *Prelude to Literacy: A Preschool Child's Encounter with Picture and Story*, Carbondale, Southern Illinois University Press, 1983.

De Mause, Lloyd, 'The Evolution of Childhood' in De Mause (ed.), *The History of Childhood*, NY, Psychohistory Press, 1974.

Henry, Jules, *Pathways to Madness*, New York, Vintage Books, 1973.

Hoffman, Sandra Josephs, 'Developing a Literary Orientation: A Parent Diary', *Children's Literature Association Quarterly*, Fall, 1983.

Hunt, Peter, 'Questions of Method and Methods of Questioning: Childist Criticism in Action', *Signal*, 45, 1984.

Keeping, Charles, *Black Dolly*, London, Hodder and Stoughton, 1983.

Lass, Bonnie, Review of *Prelude to Literacy*. *The Reading Teacher*, 1984.

Lowe, Virginia, 'Carol, Cushla and Rebecca', *Signal*, 24, 1977.

Mikkelsen, Nina, 1984: 'Sendak, Snow-White and the Child as Literary Critic'. Paper given at MLA 100, Washington, DC; revised version to appear in *Language Arts*, 1985.

Noble, Grant, Review of *Prelude to Literacy*, U. of New England (Australia) *Bulletin*, 54, 1984.

Steedman, Carolyn, *The Tidy House: Little Girls Writing*, London, Virago, 1982.

Whalen-Levitt, Peggy, 'Carol, Cushla, Rebecca, Anna, Dan and Ben', *Children's Literature Association Quarterly*, Winter, 1980.

White, Dorothy, *Books Before Five*, Oxford University Press, 1954; repr. Macmillan Educational, 1984.

Wood, Joyce and Francis, Frank, *Grandmother Lucy and her Hats*, London, Collins, 1968.

Illustration is a remarkably unconsidered area of children's literature – probably because there is no adequate theory attached to it; until recently it has remained very much on the periphery of both literary and graphic-art criticism. And yet it has both a distinguished history and a remarkably vibrant present, with some of the most distinctive talents in art and illustration working in the field. William Feaver indicates its range:

Children's book illustration is more than a publishing speciality. It is part of a wider popular culture. The leading figures, the fairy godmothers, the wicked uncles, the freaks, ogres, clowns and heroes parade as not so much literary creatures as a troupe of performers. Many of their exploits, outrages, role-reversals, comic turns, magical transformations and glittering finales entered books via theatre and sideshow. They took shape in the early nineteenth century, at the same time as the circus and pantomime were fomulated in England and France, and in parallel terms. Death-defying acrobats climbed ladders to the moon, villains lurked with daggers drawn, Puss in Boots proffered advice, Punch thumped Judy, the ringmaster held sway. With a crack of the whip and a clearing of the throat to bring the audience to order and the troupe to heel, with 'Once upon a Time', the story performances began. The feats were recorded penny plain, tuppence coloured, on broadsheets, a stream of ephemera that was to widen to include stickers and trade cards, cigarette cards, and pin-ups.

Children's book illustration is suspended in this welter of imagery, occasionally bobbing into fine art waters but more often drifting in commercial shallows. A tiny proportion survives to become classic. The fittest, not necessarily the most deserving. Noddy and Superman remain, unaffected by condemnations of their characters and appearance. Tenniel's portrayal of the Mad Hatter has outlived all others. Peter Rabbit, Mickey Mouse and Babar seem imperishable. Hoffmann's 'Little Suck-a-Thumb', 'Johnny Head-in-Air' and

'Struwwelpeter' have remained in print continuously ever since they first appeared in 1845. Edward Lear's limerick personalities have persisted since 1846. Survival depends on continuing demand. Ultimately children's tastes, not adult strictures, determine which shall be immortal.

But the point about the child crying for the moon is that it cannot know exactly what it wants in advance. Both Hoffmann and Lear made their drawings for particular children – Hoffmann's three-year-old son, Lord Derby's family – an ideal situation. Inevitably, however, *Struwwelpeter* and *The Book of Nonsense* were inspired and shaped to a great extent by the imagery their creators had been brought up on. They are caricatured chapbooks. Blake's *Songs of Innocence and Experience* too are, recognizably enough, based on chapbook formulae, relief-etchings substituted for the usual artless woodcuts: neo-classicized a little, transfigured overall.

In this relay of imagery from childhood to childhood, themes snowball, conventions proliferate. But each generation has to feed off what adults envisage, publish and see fit to buy. (*When We Were Young; Two Centuries of Children's Book Illustration,* Thames and Hudson, 1977, pp. 8–9)

The interesting situation of illustration today is summed up by Jane Doonan:

Over the past twenty years, one of the most spectacular areas of change and growth in children's literature has been in the development of the picturebook. Formerly the prerogative of the very young, picturebooks generally were intended to be put aside outgrown, once reading skills had been acquired. The child graduated from picturebooks to books with only a frontispiece and the occasional plate to enliven the text visually. But now there has emerged a new type of picturebook, one which is capable of engaging the interest of children well over the age of the learner-reader. What is more, since comprehending a picture is not the same process as reading a text, these picturebooks can intrigue any non-reader, child or adult, who is prepared to think about what may be made from a sequence of pictures.

One of the reasons why these new picturebooks for the not-so-young have wide appeal is that they have themes which are challenging and are rich with underlying messages, some of which would formerly have been associated with adult experience. For example, Michael Foreman's themes have encompassed conservation, conflicts between rich and poor countries, and the search for self; Charles Keeping's work reflects an unglamorous, though warm, view of the life of the inner city; John Burningham explores the double life led by children in relation to their elders, and one of his picturebooks moves with sensibility towards illness and death; Raymond Briggs takes satirical tilts at bureaucracy, education and the consumer society. The picturebook artists are equally uncompromising in their styles, which belong to adult art expression. We can find examples of Expressionism, Symbolism, Surrealism, Romanticism, and techniques as varied as *cloissonisme* and collage. Yet these picturebooks in their totality are nevertheless authentic 'children's books'. (from 'The Object Lesson: Picture Books of Anthony Browne', *Word and Image*, vol. 22, April–June, 1986, p. 159)

A similar approach has been taken by Elaine Moss in Picture Books for Young People, 9–13 *(Thimble Press, 2nd edn, 1985), and in her articles 'Them's for the infants, Miss' (Signal, 26, May, 1978; 27, September, 1978).*

There have been some attempts to describe the picture-book in the language of literary criticism, such as Paul G. Arakelian's 'Text and Illustration: a Stylistic Analysis of Books by Sendak and Meyer' (Children's Literature Association Quarterly, *10:3, Fall, 1985, pp. 122–7). Patricia Cianciolo's* Illustrations in Children's Books *(William C. Brown, Dubuque, Iowa, 2nd edn, 1970), tends to be somewhat prescriptive.*

Perhaps the best exposition in theory so far is the article by William Moebius, who is, significantly enough, a scholar in comparative literature. The article concludes with a detailed analysis of Bernard Waber's Ira Sleeps Over, *which has been omitted here.*

William Moebius
'Introduction to Picturebook Codes', *Word & Image*,
vol. 2, no. 2 (April–June 1986), pp. 141–51, 158

It is easy to be captivated by the lovable and endearing creatures that inhabit the modern picturebook. Whether our taste for picturebooks was formed by the work of Beatrix Potter[1] or by that of her distinguished successors, we know, even if we often disavow it, this infatuation with the image of her Mrs Tiggy-Winkle (a hedgehog), Mary Chalmers' Harry (a cat) or Cyndy Szekeres' Pippa Mouse, Ernest Shepard's or William Pene du Bois' bears, Clement Hurd's rabbits, or Bernard Waber's Lyle (a crocodile) and Arthur (an anteater). Disarmed, entangled in a net of affection, we are almost ready to eat, as it were, out of the handling of the illustrator.

The story 'behind' the image, a story often supplied by the illustrator, may lead us to form our attachment to such images; is it possible that the sweetness of Raphael's Madonna is made sweeter by the story of Jesus, or the poignancy of Rembrandt's self-portraits by the story of Rembrandt's own life? The story in the child's picturebook may have no such scriptural or historical pre-existence; it unfolds for us just now, a variety-show of images and texts. We anticipate the next while looking at the one before, we laugh now that we see what we had not noticed or expected before, we let our eyes wander off a familiar character's face to a puzzling word on the page and back again.[2] Unlike the framed settings of a Biblical text of a Raphael or Rembrandt, the pictures in a picturebook cannot hang by themselves; picturebook texts do not fare well when they are extracted and anthologized in various bibles of children's literature.[3] Each works with the other in a bound sequence of images/text, inseparable in our reading experience one from the other. In a contemporary artbook, we would be encouraged to read a succession of figures by Picasso, or of portrait-landscapes by the Douanier Rousseau as a record of each artist's creative development.[4] In the picturebook, we read images and text together as the mutually complementary story of a consciousness, of a Lyle the Crocodile's ways of being, his growing and suffering in the world.

Each page affords what Barbara Bader, the pioneer historian of the genre in its American development, has called an 'opening';[5] implied, of course, is a closing, a deliberate shutting out of what came before, and a constant withholding of what is to come.[6] Unlike a published reproduction of a mural or a frieze, upon which the eye can wander, scanning a wide field for pattern, for signs of unity, the picturebook opening allows only limited exposures. Each page, if read at the speed of a slow reader, has only a minute or less to impress itself on our attention, to earn a place in our memory, as the story compels us forward, in what Bader, borrowing from Rémy Charlip, calls 'the drama of the turning of the page'.[7] Even as H. A. Rey or Bernard Waber make introductions ('This is George. He lived in Africa . . . ';

'This is the house. / The house on / East 88th Street'), what they introduce remains elusive, images lost, tracked down, and lost again and again.

We can pour emotion and affection into these pages, if we choose, under the license of our second childhood; or, as I wish to do here, we can watch more closely, looking past the lovable expression on the monkey's or anteater's face, and attend to elements of design and expression that comprise what we might call 'codes'.[8] To do this is not to deny anyone the emotional truth of the image, a sensitive issue to many adults who admire children's books as the last frontier of innocence. Dorfman and Mattelart, in introducing their icon-smashing *How to Read Donald Duck*, state rather unequivocally: 'For the adult, in protecting his dream-image of youth, hides the fear that to penetrate it would destroy his dreams and reveal the reality it conceals'.[9] I make no claims to revealing realities hidden behind a screen of text and illustration, not do I seek to destroy any dream-images. Close study of the picturebook may generate more dream-images, more for the waking imagination to contemplate, not all of it pleasant or 'delightful'.[10]

Some historical considerations first. Readers of either of two recent, lavishly illustrated histories of the picturebook or its parent, the illustrated book for children, will recall the attention given by both Susan Meyer and Barbara Bader to developments in media and printing techniques; out of each technical advancement, certain picturebook artists found a personal style. But more to our point, both historians also give rather detailed accounts of how, from Edmund Evans on, the making of the picturebook was seen more and more to require an integral relationship between picture and word, a 'total design'. Rather than being an album of pictures, or a text with some 'tipped-in' illustrations, the picturebook was, after Edmund Evans, conceived of as a whole 'product'. Text was 'script' or libretto (sometimes, as we shall see, better seen as footnote, or even as decorative flourish). Cover, endpapers, title-page design, all were carefully chosen elements of a whole, an experience wrapped, not without conscious intention, as a gift.[11] Yet, as Bader's treatment of the subject reveals, distinctions were still to be made, almost 100 years after Evans' first publishing efforts, between 'illustration-as-communication' and 'illustration-as-art'.[12] In Bader's aesthetics, it appears that an emphasis on design is linked to the communicability of messages. Tomi Ungerer, a contemporary, is 'more the designer'.[13] Of Marcia Brown's work, she writes, 'and the design itself tells much of the story'.[14] While Bader's work investigates the development of the 'design' factors, allowing the work of former Disney artists Bill Peet and Hardie Gramatky a place in the development of the picturebook alongside the work of Wanda Gág, Margaret Wise Brown and Feodor Rojankovsky, it does not elaborate a poetics of the picturebook, except in passing reference to what a certain illustration 'does' for the text.

Meyer's work largely pays tribute to what Bader would call 'illustration-as-art', the tradition of Caldecott and Pyle, of Kay Nielsen and N. C. Wyeth. But Meyer singles out Walter Crane and W. W. Denslow, for whom 'the words themselves were part of the total picture, exquisitely designed letterforms integrated within the format of the unit of a decorated book'.[15] Devoting her final chapter to W. W. Denslow, 'a very different kind of American' from N. C. Wyeth,[16] Meyer tries to give her reader the sense of a different tradition, one which would demand that the picturebook be 'an object of beauty, designed carefully from cover to cover, with attention to every detail, including endpapers, frontis and title page, typography and illustrations'.[17]

No approach to the picturebook can overlook the importance of medium and design as a part of the reader's experience. Nor can we pretend to be unaffected by pictures we encounter in picturebooks that could be cut out, framed and placed over the fireplace, such as N. C. Wyeth's or Kay Nielsen's. Yet I believe that in the picturebook what matters is something more than the artist's mastery of materials and technique, or the felicity of the book's design. These may prove attractive features to some readers, and may even foster an appreciation of 'good' books, of 'objects of beauty' in younger readers. By focusing attention on codes in the picturebook, we are no less concerned with dignifying the artist's creation. We are, as it were, making soundings in the harbour of 'design-as-communication', marking the deeper channels of a modern art-form.

Such soundings must begin simply enough with the *world* as it is depicted in the picturebook, of what has been called the 'presented world'.[18] By using the word 'depict' I mean to include verbal as well as pictorial elements. What is presented in the text usually obeys certain conventions of recognizability and continuity. We depend on a number of stable visual cues, so that we can say 'There goes Curious George again', or ask 'Isn't he there behind that bush'? Whenever we ask 'Who's that'? of a picturebook character, we expect the answer to hold for that image during the entire story, unless we are alerted to a metamorphosis. We expect George to keep looking like George, and not like any monkey or anthropomorph, unless we are led to believe that George will now simulate such another. To remain recognizable, a character need only reveal a few signal traits such as curly hair (Ira), a proboscis (Arthur) a striped tail (Frances) or a blue jacket (Peter Rabbit). These metonyms of personality, species, gender, character type constitute elements of a semic code, but may also play a role in action, as the main character undergoes an identity crisis related to the presence or absence of a primary feature.

Characters remain recognizable despite the omission of particular features, lips, eyebrows, etc., we know they would possess if they were to step out of the book. And the world they inhabit remains imaginable even though it is sometimes not depicted at all at a given opening. What we refer to as the 'blank face' of the picturebook character might as well also apply to the carefully managed *'blanchissage'* of the world in certain illustrations.

Between text and picture, or among pictures themselves, we may experience a sort of semic slippage, where word and image seem to send conflicting, perhaps contradictory messages about the 'who' or the 'what' of the story. Here is a kind of 'plate tectonics' of the picturebook, where word and image constitute separate plates sliding and scraping along against each other. Let's look, for an example, at the cover and title page of *Where the Wild Things Are*.[19] The front cover features the title of the book like a headline across the top; reading down the page into the picture, our eye falls on a seated animal-like creature who is dozing off in the foreground at one corner of the page. Behind this creature runs a stream and a fringe of palm-like trees. The expression 'Wild Things' in the headline is generic, almost too abstract. What is a wild thing? In no bestiary will we encounter quite the specimen of 'wildness' shown here, bull's head and human feet, sporting a one-piece blue fur suit, sitting like a Manet gentleman in *Le Déjeuner sur l'herbe*. Perhaps we will be reminded of a Seurat or a Douanier Rousseau. Stillness and quiet prevail. We turn to the title-spread. Here, not quite so high, is the same expression 'Wild Things'. But now, in addition to two others of the original furry breed, pictured on the left, comes a new figure dancing onto the page from the right. Is this too a wild thing? It looks like a boy in some sort of wolf suit . . . Suddenly the title has acquired the status of a banner above a rogue's gallery. The images on both the cover and title page each angle for our respect under the firm, immutable authority of the inscription *Where the Wild Things Are*. But between these images lies a buffer zone, an undefined 'wilderness'. What Roland Barthes has called the 'reference code' is probably also active here, as we attempt to cross this buffer zone. Only later may we discover that Max has earned the appellation 'wild thing' from his mother, thanks to his 'mischief of one kind / or another'; the benign creature with the horns is 'wild' only in appearance, and is easily tamed by Max, 'the wildest thing of all'. In order to make this distinction of kind, we must first have had some acquaintance with the different connotations of the word 'wild' outside the text. The cover and title-page have hardly told us everything necessary to sort out the meaning of the 'wild thing'. The unresolved question of 'What is a wild thing?' coupled with the hint that not all 'wild things' think or act alike, prompts us to read on, to turn up or over new evidence, to become the loyal subjects of the hermeneutic code.

The convention of recognizability operates also in cases in which the name of the character is made to apply to an object that bears no physical resemblance to that character. The verbal text maintains the continuity of character's name and feeling, keeps the inner secret; the pictorial version presents two or more manifestations. Sylvester, in *Sylvester and the Magic Pebble*, must be distinguished from the large rock he becomes, even during the period in which he is indistinguishable from that rock.

In playing with the convention of recognizability, some picturebooks enable the reader to build a network of associations between two vastly different referents, as say between Sylvester and the rock, or between Max the devouring monster who says to his mother 'I'll eat you up' and the wild things that cry out at Max's departure, 'We'll eat you up, we love you so.' These associations arise in the active imagination only, and are not usually outright in the text. If we declare that 'Sylvester is now a rock',[20] we may mean superficially that on the page at this moment Sylvester, a donkey, has been turned into a rock. But the rock is originally Sylvester's *idea* of a defence against a lion. And as the seasons change around him, the rock reinforces *our idea* of the durable, patient, somewhat stolid personality of the donkey. And as it stands by itself in the field, the rock also conveys a sense of its own isolation, and gives tangible form to the idea of loneliness. When angry Max tells his mother 'I'll eat you up', we cannot help but take him at his word. After all, he is wearing a wolf-suit and a picture of a toothy monster bears his scrawled signature; even the Scottish terrier beats a retreat before this little devil. Maybe he would take a bite out if his mother. Only later, when at his parting from them, the beasts make 'We'll eat you up' the terms of an endearment, do we catch up with the metaphorical possibility of the phrase or the action it describes.

Nevertheless, the plain, the literal sense is the first we connect with in most picturebooks. As such, we usually attribute a plain, literal point of view to the main characters, who as problem-solvers seek plain, practical solutions to their problems, a supply of food, for example.[21] Yet the best picturebooks can and do portray the intangible and invisible, ideas and concepts such as love, responsibility, a truth beyond the individual, ideas that escape easy definition in pictures or words. With her lens as historian, Bader sees 'a new non-imitative way of working generally, a way of expressing intangibles, communicating emotion, sensation – one which invited the viewer, too, to see things in a new way'.[22] After Max has enjoyed his fling with the wild things, and exercised his enormous power over them, he falls into a reverie of a world that neither he nor the reader can see, a world 'where someone loved him best of all'. Max's mother never does appear in *Where the Wild Things Are*, except as represented by her tokens, shown in the final illustration, a three-layer cake, a glass of milk, a bowl of something steaming. On the final page, without a picture, the text tells us 'And it was still hot.' Here the 'it' emerges as unspeakable and unseeable motherlove. Likewise, 'rock' temporarily replaces Sylvester. Literally petrified, made to suffer through the seasons without companionship, movement, or speech, Sylvester, once restored to donkey shape, retains certain qualities of rockhood not readily apparent on the face of a jubilant donkey. He can no longer be quite as easily shaken or frightened, nor ever so quick to use magical formulas to protect himself.

That so many picturebook characters come, in the end, to recognize or to experience the value of the intangible over the tangible, of what is 'loved best of all' over what is closest at hand, the unseen over the seen, deserves an essay of its own. Here I would offer just two observations in passing. The first is that such a pattern of story (and pattern of reader response, from dependence on the plain and literal to the development of a sense of independence in the face of individually discovered yet intangible meanings) accords with a pattern of cognitive development described by Piaget in terms of the passage from preoperational and concrete operational thought to formal operations, from the various 'realisms' to the recognition of symbol.[23] Second, I would point out that the frequent depiction in picturebooks of gates, doors, windows and stairs, of roads and waterways, and the changing representation of light, artificial and natural, to accord with different degrees of character understanding, are not accidental or fortuitous phenomena, but downright basic to the symbolic force of the story. A character who looks out the window or stands in the door, as Max does in *Where the Wild Things Are*, is implicated in the unspoken meanings of thresholds. Whether stairs, steps or extended ramp, the incline may provide a measure of the character's stature or of progress towards a depth or height of understanding or confusion. There is nothing doctrinaire about such pronouncements. Nothing should tie interpretation of stairways or doorways and such in picturebooks to a single intention or effect. Such pieces of the symbolic code work differently in different stories, and will lend themselves to different interpretations. But they should not be overlooked.

'The presented word' may also bear the marks of 'presented worlds' in other texts. For example, Sendak plays with the familiar image of 'The Thinker',[24] or, more subtly, alludes to Rodin's Adam in the final illustration of *Where the Wild Things Are*, which shows Max, hand on forehead, striding into his room, still wearing his wolf-suit, but clearly emerging as a young man. The phenomenon of intertextuality is more common in the picturebook than might appear. Series books such as Waber's about Lyle, Rey's about Curious George, or Duvoisin's about Petunia, would seem to depend on it; yet they do each stand alone. In Waber, at a point somewhere after the middle, we sometimes encounter a plethora of signs borrowed from other places, rubber stamps (in *Ira Sleeps Over*) or political signs (in *Lyle Finds his Mother*). And it is not unlikely for a character to be found reading a book, the title of which is readable within the illustration.[25] We might treat such examples of intertextuality as tests of the reader's knowledge of the world of texts.

Each of the foregoing aspects of 'the presented world' requires our prior knowledge of the world outside the text for adequate recognition. The picturebook poses the challenge 'How much of the world to you know'? at the outset, and asks us, like Chukovsky's child before the nonsense-verse, to prove our knowledge of reality by affirming the resemblance of what we see on the page to some figure already stored in consciousness.

But the picturebook also asks us 'How much do you see'? To help us in this respect, it is likely to contain figures who represent points of view other than those of the main character. It may do this by editorializing in the text, or by depicting tacit witnesses on the fringes or in the foreground or background of the picture. Sometimes, the text will somewhat heavy-handedly ask the reader to look. In Rey's *Curious George*, a butterfly and a cat offer the disengaged viewpoint, not passing judgment as the narrator, in league with the 'man in the yellow hat', but smiling out at the reader, provoking our sympathy for George, for all living things, regardless of their moral aptitudes. Clement Hurd moves mice about the bedroom in *Goodnight Moon*.

Even as early as Wilhelm Busch, we see animals in complicity with readers as the geese, backs to reader, gobble up the milled remains of Max and Moritz. From the grand final reception in Tibor Gergely's classic *Scuffy the Tugboat*, to that in Arnold Lobel's 'A Swim' or 'The Dream', the eye of the beholder in the text affords a vantage point for the wandering eye of the reader.[26]

As specific onlookers in the text tease us with their inside view, with what they see, we may ask ourselves, again, what indeed do we see? As Gombrich once pointed out, 'we are all inclined to judge pictures by what we *know* rather than by what we *see*'.[27] It is here that we may sketch out for further study the operation of certain graphic codes. These serve not so much to indicate the artist's command of the medium, or to demonstrate the artist's grasp of an ineffable beauty, as to enhance the reader's feeling comprehension of events and emotions. Graphic codes do not depend on the relation of objects to each other in a world outside the text; these we would call 'iconographic'.[28] The images of a child looking out of a window or of a boat winding its way down a watercourse belong to such inconographic codes. To be able to read a graphic code we must consider the disposition of objects on the page, the handling of line and colour, we must examine the 'presentational process'.[29] It would be misleading and destructive of the possibility of an 'open text' to say that within the graphic codes this particular gesture means one thing or another, regardless of the specific text. We must speak of 'dominances' and 'probabilities', to borrow from the language of de Beaugrande.[30] My intention in the following discussion is to toss out some leads, and to let each reader conduct research according to the demands of specific texts.

THE CODES OF POSITION, SIZE AND DIMINISHING RETURNS

The position of the subject on the page, what some might call the 'ham' factor, constitutes a code. It often matters whether the main character is depicted high or low on the page, in the centre or on the fringe, on the lefthand side or the right. Height on the page may be an indication of an ecstatic condition (as in *Curious George*) or dream-vision (as in Daugherty's *Andy and the Lion*) or a mark of social status or power, or of a positive self-image. Being low on the page is often by contrast a signal of low spirits, 'the pits', or of unfavourable social status. These figures may be strengthened or weakened depending on whether the character is centred or in the margin, large ('close-up') or small ('distanced') (we here introduce the code of size), or presented in one or in more than one scene on the same page (the code of 'diminishing returns'). The more frequently the same character is depicted on the same page, the less likely that character is to be in control of a situation, even if in the centre. Whenever Curious George is shown in a succession of vignettes on the same page or facing pages, he is probably having fun and about to lose his freedom. In such a succession of vignettes, those at the top of the page may signal a more competent character than those at the bottom. A character that is on the margin, 'distanced' or reduced in size on the page, and near the bottom will generally be understood to possess fewer advantages than the one that is large and centred. Large size alone is not a sufficient criterion for the reading of advantage; it may be a figure of an overblown ego.

As with the stage, it matters whether the actors are shown on the left or the right. A character shown on the left page is *likely* to be in a more secure, albeit potentially confined space than one shown on the right, who is likely to be moving into a situation of risk or adventure. The left-hand page will complete a thought, let us know that we can go on, that the thinking of the previous page is complete. In the *Story about Ping*, the duck family moves across the page to the right as they leave the safety of the boat in the morning, and boards the boat from right to left in the evening. When Ping finally returns from his wanderings, he moves up the plank to the right, not the left, as the boat has now become an adventure unto itself, a wise-eyed boat worth inhabiting, and no longer quite to be taken for granted.

CODES OF PERSPECTIVE

Supplementing the codes of position, size and diminishing returns are those of perspective, in which we follow the presence or absence of horizon or horizontals, vanishing points, and contrasts between façades and depths. Where it has been present earlier, the sudden absence of a horizon, of a clear demarcation between 'above' and 'below' is likely to spell danger or trouble, as in Donald Carrick's illustration of Berniece Freschet's *Bear Mouse*, in which the stratified lines of the mouse's underground burrows and the snowline give way to an utterly white background as a hawk attacks the mouse. See also *The Story About Ping*: when the horizon disappears, Ping is about to get into trouble, to lose perspective. The play of the horizon can be complicated if there is a vanishing point, or if above the horizon there is sheer open space. Either complication may place the reader along with the character in a state of suspense. What lies 'beyond'? When

Ping falls asleep in the bulrushes after losing track of his boat-home, or when he stands in shallow water, his boat-home in sight and a spanking in the offing, sheer open space covers the horizon.

A character located within a two-dimensional façade is likely to be less 'open-minded', less able to give imaginative scope to desire than one pictured within a three-dimensional 'depth'. In *Where the Wild Things Are*, the frustrated feelings of Max begin to find an outlet with the appearance of a window at the back; there is even a crescent moon, for more depth.

THE CODES OF THE FRAME AND OF THE RIGHT AND ROUND

The code of the frame enables the reader to identify with a world inside and outside the story. Framed, the illustration provides a limited glimpse 'into' a world. Unframed, the illustration constitutes a total experience, the view from 'within'. *Where the Wild Things Are* demonstrates this point with considerable force, as Max's universe expands from the small, framed picture of himself in a room to the unframed doublespread of himself in the place where the wild things live. As the frame usually marks a limit beyond which text cannot go, or from which image cannot escape, we may associate a sense of violation or of the forbidden or of the miraculous with the breaking of the frame, as when the ocean-side tree spreads over the text as Max 'sailed off through night and day', or with the frame that blocks or screens out a part of the subject, as it does Petunia's head in her moment of extreme hubris, or at moments in which text suddenly intrudes itself into the picture, as in *Andy and the Lion*, when after 23 successive openings with text on the lefthand page and picture on the right, the text 'CAME' under the left side of a doublepage spread and 'OUT' under the righthand *underline* Andy's successful removal of the thorn.

I find it useful to relate the code of the frame to the code of round vs. rectilinear shapes. A character framed in a series of circular enclosures is more likely to be secure and content than one framed in a series of utterly rectangular objects. Often, an emphasis on rectangular shapes is coupled with a problem, or with an encounter with the disadvantages of discipline or civilized life. In the *Story About Ping*, Ping is held captive in an inverted basket, which appears on the page in broad bands at right-angles to one another.

One other aspect of the frame must be mentioned. The picturebook provides a temporal as well as a spatial frame. It has an opening and a closing page, a cover with two sides. What the front and back pages say is often mutually complementary, symmetrical even, as in *Curious George*, who begins and ends his story in a tree. And given the presence of the outer frame or covering, the 'heart' or 'core' of the book lies somewhere in its middle, in the wild things' wordless dance, or in the proliferation of verbal signs (Waber).

THE CODES OF LINE AND CAPILLARITY

The intensity of a character's experience may be represented by the thickness of thinness of lines, by their smoothness or jaggedness, by their sheer number or profusion or by their spareness, and by whether they run parallel to each other or at sharp angles. Thin, spare lines may suggest mobility and speed, thick, blurred or puffy lines, paralysis or a comfortable stasis. Jagged lines and those that run at sharp or odd angles to each other usually accompany troubled emotions or an endangered life, as when Ping fights for freedom from his captor in the water, or Bear Mouse eludes the diving hawk. Smooth and parallel lines, such as those of the junk Ping calls home, or of Bear Mouse's burrow suggest a settled, orderly world. What I call the code of capillarity refers to the presence or absence of capillary-like squiggles or bundles; an abundance of such marks often signals vitality or even a surfeit of energy, rendering the scene crowded, nervous, busy, as if each line were a living organism, part of a giant audience. Swabs of plain colour provide relief from such jungles of line.[31] It is interesting to watch the gradual progress towards a simple, painted backdrop in *Where the Wild Things Are*. Max begins his story in a room, the back wall of which is represented by myriad fine cross-hatchings. Draped over a line of tied handkerchiefs, a segmented or interrupted line, is a bedspread with a pattern of pink flowers. The cross-hatchings of the wall-covering, the knotted handkerchiefs, the pattern on the bedspread contribute to a high degree of capillarity, of nervous energy, as, of course, does the anger on Max's face. Once Max is shut up in his room three pages later, the cross-hatchings seem less complicated, and the top of the pink bedspread and the blue sky visible through the window show few traces of such capillarity. At the point a few pages on where Max has begun his moondance, the cross-hatched backdrop has disappeared, to be replaced by a smooth, yet white, speckled sky. Max has moved into a calm state from an anxious one, into a position of command from one of frustration.

THE CODE OF COLOUR

While we may attribute colour-coding to factors outside the text, we should not overlook what colour can say inside the text. Apart from the traditional associations of certain colours with certain moods or feelings, and apart from the association of bright colours with exhilaration and discovery, and of dark colours with disappointment and confusion,[32] we need to be sensitive to colour as a linkage among different objects. In the *Story About Ping*, for example, the Yangtze and the uniforms of the Chinese fishermen are blue, the duck and the sunlight, yellow. Plunging into the depths of blue leads Ping into the clutches of the men in blue. Disobedience is associated with a blue captivity, freedom with yellow and white.

The graphic codes as we have outlined them above are interactive, simultaneous, though not always congruous with the codes of the verbal text, or of the presented world. As we have noted elswhere,[33] at a glorious moment in *Curious George* in which George is depicted as central on the page, of medium size, associated with a round shape (the balloon) and contained within one, all indications of positive feelings fraught with uncertainty (it is the righthand page), the text tells us that George was 'afraid' and indeed George does hover high above the ground in that 'presented world'. But George is smiling broadly, confirming the message of the graphic code, unperturbed by the narrator's alarmism . . .

[*Moebius then examines in detail Bernard Waber's* Ira Sleeps Over]

Such a reading as this is never complete. Our hope is always that we will never read the same book twice in quite the same way. And that any reader will be willing to read picturebooks like *Ira Sleeps Over* over and over again. Soft and endearing as many picturebook characters may be, they exist in tougher environments than we might imagine, blank spaces of fear. It is up to us to discover their ways to meaning and form, to being-in-the-world. Let us take them with us, not merely as the small fry charitable adults chuckle at, but as figures of our own dynamic confusion and search for order.

NOTES

1   Do I speak only for myself? I wonder how many who enjoy picturebooks today discovered them not in the arcadia of childhood, but in the straits of early parenthood. The formation of our taste then would depend on a joint enterprise between parent and child, and not on our own prefer-

ences alone. We could speak of 'households of taste'. For mine, then, the works of Beatrix Potter marked the beginning.

2   For some of the philosophical implications of such a process, Irving Massey's 'Words and Images: Harmony and Dissonance', *Georgia Review*, 34 (1980), pp. 375–95, provides a fine introduction. 'Thinking consists of a constant alternation between image-making and word-making' (p. 388).

3   In an interview, 'The Artist as Author: the Strength of the Double Vision', in Margaret Meek, Aidan Warlow and Griselda Barton (eds), *The Cool Web: The Patterns of Children's Reading* (New York: Atheneum, 1978), Maurice Sendak has remarked that 'in the United States we work to bring pictures and words together to achieve a wholeness in the book, which I was very surprised to find is not at all important in many European countries' (p. 252). Whether or not this view is representative, it is not reflected in the editorial practice of American anthologizers of children's books. In Judith Saltman (ed.), *Riverside Anthology of Children's Literature*, 6th edn (Boston: Houghton Mifflin, 1985), Steig's *Sylvester and the Magic Pebble* is reprinted with but a single illustration. In Francelia Butler (ed.), *Sharing Literature with Children: A Thematic Anthology* (New York: David McKay, 1977) Potter's 'The Tale of Two Bad Mice' appears as text alone.

4   See William Rubin (ed.), *Pablo Picasso: A Retrospective* (New York: Museum of Modern Art, 1980) and Yann le Pichon, *The World of Henri Rousseau*, tr. by Joachim Neugroschel (New York: Viking, 1982). In the Picasso volume, the editor notes (p. 13) that 'the photographs accompanying the chronology are intended to document events in Picasso's life'. In the Rousseau, le Pichon offers the following preliminary explanation (p. 19): 'Although slightly arbitrary, the thematic classification of Rousseau's works allows a better analysis of his biographical and iconographical inspiration. The illustrations are not always – indeed, may be anything but – the direct sources of his paintings. They are sometimes offered as indirect influences, as documents on Rousseau's ambience, sometimes ulterior, but as close as possible to the painter, his life, his mentality, the people surrounding him.'

5   Barbara Bader, *American Picturebooks; From Noah's Ark to the Beast Within* (New York: Macmillan, 1976), pp. 155, 316.

6   Cf. Massey, 'Words and Images', p. 376: 'Each act of vision is detached from other acts of vision; we do not see continuously. We see one thing, and then another. There is a closure in each experience of sight.' See also Roland Barthes, *S/Z*, tr. by Richard Miller (New York: Hill & Wang, 1974), p. 11: 'To read is to find meanings, and to find meanings is to name them; but these named meanings are swept toward other names; names call to each other, reassemble, and their grouping calls for further naming: I name, I unname, I rename: so the text passes: it is a nomination in the course of becoming, a tireless approximation, a metonymic labor.'

7   Bader, *American Picturebooks*, p. 359.

8   I wish to adopt Barthes' notion of the code as both a perspective of quotations and a force or voice, as he proposes in *S/Z*, pp. 20–1. In the

ensuing discussion of 'presented world', I cheerfully and gratefully lift from the reading of *S/Z* notions that I find valuable in the reading of the picturebook.

9 Ariel Dorfman and Armand Mattelart, *How to Read Donald Duck*, tr. by David Kunzle (New York: International General, 1975), p. 31. This brilliantly argued book deserves a wider circulation.

10 In Lucy Robin, 'The Astonished Witness Disclosed: An Interview with Arnold Lobel', *Children's Literature in Education*, 15, 4 (1984), pp. 191–7, Lobel declares (p. 194), 'And yet children's books, the best of them, are not delightful. My favourites, anyway, strike deep. The artists that do the best ones are able to make them delightful on one level, but that's just the whipped cream on top. Underneath there is something much more.'

11 For a more detailed summary, see Susan E. Meyer, *A Treasury of the Great Children's Book Illustrators* (New York: Abrams, 1983), pp. 37–8.

12 Bader, *American Picturebooks*, p. 289.

13 ibid., p. 547.

14 ibid., p. 322.

15 Meyer, *Treasury*, p. 43.

16 ibid., p. 249.

17 ibid., p. 256.

18 I follow Horst Ruthrof's distinction between 'presented world' and 'presentational process' as argued in *The Reader's Construction of Narrative* (London: Routledge & Kegan Paul, 1981).

19 For related insights into the workings of *Where the Wild Things Are* and other picturebooks, see Sonia Landes, 'Picturebooks as Literature', *Children's Literature Association Quarterly*, 10, 2 (1985), pp. 51–4. The issue reached me only after this essay had been completed. I am delighted to see confirmation, some of it uncanny, of ideas put forth here.

20 Whether or not young children can grasp the metaphorical significance of such a substitution is a matter of debate. See, for example, Ellen Winner, Anne K. Rosenteil and Howard Gardner, 'The Development of Metaphoric Understanding', *Developmental Psychology*, 12, 4 (1976), pp. 289–97; and Janice H. Dressel, 'Abstraction in Illustration: Is It Appropriate for Children?', *Children's Literature in Education*, 15, 2 (1984), pp. 103–12.

21 It is not my intention to read every picturebook narrative as a study in problem-solving. But in the many instances in which a picturebook character or community does have a problem, I find that the usual first remedy involves the manipulation of objects, to make the world a better place for the ego, etc. The book itself usually points to remedies beyond the concrete and factual.

22 Bader, *American Picturebooks*, p. 225; see also pp. 397–9.

23 See n. 18 above, and Charles Sarland's excellent 'Piaget, Blyton, and Story: Children's Play and the Reading Process', *Children's Literature in Education*, 16, 2 (1985), pp. 102–9.

24 Note the cover and the 17th opening of *Where the Wild Things Are*. Sendak's eclecticism is well known.

25 Observed by Barbara Kiefer in 'The Responses of Children in a Combination First/Second Grade to Picture Books in a Variety of Artistic Styles', *Journal of Research and Development in Education*, 16, 3

(1983), pp. 14–20, one young reader (p. 17) 'pointed out a tiny book lying on the floor in one double-page spread of Schulevitz's *Oh What a Noise* (1971). The book is less than one inch wide, yet Peter noticed that the title written on its spine was the same as the title of the book.'

26 Philippe Hamon, 'Pour un statut sémiologique du personnage', *Littérature*, 6 (1972), pp. 86–110, distinguishes for us (p. 95) 'une catégorie de *personnages-embrayeurs*', of characters who 'link us up' with what is happening in the text: 'Ils sont les marques de la présence en text de l'auteur, du lecteur, ou de leurs délégués . . .' See also Bader, *American Picturebooks*, p. 456.

27 E. H. Gombrich, *The Story of Art* (Oxford: Phaidon, 1966), p. 387.

28 To read inconographical codes, we need to know much more, often, than the text can tell us about symbolic usages. We acquire our knowledge of these figures from sources outside the text, from economic and political data, as Dorfman and Mattelart do in their analysis of the inconography of Donald Duck, from the symbolism of ritual or dream, from mythical and literary sources, etc.

29 Elsewhere (Olga Richard, 'The Visual Language of the Picturebook', *Wilson Library Bulletin* 44, December, 1969, pp. 434–47) we are taught, after Gyorgy Kepes, to attend to 'the Elements of Art', namely 'color, shape, line, texture and the arrangement of these within a unified picture plane' (p. 436). But as in the 'Picturebooks: Stories for the Eye' chapter (pp. 167–8) of Saltman's *Riverside Anthology*, the purpose of such attention is, by providing a descriptive vocabulary, to help us appreciate the individual styles of different illustrators. The most elaborate of such approaches that I have seen is that of Ottilie Dinges, who offers an extensive 'grid' ('*Raster*') for the linguistic and graphic analysis of picturebooks in 'Fragen über Fragen um das Bilderbuch – und eine Spielregel dazu/oder/Hermeneutische Fragestellungen zu einer umfassenden Ästhetik and Didaktik des Bilderbuches', in Helmut Fischer and Reinhard Stach (eds), *Aspekte der Vermittlung von Jugend-literatur* (Essen: Arbeitskreis Das gute Jugendbuch e.V., 1980), pp. 63–9.

30 See Robert de Beaugrande and Wolfgang Dressler, *Introduction to Text Linguistics* (London: Longman, 1981), pp. xivff. '*Probabilistic* models are more adequate and realistic than *deterministic* ones . . . *Dominances* can offer more realistic classifications than can *strict categories*.'

31 Compare Meyer, *Treasury*, p. 30, for whom cross-hatching, a technical advance on the path towards a 'more truly realistic' method, is seen to render 'a semblance of modeling', with Landes, 'Picturebooks', p. 53, who can say of a section of *Where the Wild Things Are*, 'No borders, no limitations, and, within the pictures, the cross-hatching of reality has disappeared and all the straight lines have been transformed into nature's curves.'

32 In terms of the contrast of the colourful and the colourless, the picturebook has evolved an entire genre, one in which an opening of colour alternates with an opening without colour. For prime examples, see Rémy Charlip, *Fortunately, Unfortunately* (New York: Parent's Magazine, 1964); and Roger Duvoisin, *A for an Ark* (New York: Lothrop, 1952).

33 '*L'Enfant terrible Comes of Age*', in Norman F. Kantor and Nathalia

King (eds.), *Notebooks in Cultural Analysis* (Durham, NC: Duke University Press, 1985), pp. 32-50.

PRIMARY SOURCES

Betty Boegehold/illustrations by Cyndy Szekeres, *Here's Pippa Again*, New York, Dell, 1975.

Margaret Wise Brown/illustrations by Clement Hurd, *Good Night Moon*, New York, Harper & Row, 1947.

Mary Chalmers, *Throw a Kiss, Harry*, New York, Harper & Row, 1958.

Gertrude Crampton/illustrations by Tibor Gergely, *Scuffy The Tugboat*, New York, Golden Press, 1946, 1955.

James Daugherty, *Andy and the Lion*, New York, Viking, 1938.

Roger Duvoisin, *Petunia*, New York, Knopf, 1950.

Marjorie Flack/illustrations by Kurt Wiese, *The Story About Ping*, New York, Viking, 1933.

Berniece Freschet/illustrations by Donald Carrick, *Bear Mouse*, New York, Scribner's, 1973.

Russell Hoban/illustrations by Garth Williams, *Bedtime for Frances*, New York, Harper & Row, 1960.

Arnold Lobel, 'A Swim', in *Frog and Toad Are Friends*, New York, Harper & Row, 1970, pp. 40-52.

Arnold Lobel, 'The Dream', in *Frog and Toad Together*, New York: Harper & Row, 1971-2, pp. 42-64.

A.A. Milne/illustrations by Ernest H. Shepard, *Winnie-the-Pooh*, New York, E.P. Dutton, 1926.

William Pene du Bois, *Bear Circus*, New York, Viking, 1971.

Beatrix Potter, *Mrs Tiggy-Winkle*, London, Frederick Warne, 1905.

H. A. Rey, *Curious George*, Boston, Houghton Mifflin, 1941.

Maurice Sendak, *Where the Wild Things Are*, New York, Harper & Row, 1963.

William Steig, *Sylvester and the Magic Pebble*, New York, Windmill/Simon & Schuster, 1969.

Bernard Waber, *The House on East 88th Street*, Boston, Houghton Mifflin, 1962.

Bernard Waber, *Lyle and the Birthday Party*, Boston, Houghton Mifflin, 1966.

Bernard Waber, *An Anteater Named Arthur*, Boston, Houghton Mifflin, 1967.

Bernard Waber, *Ira Sleeps Over*, Boston, Houghton Mifflin, 1972.

Bernard Waber, *Lyle Finds His Mother*, Boston, Houghton Mifflin, 1974.

4

Directions in children's literature criticism

I have suggested that one of the great strengths of children's literature criticism is that it is necessarily eclectic, and, by being so, often finds itself on the leading edge of critical developments – as we have seen from the work of Benton and Crago. In this section, I would like to take two significant articles which point forward to the ways in which children's literature criticism may develop.

The first is an exposition of feminist theory which points out, through the examination of two important children's books, the similarities between children's literature and women's literature. It is a radical and inspired piece which, to borrow Lissa Paul's own words, breathes life 'into what was becoming the moribund discipline of literary criticism'.

Lissa Paul
'Enigma Variations: What Feminist Theory Knows About Children's Literature', *Signal*, 54 (September 1987), pp. 186–201

One thing is certain. The fault lies with *Foreign Affairs* by Alison Lurie. And with a friend who gave me the book. I read it immediately, and in my habitually academic way said that I really liked it because it was a book about masquerade. Then, casting about for a suitable example to support my thesis, I went on: 'especially the raincoat'. 'Yes,' said Nick, 'his [Chuck, the hero's] green plastic-bag packaged raincoat – the one that looks like a dead fish.' That stopped me. I had meant her [Vinnie, the heroine's] raincoat, not his – her new silvery-blue, shimmering silk, extravagantly expensive designer raincoat that makes her feel taller and look like a Druid.

If you haven't read *Foreign Affairs*, don't worry – though it is a terrific book and, as Vinnie is a specialist in children's literature, probably insider's reading for people who read *Signal*. This article is not about *Foreign Affairs* or raincoats or masquerades. At least not exactly. It is about what I saw in that raincoat exchange of words: how very different Nick's reading was from mine – how the words 'masquerade' and 'raincoat' precipitated quite separate constellations of meaning for each of us.[1]

For one brightly lit moment I caught a glimpse of the doubleness in words and things: raincoats keeping the rain out, but also disguising spies, movie stars, flashers, and other people with something to hide. I saw raincoats concealing and revealing identity and meaning – very like words. And in that initial net of double meanings, I caught something else: something with powerful implications about the content and language of children's literature and children's literature criticism; something to do with 'inside' stories; something of our own fractured sense of the distinctions between self and other; something in tune with our particular moment in Western culture – something articulated in feminist theory.

Bad luck, I thought. It's all very well to have an epiphany, but telling someone else about it is another matter entirely. Though I had understood the need for people – male and female, adult and child – to speak each other's languages and wear each other's clothes, I knew that it would take a long time even to begin to describe, word by word, what had been visible in that moment of illumination. And critics, as Frank Kermode observes in *The Genesis of Secrecy*, prefer enigmas to muddles.

Maybe that is why the idea of masquerade caught me so strongly. I write fiction masquerading as criticism: a mode of discourse that hides and reveals my personal pleasure in a text inside a raincoat of scholarly language. Hence, my 'Enigma Variations'. Both the title and the structure are borrowed (or stolen) from Edward Elgar. He composed thirteen variations, fourteen if you count his own self-portrait. To communicate my epiphany as an enigma rather than a muddle, I have written only two variations, 'The Plot' (pp. 158–64) and 'Dumb Bunnies' ('A Revisionist Re-reading of *Watership Down*', *Signal*, 56, May 1988, pp. 113–22.) – though three variations might be closer to the truth, if you count my self-portrait that runs like Elgar's 'dark saying' through the whole. And the theme I've composed is the common ground between women's literature and children's literature: a theme that lies in a shared content (the enclosed, interior scenes of the action); and in a shared language (of otherness).

There is good reason for appropriating feminist theory to children's literature. Both women's literature and children's literature are devalued and regarded as marginal or peripheral by the literary and educational communities. Feminist critics are beginning to change that. By tracing the history of women's writing, especially in the nineteenth century, feminist critics are giving definition and value to women in literature and literature by women. As it happens, the forms of physical, economic and linguistic entrapment that feminist critics have been revealing in women's literature match the images of entrapment in children's literature.

The similarity is not surprising. After all, the nineteenth century, give or take a few decades either side, corresponds to 'The Golden Age of Children's Literature', to the age of Lewis Carroll, and Kenneth Grahame, and George MacDonald, and to the age when traditional folktales and fairy tales were gathered up into the children's literature canon.

INSIDE STORIES

Children, like women, are lumped together as helpless and dependent; creatures to be kept away from the scene of the action, and who otherwise ought not to be seen or heard. But women make up more than half of the population of the world – and all of us once were children. It is almost inconceivable that women and children have been invisible and voiceless for so long.

There. Now I've named the twin problems feminist critics have: how do you know something is invisible if you can't see it? And how do you know something is inaudible if you can't hear it?

Adrienne Rich, American poet and critic, says in 'When We Dead Awaken: Writing as Re-vision', that feminist critics are engaged in an act of re-vision, that they are waking up, seeing, as if for the first time, all the repressed anger and pain that they have been keeping silent about for so long. Along with other feminist critics Rich is attempting to renegotiate the status quo: to 'review', reimagine, rethink, rewrite, revise and reinterpret' the physical, economic and linguistic entrapment experienced as normal by women and children for roughly, as feminist critic Sandra Gilbert says, 'a thousand years of Western culture'.[2] A frightening prospect, but not a hopeless one. Children's literature, in fact, provides some helpful hints on transcending traps.

Women in literature are disproportionately shown as physically trapped in rooms, attics, in their father's houses, or in their husband's. In those enclosed spaces women go mad or silent, or they die. *Jane Eyre* is the prototypical story of this 'madwoman in the attic'. But the protagonists in children's literature transcend, and, for the most part, win, even when the endings of stories are not conventionally happy. Though they have to deal with the same (often overlapping) forms of physical, economic and linguistic entrapment that women do, they are not yet closed in by the rules of adulthood. To illustrate I'm going to draw a few miniatures, naming the hidden stories feminist criticism has been revealing about the contents of traps and the preferred (deceitful) means of escape, but I'll draw the examples from traditional folk and fairy tales and from children's literature. Forgive the thumbnail-sketchiness of the examples, they are not intended as *trompe-l'œil* portraits.

Unlike men, women and children can't stray very far from the bounds of home and gardens (at least, not unaccompanied) for technicolor epic adventures on the scale of, say, *The Odyssey*. So physical entrapment (often connected with economic dependence) is just a fact of life. In 'Rumpelstiltskin' or 'The Three Spinners', for instance, the protagonists are locked in rooms with mountains of spinning to do. To seek their fortunes in the outside world is simply not an option. Though they cry (a perfectly normal response) about their fates at first, they manage to free themselves from both their rooms and their spinning, with a little help from their friends, and with a little trickery and subversion.

Child protagonists from authored texts tend to be equally inventive when it comes to subverting traps and punishment: Max transforms his room (the scene of his punishment) into the land of the wild things (the scene of his power); Colin and Mary transform the dead garden of Misselthwaite Manor into a blooming, secret one; and Anne (of Green Gables) turns each of the scenes of her early childhood abuse into places of beauty and pleasure. These child protagonists create options that are simply unthinkable to grown-ups whose conditioned responses have already closed in on them. That is one of the reasons why these stories are of value to us as adults. The reader, or listener, looks at life from a very cramped vantage – rooms without views all right, but not without adventures, and not without options. Even a boy who is only as thickasathumb can live an exciting life, and outwit the world from inside a horse's ear, a mouse hole, a snail shell, a cow's belly and a wolf's belly.

Because women and children generally have to stay at home without the affairs of state to worry about, their stories tend to focus on the contents of their traps, the minute and mundane features of everyday life around which their lives revolve: household effects, food, clothes, sewing, interior decorating, and nuances of social relationships. These homely details have been redeemed by feminist critics (see Annette Kolodny, 'A Map for Rereading', in *New Feminist Criticism*) as having interest; as being as worthy for critical attention as descriptions of battles or card games or beer drinking.

Harriet (the spy) understands very well that adventure stores are as available inside as they are outside. Although she goes out to follow her spy route, she peeks into the enclosed private spaces of lives of the people on it. She knows how to read the signs. The barrenness of the Robinsons' lives is revealed in their silence and in their monstrous sculpture of a nameless baby. And the tenderness of Harrison Withers is revealed when he addresses each of his twenty-six cats, by name.

The stories Harriet tells are secret stores, founded on voyeurism and gossip. Her adventures are more suited to *Family Circle* than James Bond; more like sociological studies of the family in contemporary urban life than adventures involving the secrets of state. They are private stories, not public, and so subject to the third kind of repression I've named as characteristic of women's stories – linguistic repression.

Harriet's secret writing is typical of the kinds of writing women and children do: small-scale stories, often in the forms of journals, diaries, letters, little poems, or romance novels. These forms are often simply regarded as insignificant, minor, in the face of the epic, grand-scale writings of Dostoyevsky or Dickens or Hemingway, stories that engage the full sweep of human endeavour – war, politics, science, philosophy, areas in which women and children have little experience. Even female writers who have secure places in the canon (Jane Austen, the Brontës, Emily Dickinson, George Eliot, and Virginia Woolf) spent most of their lives feeling not quite a part of the literary establishment (Jane Austen hid her writing if anyone walked into the room, Emily Dickinson published only a few poems in her lifetime).

In children's literature the most famous repressed writer is, I think, the little woman Jo March, Louisa Alcott's *alter ego*. Jo is, in fact, the perfect nineteenth-century embodiment of physical, economic and linguistic entrapment. She is shut up in her attic, secretly writing romance fiction (to support the family) while her pretentious father holds court in the main-floor study. She is made to feel ashamed of her writing by her husband/father, Professor Bhaer, and to give it up in favour of a really useful profession – raising boys. Dependence is treated as the preferred occupation.

Work and money are the keys to freedom, and women and children don't have much access to either. Unlike adventure stories, or fairy tales where men go out to seek their fortunes, women just have to hope that fortune smiles upon them. In *The Dialectic of Sex* Shulamith Firestone says that women and children live in a condition of 'privileged slavery' under a demoralizing system of patronage:

the individual eventually appears to be a different kind of human animal with its own peculiar set of laws and behaviour ('I'll never understand women!' . . . 'You don't know a thing about child psychology!')

Contemporary slang reflects this animal state: children are 'mice', 'rabbits', 'kittens', women are called 'chicks' (in England), 'birds', 'hens', 'dumb clucks', 'silly geese', 'old mares', 'bitches'

. . .

Because the class oppression of women and children is couched in the phraseology of 'cute' it is much harder to fight than open oppression. What child can answer back when some inane aunt falls all over him or some stranger decides to pat his behind and gurgle baby talk? . . . Because it makes them uncomfortable to know that the woman or the child or the black or the workman is grumbling, the oppressed groups must also appear to *like* their oppression – smiling and simpering though they may feel like hell inside. The smile is the child/woman equivalent of the shuffle; it indicates acquiescence of the victim to his own oppression. (pp. 100–1)

The repression about which Firestone writes is easily carried out because women and children are, generally, smaller and weaker than men, regarded as 'other' and so open to abuse. It is not surprising, then, that difficulty being seen and heard is experienced by small protagonists – from Treehorn (who is accused of shirking, when his real problem is that he is shrinking, and no one seems to notice) to Jacob Two-Two (who has to say everything twice to be heard). What makes these characters so engaging is that, despite being small and weak, they win over powers that be. The story is familiar. It is Jack-the-Giant-Killer and David and Goliath. It is the trickster's story. It is also the heroine's story, and the child's.

The quickening of academic interest in women's and children's literature testifies that something in their stories is in touch with the temper of our time. Trickster stories express a contemporary reality; powerlessness is no longer a condition experienced primarily by women, children and other oppressed people. It is a condition we all recognize. And with the new consciousness of the value of the small, weak and powerless protagonist, there is a renewed interest in a survival tactic that has long been out of favour. Deceit.

Deceit, fraud, guile and other forms of trickery have been out of favour for the last thousand (or more) years of Western culture. That wasn't always the case. Tricksters – from mythic Raven and Anansi,

153

to the folk heroes Brer Rabbit and Tolkien's Bilbo Baggins – have all been revered as culture heroes, valued for their craftiness. As deceit isn't a manly virtue, it has been relegated to a lower-order survival tactic, somewhere well below the dignity accorded to man who fights for his honour, or for 'truth, justice and the American way'.

Academic interest in the tactics of the heroine has generated interest in deceit. In 'Our Lady of Pain: Heroes and Heroines of Romance' (from *The Secular Scripture*) Northrop Frye, taking his terms from Dante, says that heroes fight through the use of 'forza', violence. They usually end up dead, and their stories are tragic more often than not. But heroines who use 'froda', fraud, survive, and their stories resolve happily.

Although 'froda' is a traditional female survival tactic, it is not successfully deployed in times and places in which women are supposed to like being trapped. In the nineteenth century, for instance, girls might start out using guile, but growing up was regarded as a process of civilizing guile out. So Anne in *Anne of Green Gables* is an engaging child, whose imagination allows her to escape from the banality of everyday existence, but in growing up, she actively chooses to stay at home (at Green Gables, on Prince Edward Island) rather than go off to university. She chooses to be trapped. Jo, in *Little Women*, undergoes much the same repressing process. She is also an engaging, even naughty, girl, but as she grows up and learns how to stifle her anger, she becomes much less interesting. For both Anne and Jo, this process is seen (overtly anyway) as a positive one. But I would be willing to bet that one of the reasons that *Anne of Green Gables* and Little Women remain such favourites is that readers intuitively understand the tension between the vital girl and the repressed woman. Even if guile gets civilized out, its traces remain.

Still, the point is that though deceit is the traditional tactic of the heroine, it is most visible in the tactics of defenceless child protagonists in children's literature – from Jack, when he meets the Giant Killer, to Jacob Two-Two, when he meets the Hooded Fang. Even *The Secret Garden*, one of the most enduring stores for children of all time, is founded on deceit. Mary and Colin know they have to keep the secret of their growing strength and capacity to survive locked inside the garden wall, until they have managed to undo all the damage done to them by misguided adults. Grown-ups (except for the rustic, childlike sort) are depicted in *The Secret Garden* as destructive and morbid – especially the doctors who prescribe debilitating 'corrective' measures for Colin. Mary and Colin lived in a world where separation between grown-ups and children was possible, and in their case, a positive asset. That separation is no longer possible.

As women and children are increasingly incorporated into the body of the culture, the culture recognizes and incorporates the value of their difference. By naming the physical, economic and linguistic traps in women's and children's literature, and by naming deceit as a survival tactic, I've been naming the previously invisible difference between 'them' (women and children) and 'us' (adults). What follows is an account of the sound of those differences.

AND OTHERNESS

Feminist critics have been writing about how hard it is to find a voice to talk about women's literature. That is because criticism has traditionally – at least in the now old-school new-critical terms – been deemed objective, and the authority of the text deemed sacrosanct. We now understand that texts don't exist in isolation, and language that pretends to be authoritative and objective is male-order language – not suited to discussions about the inscapes of women's stories.

Male-order criticism is pointed towards the one penetrating strategy that removes even the last G-string of mystery and lays bare the text. But it doesn't quite work; the emperor's magic new clothes degenerate into a low-brow skinflick. Bare texts don't allow for the kind of intellectual play upon which readers (especially critics) thrive. Feminist criticism, on the other hand, is about keeping the voyeur's attention and imagination engaged while the clothes are being taken off. Critical interest centres on the play of meaning, not the sadly naked revelation of meaning.

But as long as the signs and language of women's literature and children's literature are foreign, other, to male-order critics, it is almost impossible to play with meaning. So one of the primary problems feminist critics and children's literature critics have is how to recognize, define, and accord value to otherness.

To make otherness less foreign, feminist critics have been bringing to the body of their critical work all the available power and light from a host of disciplines: semiotic theory to make the signs of otherness visible; linguistic theory to identify the difference between male language and female language; Marxist theory to name the economic entrapment of women and children as comparable to that experienced by the lower classes in class-defined societies; communication theory to focus on the implications of the shift from a print-based, cause-and-effect (essentially male-order) mode of discourse to an audio/visual, storytelling (essentially female) mode of discourse; reader-response theory to give value to the subjective response to texts, and to acknowledge the cultural, social and gender differences between readers, cultural anthropology to explore otherness as a way for us to test the points of likeness and difference between ourselves and others more clearly; psychoanalytic theory to explain the discomfort experienced when we divide 'them' from 'us'. (For reference to specific texts, see 'Useful books', pp. 164-6.)

The capacity to bring together a 'hard body' of critical theory in a 'user friendly', often warm and funny, way is what marks feminist criticism. And I hope it marks my criticism too: the capacity to write with 'hard body' (from a North American predilection for life in the gym) and *jouissance* (Roland Barthes uses the term in *The Pleasure of the Text*; it translates roughly as pleasure – multiple, female orgasmic pleasure). The rewards of writing criticism with this mixture of pain and pleasure make it well worth doing. By bringing scholarship from a variety of disciplines to literary study, and by addressing points of likeness and difference between ourselves and others, feminist critics have breathed life into what was becoming the moribund discipline of literary criticism.

Feminist critics aren't the only ones bringing a range of critical insights into the study of literary texts. The 'impressionistic' criticism (as Nancy Chambers calls it) and 'emotional' criticism (as Eleanor Cameron calls it) that has weakened children's literature criticism for so long is being challenged by something more vigorous and resonant: Aidan Chambers, Hugh Crago and Roger Sale have been bringing various forms of reader-response theory to children's literature, focusing on the points of contact between child-reading and adult-reading; Carolyn Steedman brings Marxist, linguistic and culture theory to writing by children; Jack Zipes draws on Marxist theory to show how fairy tales betray our social values; Peter Hunt is developing what he calls 'childist' (the term sits uncomfortably with me because, I suspect, it maintains them-and-us distinctions) criticism, drawing on the 're-seeing' of the culture; and Eleanor Cameron is bringing a 'wrinkled brow and cool fresh eye' (borrowing her terms from Robert Lowell on Randall Jarrell) to children's literature. I like her approach because she possesses the kind of double-vision that I think is essential in children's literature criticism: the capacity to move freely 'between intuitive thinking and logic' and between adult experience and the freshness of child vision. Cameron says that 'the critic worth reading neither destroys nor chews to shreds; one tries to reveal'. If we are good critics or visionaries, or good sibyls, or good at hermeneutics and semiotics, then we read the signs and interpret them.

In children's literature, the critical issue no longer involves clarifying distinctions between them (children) and us (grown-ups). It involves looking for the kind of double-vision that Eleanor Cameron advocates and that Aidan Chambers ('All of a Tremble to See His Danger') sees actively operating in *Huckleberry Finn*, when Mark Twain 'stays true to the adolescent self he once openly was and still secretly is' but 'takes with him into his novel the knowledge of life he has acquired since, and transposes it by his craft skill into knowledge that a teenager can discover'. What Aidan reveals is the capacity of the adolescent novel to hold open the signs of the future for the adolescent looking forward, and the signs of the past for the grown-up looking back.

If one of the critical tasks is to look at children's literature as something that keeps childhood and adolescence alive within us, then objective them-and-us conventional approaches to texts look sadly dated. The approach we need is closer to one Richard Shweder, a cultural anthropologist, says is suited to good ethnography: casuistry ('adroit rationalization') to make familiar 'what at first seemed strange, the other' and estranges us 'from what we thought we knew, ourselves'.[3] Simply put, Shweder advocates deceit as a useful tactic for exploring the play of likeness and difference between self and other. It is a language of deceit that tells the truth (reminiscent of raincoats).

As an adult, and as a critic, someone who shares books with children (and with adults who share books with children), I'm responsible. I'm responsible for finding a language that speaks the cultural and aesthetic values of our society in an intelligible way. For me, that is a mode of discourse that incorporates both the *jouissance* of mimetic, storytelling language and the hard body of critical theory: a critical stance that acknowledges both the seriousness and the pleasure of the audience and the text. This only happens if we understand that we explore texts not because the child is the father of the man (or the mother of the woman, one might say, though that seems not to carry the same weight) but because there is something alive in us worth exploring.

THE PLOT – READING THE SIGNS IN *THE SECRET GARDEN* AND *THE CHANGEOVER*

I was disappointed by Humphrey Carpenter's *Secret Gardens; The Golden Age of Children's Literature*.[4] When I first encountered it, I eagerly anticipated a book that would give me some keys to *The Secret Garden*, reasons why the story continues to resonate so strongly in me, even though I intensely dislike the way it turns from Mary's story into Colin's (a feeling I know I share with other readers, especially women). Carpenter hits on the right sign: the secret garden itself is the key to the story and to the Golden Age of children's literature. But he doesn't understand the meaning of the sign. He doesn't understand what I now know: the secret garden is a plot.

Plot, says Peter Brooks in *Reading for the Plot: Design and Intention in Narrative*,[5] is both the scene of the action and the plan of action, the location and the scheme of a story. The ways that the events of the story are worked out (and the ways the reader reads them) depend on the interpretation of the signs. Humphrey Carpenter's account of secret gardens is disappointing because he depicts the kingpins of the Golden Age of children's literature (especially Kingsley, Carroll, Alcott, and Barrie) as social misfits stuck in some sort of adolescent never-never land. What he doesn't do is explain why their stories remain so compelling. He doesn't explain that they had understood the secret of their secret gardens: the tension between Victorian repression and the archetypal transcendence of a quest romance. They had worked out ways of transforming the repression of their lives into the transcendence of their art. And the traces of their success remain as accessible to readers now as they were then.

In the first part of 'Enigma Variations', I tried to make the signs of feminist poetics (as applicable to children's literature) visible and audible: the physical, economic, and linguistic entrapment of women and children as revealed in the enclosed spaces and small-scale, secret stories of the texts. This part of 'Enigma Variations', 'The Plot', is about what those signs mean. I'm going to use Frances Hodgson Burnett's *The Secret Garden* (1911) and *The Changeover: A Supernatural Romance* by Margaret Mahy (1984)[6] as paradigmatic texts. Both stories tell of the identity quests of their respective protagonists, and both stories locate the scene of the action and the plan of action in enclosed, secret gardens. As in the first part of 'Enigma Variations' I'm going to suggest that there has been a shift in children's literature: from Golden Age entrapment to the transcendence in the young adult fiction of the 1980s.

I've always felt *The Secret Garden* to be as much a monument to the British Empire as are the Crystal Palace and Queen Victoria herself. There is something so compelling about the story that I am prepared to suspend my annoyance with the ending, with the way

Burnett puts priggish little Colin front and centre and relegates Mary to the sidelines. My problem is that I have to acknowledge, reluctantly, that Burnett wrote the only possible ending to the story. Like it or not, Burnett got the plot right.

One of the most telling scenes occurs at the end of the book when Colin comes bursting out of the garden, almost knocking his bewildered father off his feet (an obviously Oedipal gesture). Mary comes second. Colin gloats about being able to beat her in a race. Social order is restored. Colin will be king of the castle (of Misselthwaite Manor in this case, displacing the pretender, his uncle Dr Craven). Mary is an also-ran. She fades quietly into the background, the perfect wallflower. The irony implicit in Mary's story is that the secret garden, the place of growth, is the place of her defeat.

Colin is a winner. He is 'Master Colin', who walks 'as strongly and steadily as any boy in Yorkshire' (p. 253). I am always dismayed by how far the story drifts from the opening sentence! There we were introduced to the sad image of Mary, who had been 'sent' to Misselthwaite Manor: 'the most disagreeable-looking child ever seen' (p. 7). As a reader, I want her to find herself, to complete her quest for selfhood. It is Mary, after all, who divines that the secret of survival is in the garden (the scene of the action) and she is the one who devises a way of acting upon her instinctive knowledge (the plan of action). It is Mary who seeks the garden, finds the key, finds the help she needs to make the garden grow, and finds in herself enough nurturing instinct to help Colin grow. But her story is gradually relinquished to (pretentious, boring) Colin. Though she formulates the plan to save him, she gets little credit. It is Colin, 'the Athlete, the Lecturer, the Scientific Discoverer' (p. 251), who stands at the end of the book to tell his story to the adoring assembly of listeners (including Mary) sitting clustered at his feet.

For Colin, growing up in the garden, being nurtured in the garden, means that he has been able to overcome the physical and emotional deprivation of his early childhood – without earning it. For Mary, growing up, outgrowing, her early childhood deprivation means learning to be a follower not a leader, learning that winning selfhood means losing self.

So, there it is, the plot of *The Secret Garden*: the key to the story is the story itself. The signs tell a thwarted story of independence, a thwarted quest romance. Its compelling attraction arises in the tension between the knowledge that the story deteriorates (as Mary's story gives way to Colin's), and the knowledge that Burnett ends the story in accordance with the social and economic truths and values of her particular time and place.

The Changeover, on the other hand, is a success story. Laura, the heroine, completes her quest without losing her story or herself to the male lead. Mahy writes out of a time and place where it is possible for a woman to succeed in a man's world, and where nurturing instincts need not be devalued in relation to science and reason: 'the Scientific Discoverer' doesn't have to suppress the gardener.

The plot traces fourteen-year-old Laura's quest to save her three-year-old brother, Jacko, from succumbing to an incubus, Carmody Braque, who is trying to renew himself (rather more stylishly than a vampire would) by sucking the life out of Jacko. To rescue her brother, Laura must fight Braque's supernatural powers in kind. She must become a witch (through a 'changeover') – aided by sixteen-year-old Sorry (the male lead, who is also a witch and the head prefect at her school) and his witch mother and grandmother.

The plot of Mahy's story, like the plot of Burnett's, is both the scene of the action and the plan of action – and it takes place in a secret garden. But whereas Mary and Colin outgrow their inner secret garden in order to take up life outside, Laura and Sorry learn to take their secret garden with them and incorporate its nurturing powers. In *The Changeover* the everyday, 'outside' world where Laura lives with her mother and brother, is a subdivision called Gardendale. In accordance with the unintentional irony common to such places, it is a perfectly ordinary, raw example of urban blight. The inner secret garden, 'Janua Caeli' (the door of heaven), is where Sorry lives with his mother and grandmother. And it is where Laura recovers her witch nature, and finds the supernatural help she needs to save Jacko.

During the course of her quest Laura finds that her inner and outer gardens are not mutually exclusive: they are, rather, 'like a holograph' in which 'every piece of the world contained the whole of the world' (p. 211). In the end, even though she outgrows her immediate need for the secret garden of Janua Caeli, she recognizes its presence all around her:

> Outside in the city, traffic lights changed colours, casting quick spells of prohibition and release. Cars hesitated, then set off again, roaring with urgency through the maze of the Gardendale subdivision, a labyrinth in which one could, after all, find a firebird's feather, or a glass slipper or the footprints of the minotaur quite as readily as in fairy tales, or the infinitely dividing paths of Looking-Glass land. (p. 214)

Throughout *The Changeover* Laura's capacity to fulfil her hero(in)ic quest is tied to an ability to read small-scale signs accurately. When she wanders with Jacko into Carmody Braque's tiny, enticing shop filled with things like 'seven owls made of walnut shells', and 'a peep-show shaped like an egg' – and the smell of stale peppermint (p. 19), she recognizes a gingerbread house of a trap. The 'faint used-peppermint smell that made her want to be sick in the gutter' that morning is one of the traces of Carmody Braque that Laura notices. She comments on it every time she is near him, or near Jacko once he is possessed. But it is another of Carmody Braque's small signs that proves almost fatal for Jacko: a rubber stamp, like the Mickey Mouse stamp that the librarian puts on Jacko's hand each week, but this one has Braque's face on it. Jacko begins to wither from the moment his hand receives Braque's image. Laura saves him by tricking Braque into receiving a stamp with her face on it – a magical, powerful stamp won through her changeover.

I like the redemptive ending of *The Changeover*. Laura's quest is personal and domestic, she fights for someone she loves. She uses the tricksterish tactics of the weak and powerless. And she doesn't boast about her success as pretentious Colin does (in a way that makes me cringe) at the end of *The Secret Garden*. The values in Mahy's book are connected with individual humanity rather than public glory. They seem to me to be positive values, especially if we assume that the truth of the story she tells both reflects and is reflected by the truths of our society.

The Secret Garden, on the other hand, has what my colleague Margaret Watson calls a 'blocked ending'.[7] The story can't end with the fairy-tale conclusion in which every protagonist gets what he or she deserves, and gets mated accordingly to his or her personal value. That's why the story (correctly) fades from Mary's quest to Colin's and denies Mary her social integration while allowing Colin his. Archetypal quest romances, or identity quests, or *Bildungsroman* patterns are supposed to be universal. But they are skewed or blurred in the Golden Age of children's literature, as they are in women's literature. The problem with a 'typical' archetypal quest that traces the hero's call to adventure, his descent underground, his battle with the enemy, and his triumphant return (as outlined by the typically male cartographers, Joseph Campbell, or C. G. Jung, or Northrop Frye, for example[8]) is that it is about turning boys into men, not girls into women, or children into people. When the quest ends, the hero gets his rewards, his property, his integrity and, often, a princess thrown in among the other goods and chattels.

A female quest doesn't look quite like that, and a story that simply exchanges a female protagonist for a male one usually ends up making the heroine look like a hero in drag. Annis Pratt, in *Archetypal Patterns in Women's Fiction*, looks at women's stories and illuminates a typical five-phase identity quest that a heroine might travel: a splitting off from family; a green-world guide; or token, a green-world lover; confrontation with parental figures; a plunge into the unconscious; and finally an integration with society.[9]

In *The Secret Garden* Mary's female identity quest more or less fizzles out: she goes through all the difficult parts, then Colin gets all the rewards promised in a male quest. The quest romance in *The Changeover* is different. The male and female quest patterns are superimposed, and the story resolves in a much more triumphant way. Margaret Mahy's choice of subtitle, 'A Supernatural Romance', speaks the multiple nature of the quest undertaken by Laura and Sorry. While Laura assumes the role of the male quest hero (she descends into the underworld, and is initiated as a witch in order to do battle with Carmody Braque), Sorry has a supporting female role (as Gatekeeper during her changeover). In accord with Pratt's female quest pattern, Laura splits off from her (divorced) parents (in contemporary children's literature, parents are often depicted, as they are here, as concerned and interested but largely ineffectual); receives green-world tokens from Sorry's mother and grandmother (they are depicted as women who love the landscape); Sorry is her green-world lover (he wants to be a kind of ranger with the Wild Life Division); she descends to do battle with Carmody Braque; and in coming to terms with her witch nature, Laura finds the maturity to be reconciled with her family.

Besides being a quest romance. *The Changeover* is a romance in the sense that it is a teen-dream love story between Sorry and Laura: good-looking sixteen-year-old male witch disguised as a prefect in love with girl (a latent witch) in fourth form who has never been kissed. That love story has something of the character of the sweet-dreams romances that Sorry – much to Laura's puzzlement – reads. Throughout *The Changeover* these cheap romances counterpoint the serious relationship between Sorry and Laura. In his pursuit of Laura, Sorry refers to them occasionally, only half in clichéd jest: 'If you had read *Wendy's Wayward Heart* ... you would recognize my expression. I'm trying to look rueful at being caught out in an act of sentimentality' (p. 96). Laura is unimpressed. Yet there is a kind of dignity to those romances because Sorry reads them to try to identify the humanity in his witch nature. And readers of *The Changeover* are consciously alerted to the fact that the conventions of sentimental romances are in operation in serious fiction.

By acknowledging that *The Changeover* is both a traditional heroic male quest romance and a sentimental woman's romance, Mahy makes her book reflect the gender-crossing and genre-crossing trends of contemporary young adult fiction – and contemporary society. Mahy 'unvents', to borrow Annis Pratt's term, the conventions of the typical quest romance in her inclusion of the female quest pattern.

Annis Pratt, in her turn, has borrowed the term 'unvention' from a woman who wanted to learn to spin her own wool, but found herself unable to follow the step-by-step male-order instructions. It was not until she actually began to work with the spindle that 'she found that her fingers already seemed to know how to perform motions arcane to her conscious mind. She coined the term "unventing" for the rediscovery of a lost skill through intuition, a bringing of latent knowledge out of oneself in contrast to "invention" from scratch.'

Laura is the kind of heroine I always wanted Mary to be. Laura unvents herself, in a way that Mary never can, in order to bring her story to a redemptive conclusion. Mahy's redemptive, feminist story is only possible in a society which at least accepts the premise that women's stories and natures are of value in and of themselves. In the same way that Laura unvents herself, 'the reading and writing of women's fiction', says Pratt, is a form of 'unvention': 'the tapping of a repository of knowledge lost from Western culture but still available to the author and recognizable to the reader deriving from a world with which she, at some level of her imagination, is already familiar' (p. 178).

The capacity (or incapacity) of the heroine to understand her own destiny is mirrored by the reader of *The Secret Garden* or *The Changeover* – or the reader of any book. In order to make meaning out of mystery, in order to understand the plot, one has to be able to read the signs. Just as Laura learns to read the signs of her life (and Mary is inhibited from reading her signs), so readers learn, unconsciously perhaps, to read the signs and plots of feminist poetics.

Story by story, the signs and plots of women's lives begin to find a rightful place, alongside the more familiar male signs, in the mind's eyes of the readers – male and female, adult and child.

NOTES

1 It is fitting that this instance of reader-response theory in action should occur in conversation with Nicholas Tucker. In *Signal* 43 Nick argues that Bruno Bettelheim's misguided homogenization of individual readers

ignores the idea (put forward by Norman Holland in *5 Readers Reading*) that 'individuals habitually react towards fiction according to their own imaginative lifestyle, and use each story to re-create their most character-istic psychological processes' (p. 35). Nick and I betrayed our individual 'identity themes', as Norman Holland would say.

2 Adrienne Rich, 'When We Dead Awaken: Writing as Re-Vision', *On Lies, Secrets, and Silence: Selected Prose 1966-1978*, Norton, 1979, p. 35; Sandra Gilbert, 'What Do Feminist Critics Want?: A Postcard from the Volcano', *The New Feminist Criticism: Essays on Women, Literature and Theory*, edited by Elaine Showalter, Pantheon, 1985, p. 32. References to other books of feminist criticism are cited below, under 'Useful books'.

3 Richard Shweder, 'Storytelling Among the Anthropologists', *New York Times Book Review*, 21 September 1986, p. 39.

4 Humphrey Carpenter, *Secret Gardens: The Golden Age of Children's Literature*, Allen & Unwin, 1985.

5 Peter Brooks, *Reading for the Plot: Design and Intention in Narrative*, Knopf, 1984, pp. 11-12.

6 Frances Hodgson Burnett, *The Secret Garden*, Puffin, 1951; and Margaret Mahy, *The Changeover: A Supernatural Romance*, Dent, 1984. Future references are to these editions and will be cited in the text.

7 Margaret Watson teaches children's literature at York University in Toronto. She made the remark in the context of Vladimir Nabokov's lecture on *Mansfield Park*. Vladimir Nabokov, *Lectures on Literature*, ed. Fredson Bowers, Harcourt Brace Jovanovich, 1980.

8 I've synthesized a 'typical' male quest from the following sources: Joseph Campbell, *Hero with a Thousand Faces*, second edition, Princeton, 1968: C. G. Jung, *Archetypes and the Collective Unconscious*, Princeton, 1969; Northrop Frye, *The Anatomy of Criticism*, Princeton, 1957, and *The Secular Scripture*, Harvard, 1976. Campbell is my main source.

9 Annis Pratt, *Archetypal Patterns in Women's Fiction*, Harvester Press, 1982, pp. 139-43. Future references are to this edition and will be cited in the text.

USEFUL BOOKS AND ARTICLES

On feminist theory

Rachel Brownstein, *Becoming a Heroine: Reading about Women in Novels*, Penguin, 1982.

Mary Eagleton (ed.), *Feminist Literary Theory*, Basil Blackwell, 1986.

Sandra Gilbert and Susan Gubar, *Madwoman in the Attic*, Yale University Press, 1979.

Elaine Marks and Isabelle de Courtivron, *New French Feminisms: An Anthology*, Schocken, 1981.

Jane Miller, *Women Writing about Men*, Virago, 1986.

Elaine Showalter, *A Literature of Their Own: British Women Novelists from Brontë to Lessing*, Princeton University Press, 1977.

Elaine Showalter (ed.), *The New Feminist Criticism*, Pantheon, 1985.

On contemporary approaches to literature

For semiotic theory, see Julia Kristeva, *Desire in Language: A Semiotic Approach to Literature and Art*, Columbia University Press, 1980.

For psychoanalytic/linguistic theory, see Juliet Mitchell and Jacqueline Rose (eds), *Feminine Sexuality: Jacques Lacan and the Ecole Freudienne*, Norton, 1982.

For Marxist theory, see Shulamith Firestone, *The Dialectic of Sex*, Morrow, 1970.

For communication theory, see Eric Havelock, *The Muse Learns to Write*, Yale University Press, 1986; Walter J. Ong, *Orality and Literacy: The Technologizing of the Word*, Methuen, 1982; Marshall McLuhan, *Understanding Media: The Extensions of Man*, New American Library, 1964.

For cultural anthropology, see Clifford Geertz, *The Interpretation of Cultures*, Basic Books, 1973; Richard Shweder and Robert A. LeVine (eds), *Culture Theory: Essays on Mind, Self and Emotion*, Cambridge University Press, 1984.

For psychoanalytic theory, see R. D. Laing, *The Politics of Experience*, Penguin, 1967; Jane Gallop, *The Daughter's Seduction: Feminism and Psychoanalysis*, Cornell University Press, 1982.

For literary theory, see Roland Barthes, *The Pleasure of the Text*, translated by Richard Miller, Farrar, Straus and Giroux, 1975; Northrop Frye, *The Secular Scripture*, Harvard University Press, 1976; Frank Kermode, *The Genesis of Secrecy: On the Interpretation of Narrative*, Harvard University Press, 1979.

On contemporary approaches to children's literature

Eleanor Cameron, 'With Wrinkled Brow and Cool Fresh Eye', *Horn Book*, May–June 1985 and July–August 1985.

Aidan Chambers, *Booktalk*, Bodley Head, 1985; 'All of a Tremble to See His Danger', *Signal*, 51, September 1986.

Peter Hunt, 'Childist Criticism: The Subculture of the Child, the Book and the Critic', *Signal*, 43, January 1984; and 'Questions of Method and Methods of Questioning Childist Criticism in Action', *Signal*, 45, September 1984.

Roger Sale, 'Child Reading and Man Reading' in *Fairy Tales and After: From Snow White to E.B. White*, Harvard University Press, 1978.

Carolyn Steedman, *The Tidy House: Little Girls Writing*, Virago, 1982.

Carolyn Steedman *et al.* (eds), *Language, Gender and Childhood*, Routledge & Kegan Paul, 1985.

Jack Zipes, *Fairy Tales and the Art of Subversion: The Classical Genre for Children and the Process of Civilization*, Wildman Press, 1983.

Margaret Meek's approach from the point of view of reading and language acquisition is similar to Benton's, but her roots seem equally to be in what is more conventionally seen as literature. This, together with her willingness to take on board such of those critical theories as seem to be useful and relevant, and her determinedly accessible style, make her work the ideal bridge between the many competing disciplines.

Margaret Meek
'What Counts as Evidence in Theories of Children's Literature?' *Theory into Practice*, vol. 21, no. 4 (Autumn 1982), pp. 284–92

If we include all the speculative thinking that goes on about children's books, of the making of theories there is no end. Reassuringly, my Oxford dictionary says I can expect 'systematic statements of general principals and laws', or 'in a loose and general sense' treat a theory as 'a hypothesis proposed as an expanation'. Having neither the time nor the wit to make laws, not yet the zealous exactitude to be exclusively systematic, I never begrudge theoretical status to anything that helps us to understand how we come to understand the principles, the categories, the criteria for judgment that make up an interaction with all literature, not only children's.

I willingly concede that most writers, critics, or straightforward readers, are bound to be theorists. I may speak loosely, and say that John Newbery's motto, 'Trade and Plumb Cake for Ever, Hurrah!' shows a theoretical understanding of the relationship of children's books to the prevailing economic and social facts related to their production and sale in the mid-eighteenth century because I know that comparable understandings underpin the appearance of most children's books throughout their history. I long for Harvey Darton's (1932) perspicacity in announcing – in the first line of his great volume – that children's books are 'works produced ostensibly to give children spontaneous pleasure', for there is no clearer or better theory than that. It allowed Darton to discuss as 'the theorists' the writers of moral tales, like Maria Edgeworth and Thomas Day, in the way that has informed and formed our thinking about children's books ever since. For all that their writings embody the child-centered educational philosophy of Rousseau, these authors are essentially, says Darton, good story tellers moved by 'human realism', a characteristic clearly marked in Darton himself.

Whatever the topic to be studied, in literature, as elsewhere, we inherit the theories of our predecessors, willy nilly: and in making our own we are bound to represent not only their earlier methods of inquiry, but also the pattern of associated constructs already existent in our own minds. Thus, I cannot speculate about children's literature without incorporating the tissues of ideas that inform my everyday thinking about literature, children, reading, writing, language, linguistics, politics, ideology, sociology, history, education, sex, psychology, art, or a combination of some or all of these, to say nothing of joy or sadness, pleasure or pain. This is a lengthy way of saying that those who would theorize do so initially about themselves. There is a sense in which I can make a theory of children's literature only for myself and encourage you to do the same.

The first excuse for doing it publicly is to look collaboratively with you at some things which go unacknowledged simply because, as bookish people, we tend to take them for granted. The second is more serious: I believe we have come to the point where the existence of a literature whose *implied* readers are not adult (although its actual writers, producers, buyers, critics, and promoters undoubtedly are) expects of serious critics and students a more systematically speculative poetics, in the Aristotelian sense of defining the thing made. Children's literature has an appreciable history and an expanding present. Look, if you will, at the size and scope of the volume called *Twentieth Century Children's Writers* (Kirkpatrick, 1978), which is about to be revised by the addition of more than 80 new authors, and ask if we might not profitably address ourselves to this matter, perhaps with more stringency than we have hitherto shown. It may be argued that our very hospitality to ideas in this field which, for all its rapid growth, is still quite young, has hindered a more systematic search for what counts as evidence of the nature of the thing we study with great zeal.

My simple beginning point is, things are changing, fast. In the past 20 years, we have outgrown the need to establish children's books as a legitimate area of study, but we are still looking through the lorgnettes of critical models now outworn in adult literature. We have had the fights of the 'book people' (those who espouse what in England is called 'Leavisite élitism' or, in the US, 'new criticism', and look for 'the good' as against 'the best' to establish criteria of selection, so that 'literature' can be separated from 'reading matter') against the 'children people' (those who support the needs of young readers and exploit the benefits of developmental psychology). Clearly, the 'book people' do not ignore children as readers; they simply find them irrelevant to the judgments made about the books (Alderson, 1969). The 'children people' certainly do not tolerate bad books for children; they prefer, however, to bring the readership into focus. We have done, as Stanley Fish (1980) explains, 'what critics always do: we saw what our interpretative principles permitted or directed us to see, and then we turned around and attributed what we had "seen" to a text and an intention' (p. 12). We are only now coming to realize that we are an interpretative community of those who read books where the readership is part of their definition. The texts we choose gain the status of literature because we are responsible for defining what counts as evidence of their worth. But it is what counts as evidence that needs reevaluation. The books are slipping through our categories of genre, narrative stance and style, text and structure, ideology, and social relevance. The new readers are, quite simply, different. Two generations of television and the prospect of boundless technological resources have seen to that. If we agree that children's literature exists, we need to examine what makes it specially *children's* nowadays.

I propose therefore to offer you a very primitive kind of theory, a *viewing* or a *sight*, of these things that must be included in revised hypothetical descriptions of literature specially designated 'children's'. If I can do this, my argument will be that earlier considerations of children's books as either picture books and fairy stories, the printed forms of earlier oral traditions, or as lesser, smaller, easier-to-read, miniaturized forms of other literatures, can be turned around. Then, literature for children may be seen as the significant model, the cultural paradigm of subsequent literature in *the experience of the reader*. Children's literature is, undeniably, the *first* literary experience, where the reader's expectations of what literature *is* are laid down.[1] Books in childhood initiate children into literature; they inaugurate certain kinds of literary competences, in Culler's phrase (1975). They offer a view of what it is to be literate. As (in my case) aging, expert *literati* we take all this for granted and assume that our early experience has a generality that stretches beyond our generation. Thus we often neglect our obligation to find a way of talking about children's literature that matches their contemporary experience of it.

Let us begin, however, by agreeing that we have gained a great deal from the study of children's literature of the past, if only because scholars have established in their field standards of research as rigorous as any literature demands. Given the notoriously ephemeral nature of publications for the young, we must be grateful for the continuous sifting and ordering of texts, the bibliographical and publishing details which now allow us to match the books with their reading public. In studies of nineteenth-century children's books, the literary historians have reaped bountiful harvests. Brian Alderson, the children's book columnist of *The Times*, said wryly in a recent paper: 'Opinions are free; facts are expensive', implying that the bibliographical exactitude demanded of someone involved, as he was, in re-editing Harvey Darton demanded more time and labor than the expressive forms of literary criticism. This is true, and I acknowledge our debt as I would for the solution of the editorial problems in Shakespeare.

But it is not only the antiquarian interest in these studies that makes them important. They also help us to understand how children's books are produced within and determined by their social and historical context. We can better appreciate, then as now, how conditions of production and distribution influence what children can and do read. It is impossible to discuss books in a social vacuum. J. S. Bratton's (1981) study of Victorian children's fiction, the books that Darton despises, shows that what we accept as literature - *Alice* and *The King of the Golden River* (Ruskin, 1841) for instance - are finely wrought fastidious exceptions. They were not read at that time by the majority of literate children whose books were Sunday school prizes, moral tales for Christian propaganda and social control. The most prolific writers of these books were women who needed the money. By showing how their author's intention was held in common, Bratton demonstrates that we can judge the skill of a writer like Hesba Stretton in interpreting and manipulating the given formula. Where once critics lumped these books together, she now exercises a more refined literary discrimination. This is only one example of how the awareness of the readers influences our judgment of the books. The presence of a literature judged to be 'popular' tells us what the literate read. It also tells us what adults offer children to read, the kinds of texts they are expected to be able to cope with, and how these relate to what adults are reading. The significantly different texts, the exceptions, like *Alice*, are then all the more exceptional. We can derive from studies of Victorian children's books a theory of children's literature that includes children reading as authors taught them to. The advantage of so doing is that it helps us to do the same for our contemporary children's books.

THE CULTURE OF CHILDHOOD

Before we do that, we have to look again to the past for what we have too easily taken for granted in our own reading and development, namely, the culture of childhood. The untimely death of Peter Opie brought me to a re-reading of *The Lore and Language of School Children* (Opie and Opie, 1959) and a recollected awareness of two traditions, the adult-transmitted and approved nursery rhymes, picture books, and fairy tales, and the oral tradition of the society of children. The first is reproduced in books as literature; the second goes underground and seems to lose itself in the business of growing up, to be outgrown. When we examine this formidable lore closely we discover it is never truly lost. For one thing, it doesn't die out, but recreates itself in each generation carrying forward the natural linguistic heritage of children, what the Opies call 'a thriving unselfconscious culture which is unnoticed by the sophisticated world. Boys', they say, 'continue to crack jokes that Swift collected from his friends in Queen Anne's time; they play tricks that lads used to play in the days of Beau Brummel; they ask riddles which were posed when Henry VIII was a boy. Young girls continue to perform a magic feat (levitation) of which Pepys heard tell . . . they hoard bus tickets and milk bottle tops in distant memory of a love-lorn girl held to ransom by a tyrannical father; they learn to cure warts (and are successful in curing them) after the manner that Francis Bacon learnt when he was young' (p. 2), and so on. This is the oral literature of a primitive society; it is also the bedrock of both common sense – 'If you make that face and the wind changes, it will stay like that' – *and* the expression of a subversive possibility – the story of a girl or boy to whom it happened.

My main concern is that this childhood culture has the *formal* characteristics of literature; and when it is learned, it is acquired holistically, as form and content, signifier and signified, metaphor and meaning. This is clear when we look at the origins of children's ability to tell and understand jokes. They tell jokes successfully before they understand them because they master the formula ('when is a door not a door? when it is ajar').[2] The formulae of childhood culture are varied yet unchanging, memorable, simple structures with manifold substitutions, like language itself. They rehearse a barter economy, set territorial bounds, teach counting. They express the basic cohesion of a group and explain the limits of authority. The passer-on becomes the author.[3] All this we know, but because it is obvious, we neglect not only its importance as symbolic truth, but also its basic importance as evidence of literary competences:

> Tell tale tit
> Your tongue shall be split

And all the dogs in London
Shall have a little bit.

As they recite and jeer, threaten, beg, count, and exercise word-calling as power against the dark, or as the fomulation of forbidden impulses, children are doing many things they will meet later in acknowledged literary forms. As language breaks the boundaries of sense,

The man in the wilderness said to me
How many strawberries grow in the sea . . .

children learn to play with what they have now mastered - their mother tongue - and to make reality what it is, and what it is not. They lay the foundations of literature, the formal language which, in our day, is written text.

We admire this widespread oral culture, marvel at its transmission, and that is that.[4] A number of things go insufficiently remarked. One is the power of the feeling that lies behind children's chants and verses. Because they are small of stature and immature in thought, believing for a number of years that they may visit Cinderella (Applebee, 1978), we ignore the immensity of their emotions which are never less than adult-sized and sometimes ungovernable. The shape of the chant, its ryhthm, and its form contain the emotion, thereby sublimating the overwhelming contents of childish consciousness to the form of art. Poems and verses become metaphors for feeling. The reciters 'extend reality the better to test it' (Jones, 1968). Pain and anger, joy and excitement move from their raw state into the ritual and magic of formal utterance that is primitive literary competence. 'Common sense', says Roy Shafer (1981), 'is our storehouse of narrative structures'.

This lore is embedded in play, the essential activity of children. It is their cultural memory, undistinguished as to means and ends, occurring, as Winnicott (1971) says, in the 'third area' between the demands and pressures of inner and outer reality. It is the *shared text* - the *first* literature of an emergent social group that is exploring the boundaries of its common world, discovering reality, discovering forms of utterance that are not communicative speech trafficking in information sharing. It is robust, alive, dialogued, repeated, rule-governed, and therefore easily transmissible across countries and cultures. The most natural current manifestation of it is the TV jingle which has the same generality, even greater transmission potential, the same fading of detail and survival of form, the same sharing of common, known texts.

It is difficult for the highly literature to understand the importance of this culture because, as we know, it seems to disappear. In fact, we replace it with books and television where it hovers just below the surface. At the same time we don't explore how, and to what extent, we *share* text. Literary theorists take Shakespeare, Milton, Danté, Blake, Dostoyevsky as common currency. Behind them stand the monumental classics of Greece and Rome and what Northrop Fyre (1982) calls the 'great code' of the Bible. When we read poems and novels, we often know what is going on in them because earlier in our lives, as children, we read the same books as the author. Now this is much less likely than it used to be. In nineteenth-century books for both children and adults, Bible cadences and stories are echoed and alluded to. Authors counted on their being recognized. But in our day the Bible is no longer a shared text across the generations. Thus the source references in Graham Oakley's picture book for children, *The Church Mouse* (1977), are reserved only for those adults who, when they read to children, have what Frank Kermode (1979) calls 'circumsized ears'; and we are bound to admit that they are the few where once they were the many.

In our concern to speed children's progess to what we believe is their literary heritage, and in our making of theories of children's books, we gradually dismiss as insignificant everything that is not 'literature' transmitted by adults. This is one of the historical consequences of living in a society where literacy is both prized and taken for granted. We believe that important *text* is prose or verse in *books*. We even disregard drama, and therefore fail to see the developmental connection between young people of 17 and 18 who flock to the National Theatre to see the *Oresteia* and the 3 million children who, twice a week, watch a TV serial about a school called Grange Hill where comparable feuds occur. The fate of the house of Atreus is a familiar literary landmark - a great, lasting dramatic text. *Grange Hill* is drama, television text - a cultural artifact that dominates contemporary childhood.

Any significant theory of children's literature cannot ignore the texts children hold in common, for on these is their view of literature founded, and from these are their literary competences developed. My roots are not in television but in books. This is a historical accident. I share familiar literary landmarks with my generation. I have constantly to remind myself that the parents of children now in school grew up with TV. The style and narrative conventions adopted by modern writers for children develop less from earlier books than from the shared texts of television, where new codes are made and learned as universally as in the medieval art of stained glass.

THE PRIMACY OF NARRATIVE

To make my next point I have to return to *The Cool Web* (Meek *et al.*, 1977). When my colleagues and I put this book together, we were inviting readers to make their own rationale for children's literature alongside ours. We wanted to make *narrative* central to the study of children learning to read and to the criticism of children's literature. We hoped children's authors would be granted their rightful place in the great tradition of story tellers, and critics would then look at how well-made stories teach children to read in ways that no basal reader could.

We anticipated things a little. Many reading teachers found the book, and the invitation to 'theorize' which it extended, irrelevant to their classroom practice because it asks them to examine their behaviour as readers instead of telling them what to do in reading lessons. But the central idea, that narrative is 'a primary act of mind', and the emphasis on the fact that we live by the stories we tell outselves about ourselves, has now become the cosmology of literature, the present practice of adult literary theory. This is partly the result of extended interest in formalism and structuralism. It is also a prevalent idea because studies of language and literature have at last intertwined to examine 'the problems of articulating a world' (Culler, 1975).

In examining narrative, literary critics are often the victims of their own bookishness, so that they ignore what could extend their awareness – picture books, for instance. (What have they made of Raymond Briggs's *When the Wind Blows*, 1982, as a commentary on a possible nuclear disaster?) In the same way, writers about children's books have ignored, on the whole, the new theoretical studies of narrative, the very thing that characterizes children's books so clearly.

My colleagues and I are studying what Harold Rosen (1982) calls 'the nurture of narrative'. Our concern is to show how storying, the central feature of the culture of childhood, is related – in all its ethnographic complexity, its sense of occasion, its rituals, its varieties of language and its awareness of linguistic registers, its cognitive power, its mythological world-making, and its celebratory strength – to the production and interpretation of that order of texts that we still want to call literature.

Narrative is primary in children, but it stays with us as a cognitive and affective habit all our lives long. As theorists and critics we have neglected what has always been there for us to explore. Thus narratology, the theoretical study of narrative, does not begin with the 'natural' story-telling of childhood, but with Sterne, Dostoyevsky, Proust, the great novel tradition. Then, suddenly, Alan Garner in The Stone Book Quartet[5] – four short texts as lucid as the dawn – tells us about his great-grandfather, and his family. In the age-old disguise and magic of fiction he links the primary oral narrative with the subtlest 'onioning' that Barthes could approve, and shows that the secrets of narrative, in all cultures and subcultures, lie with children making sense of their world. They learn their history, their *mythos*, from the places where they live or in the strangeness of exile, and they learn it from adults who take the time and the trouble to tell it to them in the way that suits the culture in which the storytelling is embedded. In the stories they hear, and later read, children inherit the verbal memory of their tribe in a way that contact with more complex narrations will never wholly erase. For most of my acquaintances *Macbeth* is a play by Shakespeare. For me it is a stern true story of retribution and penance played out against a familiar landscape on the coast of Fife where I was born, within walking distance of a ruin called Macduff Castle. From the stories we hear as children we inherit the feeling mode, the truth value, the codes, the rhetoric, the transmission techniques that tell us who we are. Ursula LeGuin (1981) says we tell tales 'because we are so organized as to take actions that prevent our dissolution into the surroundings'; and Maurice Sendak reports that stories, such as Mickey Mouse tales, helped him 'to get through the day'.[6] Whatever else our theorizing does, it must not neglect such powerful statements of primary feelings.

Critics of children's literature are notoriously unlettered about the features of children's starting-points when they relate storying, the natural cognitive habit, to Story, the art form developed from it. Elaine Moss (1981) has shown quite conclusively how poorly adult critics read picture books which are at once children's primary reading and subtle semiotic systems. A picture book invites all kinds of reading and allows the invention of a set of stories rather than a single story. Picture books alone, with their differing perspectives and points of view, the variety of artists' techniques and ways of teaching conventions of image and text, offer us a chance and the means to produce a whole poetics of literature that no one disputes is undoubtedly children's. I hope I may be forgiven by those who have devoted their lives to this field in order to educate me when I say I am amazed by how little I know, yet I still base a whole rationale for my view of the teaching of reading on the fox and the goat in *Rosie's Walk*.[7] There is scope now, I think, for a new *Cool Web*, a revised pattern of children's reading, but I am, without any modesty, proposing that it should be spun off the central tenet of the first.

In moving toward new theories of children's literature, we may have to shift our emphases somewhat. Few critics will ever stop looking for 'the best' of anything, but as one who spends a great deal of time escaping from the awarding of prizes, I know I lack the absolutism this demands. I am essentially collaborative rather than competitive in my intellectual life, agreeing as I do with Northrop Frye (1982) that evaluation is 'a minor and subordinate function of the critical process, at best an incidental by-product, which should never be allowed to take priority over scholarship' (p. xvi). Too refined evaluation winds us down into smaller and smaller categories of what I still think of as marks for good conduct. Instead let me admire craftsmanship and honest making. I think I recognize these.

Then, for all that I want to include children as readers, I have to take a rest from *response*; or rather, I need to skirt round the word in order to go forward. There is no doubt that readers are moved by what they read and that the nature of this shifting inside oneself is the result of something in the text and one's set toward it. But behind the crude notion of response lies a psychological model to which I cannot subscribe, one that treats the tale or books as simply a stimulus. My belief is that reading is an interactive process, as Iser (1978) defines it. Studies of children's responses to literature usually seek to link what young readers say about the books they read to a theory or a model of cognitive or affective development, or to prove something about the 'suitability' of a story or a theme for children of a given age. The adult asks questions about the story; the children 'respond'. Left to comment on their own, without the stimulus of a question, children often choose to talk about quite other aspects of a tale than those that preoccupy their elders. Here are four lines of transcript from the unsupervised conversation of six-year olds about *The Shrinking of Treehorn* (Heide, 1975).[8]

Brett: I don't really like shrinking, I want to grow up, not shrink.
Carolyn: How do you think it would feel, to shrink?
Ian: Frightening.
Nathan: (the smallest boy) People would say: 'Out the way, titch'.

The first three children are speculating: the fourth is producing his experience for the group. Together they are assimilating 'virtual experience' in Susanne Langer's (1953, p. 212) terms. They are discussing language and possibilities. (Humans get larger; can they get smaller?) They create a tissue of collaborative understandings for each other in a way that no single question from an adult makes possible.

We still do not know how they take on the author's view of Treehorn. Are they amused or afraid? What ways of telling are they noticing? How are they learning to read a funny story? We have so taken the conventions of story telling for children for granted that we have forgotten how a book like *The Shrinking of Treehorn* not only amuses its readers, but also teaches them how a funny story *is to be read*. In that children's literature gives its readers their earliest experience of literature, it also teaches them the reading lessons they need in order to become readers of this literature.

Thus, when authors choose to write for children, there is every chance that they may be intrigued by the prospect of creating literary artifacts for *new* readers, to whom they can teach how their story is to be read. The author can experiment, because the reader's expectations are based not on literary experience, but on a prospective reading adventure with the possibility of surprise. In this sense, that is, that they experiment on behalf of new readers, authors of children's books who are genuinely exploring the relationship of form and content can say that they write for themselves. The problem facing adult critics is that they know only too well what most storytellers are up to. They are no longer anticipating either adventure or surprise.

What we need is an analysis of narrative discourse which does not say that children's stories are simpler forms of adult telling, but insists that they are the primary kinds and structures of later tellings. The authors whose work in children's literature we admire, poise adjectives, calculate sentence length, leave gaps in texts, choose metaphors, all with poetic discipline. They counterpoint tense and time, reading time and virtual memory.

Simple scrutiny shows how closely contemporary writing for children is linked to the narratives being seen on television. Authors no longer tag their dialogue with 'he said' or 'murmured Monica'. The first chapter of a children's story plunges the reader headlong into the action; explanations wait until the second chapter, when the reader is hooked into what is happening – a good TV device. We are still no nearer understanding exactly *how* a children's book creates the 'illusion of a world' that evokes the literary belief that Tolkien speaks of, but Frank Smith suggests that this is the whole basis of understanding.[9] Susanne Langer (1953) saw that in children's stories lay the paradigm of the adult novel. She says of Kipling's *Jungle Book*:

These juvenile stories are the most skilful poetic creations. I have cited them because their magic is fairly *easy to analyse* and the analysis reveals what may, in fact, be found in any well told story - that the whole fabric of illusory events takes its appearance from the way the statements which actually compose the story are worded, the way the sentences flow, stop, repeat, stand alone etc., the concentrations and expansions of statement, the changed or denuded words. The ways of telling make the place, the action, the characters in fiction. (pp. 297–8)

'Fairly easy to analyse . . . ' I wonder why we haven't tried harder to do it. Susanne Langer says the secret is in the voice on the page, when Kipling says, 'O best beloved' - a textual device for inviting young readers into the tale so that they become both the teller and the told. How little we attend to the voice of the narrator in assessing books for children. We have been too preoccupied with the cult of the author. Is it not surprising how scantily we have studied the narrative discourse of children's literature outside the fairy tale? Or when we do it, are we not still caught in the traps of old critical practice - the diversification of the descriptive adjective - so that we applaud as the best critic not the one who comes closest to the text in order to offer us a poetics of its structure, but the one with the best dictionary or thesaurus, or the most winsome style. If we were really serious about a theory of children's literature, we should have analyzed the conventions and figures of texts and how these change as children change.

Perhaps, for all our care, we have been under-reading children's books, especially the most recent ones. We have enjoyed them, promoted them, been glad when they were 'relevant' to the lives of modern children. But we may not have been the best masters of a literature that has the culture of childhood as part of its definition and the reader's experience of it as something to explore. We have no Propp, no Saussure of children's reading, Barthes (1976) says; nor have we a Genette (1980) to analyse the discourse that makes children's literature what it is. We have not yet described how an author organizes a text that teaches an inexperienced reader how to read it. Literature, not reading lessons, teaches children to read in ways that no basal reader can, because literature is read, if at all, with passion, with desire.

NEW QUESTIONS NEEDED

We need to ask new questions. Are all readings of a story as idiosyncratic as adults claim? *How* do some children become insiders, walking around inside a story so that they tell their own alongside the author's, as Iser (1978) suggests. Good readers, we say, read fast. What do 'over-readers', the slow ones, notice that we, the experienced, miss? How do readers, experienced or inexperienced, know what kind of story they are handling, what kind of invitation they are accepting, when they begin to read? Iser says: 'Fictional language provides instructions for the building of a situation and so for the production of an imaginary object.' How do readers obey these instructions? Will you believe me if I tell you that these competences are generally learned by children when they first read books that are undoubtedly not 'the best'? Louise Rosenblatt (1978) forcibly reminds us that 'the social and intellectual atmosphere that sets up "good literature" as almost by definition works accessible only to the elitist critic or literary historian leads the average reader to assume that he is not capable of participating in them' (p. 142).

How, I wonder, do you respond to my suggestion that we have neglected *potential* readers for too long? We have often despised what they choose because we can't bear its banality. In so doing, we have not really seen the inexperienced reader building an imaginary object, and so we don't know what the next step for any one child is on the road to Jane Austen and Dostoyevsky because we haven't looked closely enough at the ways successful authors – whether we like them or not – code their reading instructions for the young. In children's reading, in children's literature, we can become aware of the conventions, the repertoires, and demonstrate how they are learned and developed as literary competences. That, in my view, would make a poetics of children's literature and children's reading. It has to be an interdisciplinary study, whereby the expert readers and the reading experts meet and enthuse each other.

We have left a great deal of neglected evidence lying around. Parents who read the same book regularly to their children know that only the 'good' ones stand up to repetition. Exactly why? The answer must lie surely in the relationship of the language to the meaning. If by literature we mean something of value, says Peter Hunt (1982), then 'the more basic the motivation touched or conjured up by a text, the more valuable that text seems to us'. His work on the relationship of *quality* and *value* in children's books seems to me an important new beginning in literary theory.

Then, we have made very little use of children's own stories beyond Arthur Applebee's assimilation of them to Piaget's and Vygotsky's studies in cognitive development. Donald Graves is looking at how reading affects narrative models in children's writing. This is one aspect of the more detailed studies we need of the development of literary competences, the mastery of language systems and conventions in texts. As I exhaustingly showed at the start, children are competent over a wide range of these in oral literature. Which ones do children's authors count on? How do authors confirm and extend the literary competences of young readers as Joyce, Beckett, and Italo Calvino persistently extend mine? To make sense of a book is to know how to read it. 'Literature', says Genette (1980), 'like any other activity of the mind, is based on conventions of which, with some exceptions, it is not aware' (p. 214). In which texts, at what age, are these conventions learned? They are rarely taught in reading lessons.

I am passionate about this need for collaborative activity because I know what concentration on the bookish child (ourselves when young) has done to children's reading. It has made children's books an insider's preoccupation. *Having read*, or knowing about, the best books has become a competitive game rather than a universal pleasure, a game that the publishers play too, so we characterize readers by what we think is suitable for them, instead of seeing how they would read if we really invited them into our world.

Finally, it is well known that every good reader has at some time been entranced by a thoroughly bad book with a strong, overarching narrative drive. Why has that never counted in theorizing? We have no convincing description of this common experience as a characteristic of writing, perhaps because we might have to exemplify it in Enid Blyton, a notoriously neglected source of evidence. Our discriminations of how the surface structures of language in children's books are linked to the natural narratives of childhood culture are in their infancy. We have no good study of children's humorous books, for example. We haven't looked for evidence readers could give us about the link between the deep feelings of childhood and their encoding in texts. The play of the text between reader and writer, in William Mayne,[10] for example, hasn't engaged us, yet Jonathan Culler (1975) says of adult literature that 'a theory of literature is a theory of reading' (p. 259). Imagine critics of children's books being able to say what authors teach children about reading, how they learn the nature of the pause in Philippa Pearce, or which sentences in Madeleine L'Engle throw the switch that moves them 'in' to the story. Why do we hold back from such engagements?

As I said at the start, storying, narrative, is now at the heart of adult literary criticism. In books for children are all the features of the starting-point for readers, writers, and critics to examine *how* a theory of literature may be a theory of reading. We have to begin again to look at the interaction of text and reader. We may first have to teach each other *how* to look, to give up old critical habits and cliches and to put new elements of what we genuinely know about children and reading into a new theoretical pattern of hypothetical description. Whatever comes out, let nothing we do stand between reader and author, for we are parasitic middlemen, when all is said and done. As usual, the poet makes less fuss and creates the image of what we seek:

> The house was quiet and the world was calm.
> The reader became the book; and summer night
> Was like the conscious being of the book.
> The house was quiet and the world was calm.
> The words were spoken as if there was no
> book,
> Except that the reader leaned above the page.
>
> (Stevens, 1964)

NOTES

1 Part of my evidence for this comes from children who have not successfully learned to read. If their earliest experience of learning at school imprints the idea that reading is hard work, they do not easily progress to the belief that it can be voluntarily engaged in for pleasure.
2 My doctoral student, Aileen Beckman of Philadelphia, has demonstrated just how uncharted are the ways of children's development in all kinds of humor.
3 For this idea I am indebted to Alison Lurie.
4 Clearly, this is not absolutely so. Ethnographic studies, such as those of Shirley Brice Heath of Stamford, have explored these sources in anthropological contexts.
5 The Stone Book Quartet by Alan Garner consists of *The Stone Book* (1976), *Granny Reardun* (1977), *The Aimer Gate* (1978), *Tom Fobble's Day* (1977). London, Collins. The order given here is the chronological order of the stories.
6 Maurice Sendak in BBC television interview May 1982.
7 Pat Hutchins, *Rosie's Walk*, London, The Bodley Head, 1968. In this story Rosie, the hen, goes for a walk around the farmyard and is pursued by a fox. The fox is not mentioned in the text. The size of the goat in the picture indicates that progress. Young readers learn quickly the bond with the author that lets them share perceptions and spectator role judgements that are nowhere expressed in words.
8 I owe this example to Pat D'Arcy and her colleagues working with children in Wiltshire.
9 Frank Smith (1982), 'A Metaphor for Literacy: Creating Worlds or Shunting Information', a paper kindly sent to me by the author.
10 William Mayne's books have always been challenging in textual terms.

REFERENCES

Alderson, Brian, 'The Irrelevance of Children to the Study of Children's Literature', *Children's Book News*, January 1969.

Applebee, Arthur, *The Child's Concept of Story*, Chicago, University of Chicago Press, 1978.

Barthes, Roland, *Sur la lecture in 'Le français aujourd'hui'*, revue de l'Association Francais des'Enseignants de Français. Paris, January 1976.

Bratton, J.S., *The Impact of Victorian Children's Fiction*, London, Croom Helm, 1981.

Briggs, Raymond, *When the Wind Blows*, London, Hamish Hamilton, 1982.

Culler, Jonathan, *Structuralist Poetics*, London, Routledge & Kegan Paul, 1975.

Darton F.J. Harvey, *Children's Books in England*, 3rd edn revised by Brian Alderson, Cambridge, Cambridge University Press, 1982. (First published in 1932.)

Fish, Stanley, *Is There a Text in this Class?* Cambridge, Mass., Harvard University Press, 1980.

Frye, Northrop, *The Great Code: The Bible and Literature*, London, The Tavistock Press, 1982.

Genette, Gerard, *Narrative Discourse*, Oxford, Basil Blackwell, 1980.

Heide, Florence Parry, *The Shrinking of Treehorn*, London, Kestrel Books, 1975. (Originally published in USA).

Hunt, Peter, 'A Critical Study of English Literature Written for Children'. Unpublished doctoral dissertation, The University of Wales, Cardiff, 1982.

Iser, Wolfgang, *The Act of Reading*, London, Routledge & Kegan Paul, 1978.

Jones, Richard, *Fantasy and Feeling in Education*, New York, New York University Press, 1968.

Kermode, Frank, *The Genesis of Secrecy*, Cambridge, Mass., Harvard University Press, 1979.

Kirkpatrick, D. L., *Twentieth Century Children's Writers*, 3rd edn London, Macmillan, 1978.

Lander, Susanne, *Feeling and Form*, London, Routledge & Kegan Paul, 1953. (Originally published in USA).

LeGuin, Ursula. 'It was a Dark and Stormy Night', In W.J.T. Mitchell (ed.), *On Narrative*, Chicago, University of Chicago Press, 1981.

Meek, Margaret, Barton, Griselda, and Warlow, Aidan, *The Cool Web: The Pattern of Children's Reading*, London, The Bodley Head, 1977.

Moss, Elaine, *Picture Books for Children 9-15*, Stroud, Gloucester, The Thimble Press, 1981.

Oakley, Graham, *The Church Mouse*, London, Macmillan, 1977.

Opie, Iona, and Opie, Peter, *The Lore and Language of School Children*, Oxford, Oxford University Press, 1959

Rosen, Harold, 'The Nurture of Narrative', In the *Proceedings of the I.R.A. Conference*, Chicago, 1982.

Rosenblatt, Louise, *The Reader, the Text, the Poem: The Transactional Theory of the Literary Work*, Carbondale, Ill., Southern Illinois University Press, 1978.

Ruskin, John, *The King of the Golden River*, East Aurora, N.Y., Roycrofter, 1841.

Shafer, Roy, 'Narration in the Psychoanalytic Dialogue. In W.J.R. Mitchell (ed.), *On Narrative*, Chicago, University of Chicago Press, 1981.

Stevens, Wallace, *Collected Poems*, New York, Knopf, 1964. (Quoted in Rosenblatt, 1978.)

Winnicott, D.W., *Playing and Reality*, London, The Tavistock Press, 1971.

5

The contemporary critical scene: a review

It would be impossible, without doubling the size of this book, to give an adequate idea of the sources available to those interested in children's literature. I merely note a selection of the most well known and most readily available, and any other writer in the field will undoubtedly see, immediately, vital omissions. Tessa Rose Chester has recently published an invaluable guide: *Sources of Information about Children's Books* (Thimble Press, Woodchester, 1989) which includes material on collections of children's and related materials, societies, and printed sources. Further material is to be found in her companion volume, *Children's Books Research. A Practical Guide to Techniques and Sources* (Thimble Press, South Woodchester, 1989). (Texts already mentioned in earlier sections of this book, in text or references, are generally omitted.)

The emphasis is upon criticism rather than reviewing, and so I have not included lists of recommended books for children. Clearly, because of the large output of texts, such reviews are necessary aids for institutional book-buyers; it is a pity if they replace individual critical efforts. In any case, there are very many review journals, or journals which include reviews, designed for different disciplines. Not only does the material rapidly date, but the details of periodicals change frequently.

I have also excluded most peripheral material, such as critical theory, which has a bearing on the subject. Some fruitful suggestions for further reading can be gleaned from the notes to the articles reprinted here, and I have noted books which have useful bibliographies.

COLLECTIONS OF ESSAYS

As a new discipline, children's literature has benefited from the

183

contemporary academic fashion of the selection or 'reader' (such as this volume). There has been some discussion as to what they might usefully contain, perhaps best summed up by the Preface to the first edition of the excellent collection, *Only Connect: Readings on Children's Literature*, Toronto, OUP, 2nd edn, 1980, edited by Sheila Egoff, G. T. Stubbs, and L. F. Ashley. The editors neatly pinpoint the major weaknesses of children's-book criticism:

> Our primary aim has been to find selections that deal with children's literature as an essential part of the whole realm of literary activity, to be discussed in the same terms and judged by the same standards that would apply to any other branch of writing. We do not subscribe to the view that the criticism of children's books calls for the adoption of a special scale of values. We looked for insight and informed contemporary thinking, and rejected any material that was too concerned with recapturing childhood . . . (p. xviii)

Other useful collections are:

Bator, Robert (ed.), *Signposts to Criticism of Children's Literature*, Chicago, American Library Association, 1983.
Meek, Margaret, *et al.* (eds) *The Cool Web: the Pattern of Children's Reading*, London, Bodley Head, 1977.
Haviland, Virginia (ed.), *Children and Literature: Views and Reviews*, New York, Scott, Foresman, 1973; London, Bodley Head, 1974.

The Children's Literature Association has produced a somewhat idiosyncratic three-volume collection, edited by Perry Nodelman, *Touchstones: Reflections on the Best of Children's Literature*, West Lafayette, Purdue University: vol. 1, on major authors (1985); vol. 2, on fairy tale, fables, myths, legends, and poetry (1987), and vol. 3, on illustrators (1988).

A single-volume collection of essays, with rather more emphasis on biography, is Jane M. Bingham's *Writers for Children: Critical Studies of Major Authors Since the Seventeenth Century*, New York, Scribner's, 1987. The inclusion of writers such as Defoe, Fenimore Cooper, Conan Doyle, Swift, and Wells, however, shows a worrying imprecision about quite what constitutes a children's author.

Innocence and Experience: Essays and Conversations on Children's Literature, New York, Lothrop, Lee and Shepard, 1987, was compiled and edited by Barbara Harrison and Gregory Maguire from ten years of summer institutes run by the Simmons College Center for the Study of Children's Literature in Boston, Mass. Its very richness and range is combined with a certain discursiveness and, perhaps, lack of focus, and it demonstrates some of the problems of bringing together many disciplines, where soft-centredness is an ever-present danger.

Unique among these collections is Lance Salway's assemblage of nineteenth-century critical texts, discussed here in Chapter 1: *A Peculiar Gift: 19th Century Writing on Books for Children*, Kestrel, 1976.

Major journals have also produced selections of essays from their pages. In the USA, the earliest were from *The Horn Book Magazine*, Boston, including *A Horn Book Sampler*, 1959, *Horn Book Papers*, 1955, 1957, and *Horn Book Reflections*, 1970, which are often more enthusiastic than rigorous, by today's standards.

In Britain, a sound collection was derived from *Use of English*: Dennis Butts' *Good Writers for Young Readers*, Hart-Davis, 1977, consisting of short essays on major writers. The major British specialist journal on children's books, *Signal*, celebrated its tenth anniversary in 1980 with a particularly strong collection, which is extremely useful as a thematic reference work: Chambers, Nancy (ed.), *The Signal Approach to Children's Books*, Kestrel.

The parallel collection from *Children's Literature in Education*: Fox, Geoff, *et al.* (eds), *Writers, Critics, and Children*, Heinemann, 1976, contains such highly influential and controversial pieces as Peter Dickinson's 'In Defence of Rubbish', David Holbrook's fierce critique of the Narnia series, 'The Problem of C. S. Lewis', and Fred Inglis' 'Reading Children's Novels: Notes on the Politics of Literature'.

I might include here Marcus Crouch's *Chosen for Children*, Library Association, 1957 and subsequent revisions, which lists the winners of the Carnegie Medal. It is perhaps more interesting for the contributions from the authors than for the generally eulogistic commentary on the books.

I have mentioned the sub-species of collections of essays by authors on their craft, or of interviews with them. The best of these – although still marked by considerable self-indulgence – is Edward Blishen's *The Thorny Paradise*, Kestrel, 1975. As Blishen notes:

> How can it be believed that to write for children is a lightweight literary task, suitably carried out by comic figures? Either literature is a single enterprise, each branch of it as honourable and as vital as any other, or there is something very wrong . . . [I]t might be argued that writing for children grows stronger and bolder as writing for adults grows more . . . inward, marked by self-doubting intricacy. (pp. 10–11)

Far more characteristic of the type are Justin Wintle and Emma Fisher's The Pied Pipers, New York and London, Paddington Press, 1974, which has some interest, and Jonathan Cott's notorious *Pipers at the Gates of Dawn*, New York, Random House, 1983, which was described by Susan Gannon as 'an opportunity lost' (*Children's Literature Association Quarterly*, Summer, 1984, vol. 9, no. 2, p. 83) and by Perry Nodelman, in a savage review as 'a prime candidate for consideration as the silliest book about children's literature ever written' (*Children's Literature*, 13, 1985, p. 204). Nodelman's review is worth reading because he defends both real children and children's books against 'the only sort of attitude towards children's literature that gets children's literature any respect in the corridors of literary power . . . that children's literature can only be important if it isn't really for children at all but actually secret pop-Zen for fuzzyminded grownups' (p. 206).

REFERENCE WORKS

Several of the books noted above could be seen as reference works. Others are noted here.

One of the earliest was Alec Ellis's *How to Find Out about Children's Books*, Pergamon, 1965, which, although much dated, still outlines a valid strategy. (Its companion volume, *A History of Children's Reading and Literature*, Pergamon, 1968, is primarily concerned with librarianship.)

Children's literature may be said to have achieved another kind of respectability with the publication of Humphrey Carpenter and Mari Prichard's *The Oxford Companion to Children's Literature*, OUP, 1984. Although inaccurate in many details, it is in most respects an elegant and impressive work, and its somewhat erratic range might be justified by the tradition of *Oxford Companions*.

There might be more reservations about *20th Century Children's Writers*, edited by Tracy Chevalier, St James, 3rd edn, 1989. As a collection of essays it is uneven, but it is bibliographically monumental and indispensable as a reference booklist.

Margery Fisher has an enviable reputation as an accessible and knowledgeable writer. Her *Who's Who in Children's Books, A Treasury of the Familiar Characters of Childhood*, Weidenfeld and Nicolson, 1975, is a splendid tribute to the discipline of children's literature. It is arranged in a way virtually calculated to irritate the academic - that is, alphabetically *by character*. This is, however, a genuinely original book, with unpretentious and shrewd judgements, and a depth of knowledge which has rarely been challenged.

Fisher's comments are even-handed and consistently clear and refreshing. Her earlier, more conventional standard works, *Intent Upon Reading*, Brockhampton, 2nd edn, 1964, and its companion, *Matters of Fact*, Brockhampton, 1972, are based upon her reviewing journal, *Growing Point*, May 1962 onward, and as a result contain rather more of the ephemeral. Nonetheless, as basic reference material, they remain useful.

As Fisher commented in *Intent Upon Reading*:

> When we write about children's books we are in a special position. We bring an experience to bear on books which are not intended primarily for us, in which we share by invitation . . . In his early years a child is willing to accept any world the writer creates, not with conscious, conscientious belief in its truth, but by participation. The critic . . . must try to achieve something of this wholeheartedness. (pp. 11, 13)

Fisher's immaculate judgement can also be found in her recent *Signal Bookguide, Classics for Children and Young People*, South Woodchester, The Thimble Press, 1986.

An American equivalent might be Zena Sutherland's *The Best of Children's Books*, 1973 and subsequent editions.

On a more ambitious scale, Gale Research has taken children's literature as an equal partner in its extensive biographical/bibliographical projects, with such titles as *Children's Book Review Index* (1975 onward), and John Cech's *American Writers for Children, 1900-1960*, 1983, which is vol. 22 of Gale's *Dictionary of Literary Biography*. Among many others which take a biographical approach are Miriam Hoffman and Eva Samuels, *Authors and Illustrators of Children's Books*, New York, Bowker, 1972.

The distinction between 'criticism' and 'bibliography' is clear, and it would be unwise to enter what is really a separate, although related field, at any length - bearing in mind, perhaps, the strictures of possibly the greatest of bibliographers, Fredson Bowers:

> We should be seriously disturbed by the lack of contact between literary critics and textual critics . . . [I]t is still a current oddity that many a literary critic has investigated the past ownership and condition of his second-hand automobile . . . more thoroughly than he has looked into the qualifications of the text on which his critical theories rest. (Fredson Bowers, *Textual and Literary Criticism*, Cambridge University Press, 1959, pp. 4-5)

Thus to cite James Fraser's *A Guide to Manuscript Collections in United States Research Libraries*, Munich, Saur, 1980, or Carolyn Field's *Special Collections in Children's Literature*, Chicago, American Library Association, 1982, is merely to gesture towards the vast output of bibliographical material.

The standard American work is probably Virginia Haviland's *Children's Literature: A Guide to Reference Sources*, Washington, Library of Congress, 1966, and supplements.

For the UK, I can do no better than to refer you to the bibliographies in Darton and Alderson's *Children's Books in England*.

HISTORY AND SURVEYS

The history of children's literature has 'stabilized' in the sense that there are now generally established historical periods and landmarks: we are now entering a period when these may well be revised, particularly in the light of political or feminist re-readings. These 'canonical' mappings of the field are represented both in books which have primarily a bibliographical and historical interest, and those which are broadly critical.

Of the first group, F. J. Harvey Darton's *Children's Books in England* is essential reading, and contains an excellent general bibliography (pp. 362-71). Also available is Percy Muir's *English Children's Books*, Batsford, 1954, 3rd impression, 1979, which was intended to supplement and update Darton, and which is more profusely illustrated (bibliography, pp. 16-19), and Eric Quale's *Early Children's Books: A Collector's Guide*, Newton Abbot, David and Charles, 1983. Quale's attitude is summed up in his 'Introduction':

A love and understanding of the often ephemeral little volumes that brought pleasure to countless children of past ages must surely be a prime requisite for successful book-hunting and the gradual building of a library whose specialist interest opens the way to research and scholarship. (p.11)

Also of interest:

Gerald Gottlieb, *Early Children's Books and their Illustrators*, New York, Pierpont Morgan Library and OUP, 1975.
Judith St John (ed.) *Osborne Collection of Early Children's Books, 1476-1910*, 2 vols., Toronto Public Library, 1975.
Mary F. Thwaite, *From Primer to Pleasure*, Library Association, 1963.
William Targ, *Bibliophile in the Nursery*, Cleveland, World, 1957.

William Sloane, *Children's Books in England and America in the 17th Century*, New York, King's Crown Press, 1955.

Historical studies are also rapidly expanding, possibly because the literary establishment has been able to accept studies of children's books as long as they do not present any awkward canonical questions. The pioneering Juvenile Library Series (General Editor, Brian Alderson) not only included editions of significant texts, but also special studies, such as M. Nancy Cutt's *Mrs Sherwood and her Books for Children*, OUP, 1974. A study of tractarian writing, in which 'much of nineteenth-century children's literature seems to be rooted', *Ministering Angels*, has been published by the same author (Five Owls Press, 1979).

Most of the books discussing these topics are marked by their readability despite the sometimes daunting nature of their material. Of particular interest are:

Summerfield, Geoffrey, *Fantasy and Reason: Children's Literature in the Eighteenth Century*, Methuen, 1984.
Bratton, J. S., *The Impact of Victorian Children's Fiction*, Croom Helm, 1981.
Avery, Gillian, *Childhood's Pattern: A Study of the Heroes and Heroines of Children's Fiction, 1770-1950*, Hodder, 1975.

In the twentieth century, surveys intended for use by librarians and others have produced several texts which lie more in the region of literary criticism than history. The most noteworthy of these (and most have a tone rather similar to that of Townsend) are Marcus Crouch's *Treasure Seekers and Borrowers. Children's Books in Britain 1900-1960*, Library Association, 1962, and *The Nesbit Tradition*, Benn, 1972; and Frank Eyre's *British Children's Books in the Twentieth Century*, Longman, rev. edn, 1971. The work of Margery Fisher has been mentioned.

CRITICAL DISCUSSIONS

'True' criticism of children's literature has developed from bibliography and history on the one hand and from specific literary, psychological, educational, or political interests on the other.

Among what might be called the 'enthusiastic' rather than the rigorous, we might note three books that frequently appear on booklists and in collections, but which are, in fact, of limited use to the student of children's literature - whatever their influence in the past:

Lillian H. Smith, *The Unreluctant Years: A Critical Approach to Children's Literature*, ALA, Chicago, 1953; New York, Viking, 1967; Paul Hazard, *Books, Children, and Men*, Boston, The Horn Book, 1944; Isabelle Jan, *On Children's Literature*, trans. and ed. Catherine Storr, Allen Lane, 1973.

To the many general critical books mentioned so far, we may add a book of anti-criticism. Elaine Moss has been very influential in her highly practical approach to reviewing, library work, and involvement with children and book selection. 'I am', she writes in *Part of the Pattern*, Bodley Head, 1986, ' . . . very happy to leave literary criticism to those who work in universities or polytechnics and who write for a committed and learned audience in respectable specialist journals. This is where real criticism belongs. That is where it is (dare I say this?) *useful*.' (p. 208) Which (despite its slightly disingenuous sleight of hand), puts the academics in their place while producing some very intelligent criticism.

The academia which Elaine Moss so distrusts might be exemplified by Zohar Shavit's theoretical *The Poetics of Children's Literature*, Athens, University of Georgia Press, 1986, or the contentious, *The Case of Peter Pan, or the Impossibility of Children's Fiction*, Macmillan, 1984, by Jacqueline Rose. Both of these are distinctively in the academic tradition, whereas Fred Inglis' *The Promise of Happiness. Value and Meaning in Children's Fiction*, CUP, 1981, brings immense individualistic energy to his investigation of 'the nature of popular culture, and the way in which these particular forms of the social imagination try to fix admired social values in a story, give them place and name and continuity' (p. xi). Nicholas Tucker's *The Child and the Book*, CUP, 1981, adds a psychological Piagetian approach to matching book and child.

The popularist tradition in writing about children's books is exemplified by Humphrey Carpenter's *Secret Gardens: The Golden Age of Children's Literature*, Allen and Unwin, 1985, which combines biographical speculation and literary criticism.

There is an American 'tradition' of producing compendious texts (usually under the guise of educational guides) which cover, lightly, very many aspects of the history, criticism, and teaching of children's literature. These can serve as competent introductions, as well as practical aids for the teacher. Good examples are May Hill Arbuthnot, *Children and Books*, 4th edn, with Zena Sutherland, Chicago, Scott Foresman, 1972; and Charlotte S. Huck, Susan Hepler, Janet Hickman, *Children's Literature in the Elementary School*, 4th edn, Holt, Rinehart, and Winston, 1987.

It would be impossible to adequately cover criticism of children's literature worldwide. I would only draw the attention of the reader to the work of Maurice Saxby and Walter McVitty in Australia, and Betty Gilderdale in New Zealand, as examples.

Also of interest:

Open University, *Literature for Children*, Milton Keynes, Open University Press, 1972.

Cameron, Eleanor, *The Green and Burning Tree: On the Writing and Enjoyment of Children's Books*, Boston, Atlantic-Little, Brown, 1969.

Selma G. Lanes, *Down the Rabbit Hole*, New York, Athenaeum, 1971.

Finally, I must mention two very significant single-author studies. The collection by Robert Phillips, *Aspects of Alice*, Penguin, 1978, which contains essays by Auden, Woolf, de la Mare, Graves, Allen Tate, Priestley, Burke, Empson, and many others, demonstrates the possible kinds of analysis which may be applied to a classic text. Neil Philip's *A Fine Anger: The Work of Alan Garner*, Collins, 1981, is distinguished as being the first in-depth monograph on a contemporary author, a fact which may signal that children's literature and its criticism has come of age.

SPECIAL TOPICS

The distinctive genres of children's literature have been receiving increasing attention.

Margery Fisher deals skilfully with the adventure story in *The Bright Face of Danger*, Hodder, 1986, and Margaret Blount, with the animal story (which covers a great deal of ground between fable, allegory, and other sub-genres) in *Animal Land: The Creatures of Children's Fiction*, Hutchinson, 1974.

Mary Cadogan and Patricia Craig's, *You're a Brick, Angela! A New Look at Girl's Fiction from 1838–1985*, is a witty and perceptive look at this singular oddity of children's literature. As they observe:

A vast body of literature already exists, much of it admirable; its effects can scarcely be overestimated. Many of the most powerful images which fascinate and obsess the adult are derived from childhood reading ... Sex-differentiated popular fiction begins here, and persists, in some cases, through teenage picture-strip weeklies to adult books and magazines. (p. 9)

See also:

Gillian Freeman, The Schoolgirl Ethic: the life and works of Angela Brazil, Allen Lane, 1976, and Isabel Quigley, *The Heirs of Tom Brown: the English School Story*, OUP, 1984.

Much of the material here is close to popular fiction, perhaps best dealt with in W. O. G. Lofts and D. J. Adley, *The Men Behind Boys Fiction*, Howard Baker, 1970, and E. S. Turner, *Boys Will Be Boys*, Michael Joseph, 3rd edn, 1975; Penguin, 1976. Sheila Ray's study of Enid Blyton, *The Blyton Phenomenon*, Deutsch, 1982, is a characteristic single-author study, with emphasis upon the sociological controversies surrounding her.

Children's literary studies tend to become involved in matters of sex, race, and class, and the most pugnacious study has been Bob Dixon's *Catching Them Young 1: Sex, Race and Class in Children's Books; 2: Politics in Children's Books*, Pluto Press, 1977, together with Robert Leeson's left-wing recasting of children's-book history in his *Reading and Righting*, Collins, 1985. These books might be usefully read in conjunction with Leeson's *Children's Books and Class Society, Past and Present*, which was edited by the Children's Rights Workshop and published by the Readers' and Writers' Publishing Co-operative, 1977, and *Sexism in Children's Books: Facts, Figures and Guidelines*, Readers' and Writers' Co-operative, 1976.

Some of the social questions surrounding children's books are summed up in a collection, Nicholas Tucker's *Suitable for Children? Controversies in Children's Literature*, Sussex University Press, 1976.

The original work on horror and violence in children's books and comics was P. M. Pickard's *I Could a Tale Unfold: Violence, Horror and Sensationalism in Stories for Children*, Tavistock, 1961, which is, perhaps surprisingly, still relevant to the 1980s.

Some of the more alarming aspects of literary censorship in this connection may be found in Edward B. Jenkinson's *Censors in the Classroom*, New York, Avon, 1982.

Myths, legends, and fairy-tales are introduced, especially for teachers, in Elizabeth Cook's *The Ordinary and the Fabulous. An Introduction to Myths, Legends, and Fairy Tales*, CUP, 1976, bibliography, pp. 123–77. More radical readings may be found in Bruno Bettelheim's *The Uses of Enchantment: The Meaning and Importance of Fairy-tales*, Thames and Hudson, 1976, which has frequently been accused of over-simplification and exaggeration in equating elements in the tales with reactions of readers. A similar charge of exaggeration has been levelled at Jack Zipes, whose *Fairy Tales and the Art of Subversion. The Classical Genre for Children and the Process of Civilization*, London, Heinemann; New York, Wildman,

1983, and Breaking the Magic Spell: Radical Theories of Folk and Fairy Tales, Heinemann Educational, 1979, have placed a new perspective on the tales. The same may be said of Zipes' *Don't Bet on the Prince*, New York, Methuen, 1986, a collection of modern feminist fairy-tales, with an illuminating introduction, and *The Trials and Tribulations of Little Red Riding Hood*, South Hadley, Mass., Bergin and Garvey, 1983.

Another major area of writing for children is that of fantasy. It may well be, as Kathryn Hume observed in *Fantasy and Mimesis*, Methuen, 1985, that fantasy 'informs the spirit of all but a small part of western literature' and that we 'are curiously blind to its presence because our traditional approaches to literature are based on mimetic assumptions' (p. 3). But there is little doubt that, for whatever reason, it represents a major part of children's literature, with close associations with folk- and fairy-tale, myth and legend.

Ann Swinfen deals with some of the initial problems of fantasy in her *A Defence of Fantasy, a Study of the Genre in English and American Literature since 1945*, RKP, 1984. Although much of her book deals with what would usually be described as 'children's literature', she dismisses the distinction in an interestingly ambiguous statement:

> It is quite clear from any prolonged study of what might be termed 'high fantasies' that to label them as children's books is grossly misleading. (p.2)

In his Introduction to a 'Special Section' on fantasy which appeared in the *Children's Literature Association Quarterly*, spring, 1987, 12.1, C. W. Sullivan III considered the definition of this field:

> Efforts in that direction, especially recently, have been prodigious, and much too much has been done in just the last fifteen years to be summarized here. But I have found the definition in Kathryn Hume's *Fantasy and Mimesis* both logical and valuable. Hume argues that all literature is the product of two impulses.

> These are *mimesis*, felt as the desire to imitate, to describe events, people, situations, and objects with such ver-isimilitude that others can share your experience; and *fantasy*, the desire to change givens and alter reality – out of boredom, play, vision, longing for something lacking, or need for metaphoric images that will bypass the audience's verbal defenses. (p.20)

And fantasy, as she further defines it, is 'the deliberate departure from the limits of what is usually accepted as real and normal' (xii); it is *any departure from consensus reality* (Hume's italics; 21).

Among this definition's strong points are, first, that it obviates the often artificially imposed distinctions between popular literature and elite/academic literature or between fantasy written for children and fantasy written for adults. Second, as Hume points out, this is an inclusive rather than exclusive definition, allowing us as readers and critics to recognize that everything beyond consensus reality contributes to the fantastic component of a given work. And third, this definition provides a meaningful way of dealing with both fantastic and the realistic (mimetic) elements in a given work, whether it is *The Lord of the Rings* or *Jane Eyre*. (pp. 6-7)

To compile a useful bibliography of writing on fantasy in a short space would be impossible. I might mention Ruth Nadelman Lynn's *Fantasy for Children*, New York, Bowker, 1983, or Hugh Crago's attempt to bring fantasy, myth, and popular culture together in his 'Terra Incognita, Cognita', in M. Trask (ed.), *Fantasy, Science Fiction. Science Materials*, Kensington, University of New South Wales, 1972, pp. 45-58, 61-6. More generally there are C. N. Manlove's *The Impulse of Fantasy*, Kent State University Press, 1983, Eric Rabkin's *The Fantastic in Literature*, Princeton, Princeton University Press, 1976, Tzvetan Todorov's *The Fantastic*, trans. Richard Howard, Cleveland and London, Case Western Reserve, 1973, W. R. Irwin's *The Game of the Impossible: A Rhetoric of Fantasy*, Urbana, University of Illinois Press, and Rosemary Jackson's *Fantasy: The Literature of Subversion*, London, Methuen, 1981 - the list could be extended massively, but as not all of these deal with fantasy in children's literature, we are left with another example of an area where our borders are unclear.

In the area of illustration, additional texts to note are Bettina Hurlimann, *Picture Book World*, OUP, 1968. *Illustrators of Children's Books, 1744-1945*, ed. Bertha E. Mahoney, 1947; *1946- 1956*, ed. Ruth Hill Viguers *et al.*, 1958, *1957-1966*, ed. Lee Kingman *et al.*, 1968, all published by The Horn Book, Boston; Cornelia Jones and Olivia R. Way, *Cobwebs to Catch Flies. Illustrated Books from Nursery and Schoolroom, 1700-1900*, Berkeley, University of California Press, 1975; Smith, Janet Adam, *Children's Illustrated Books*, Collins, 1948.

And we may conclude this brief survey by returning to Geoffrey Trease:

The past forty years have seen a miraculous flowering of children's books and a welcome improvement in the status of their writers, but there is still a tendency to patronize them as second-class citizens in the commonwealth of letters. They deserve better. There is nothing easy about writing for the young. Boswell admitted that long ago, when he made one of his many unfulfilled resolutions, in this case to write some day 'a little story-book' like the ones he had enjoyed as a boy.

'It will not be an easy task for me', he noted, 'it will require much nature and simplicity and a great acquaintance with the humours and traditions of the English common people. I shall be happy to succeed, for he who pleases children will be remembered with pleasure by men.' (p. 112)